D0951866

AN UNLIKELY TRUST

ALSO BY GERARD HELFERICH

Humboldt's Cosmos: Alexander von Humboldt and the Latin American Journey That Changed the Way We See the World

High Cotton: Four Seasons in the Mississippi Delta

Stone of Kings: In Search of the Lost Jade of the Maya

Theodore Roosevelt and the Assassin: Madness, Vengeance, and the Campaign of 1912

AN UNLIKELY TRUST

Theodore Roosevelt, J. P. Morgan, and the
Improbable Partnership That Remade American Business

GERARD HELFERICH

Guilford, Connecticut

An imprint of Globe Pequot

Distributed by NATIONAL BOOK NETWORK

Copyright © 2018 by Gerard Helferich

British Library Cataloguing in Publication Information available

Library of Congress Cataloging-in-Publication Data

Names: Helferich, Gerard, author.
Title: An unlikely trust : Theodore Roosevelt, J. P. Morgan, and the improbable partnership that remade American business / Gerard Helferich.
Description: Guilford, Conn. : Lyons Press, [2017] | Includes bibliographical references and index.
Identifiers: LCCN 2017034240 (print) | LCCN 2017033328 (ebook) | ISBN 9781493025787 (ebook) | ISBN 9781493025770 (hardcover) | ISBN 9781493025787 (e-book)
Subjects: LCSH: United States—Economic conditions—1865-1918. | United States—Economic policy—To 1933. | Roosevelt, Theodore, 1858-1919. | Morgan, J. Pierpont (John Pierpont), 1837-1913.
Classification: LCC HC106 (print) | LCC HC106 .H43 2017 (ebook) | DDC 330.973/0911—dc23
LC record available at https://lccn.loc.gov/2017034240

♾️™ The paper used in this publication meets the minimum requirements of American National Standard for Information Sciences—Permanence of Paper for Printed Library Materials, ANSI/NISO Z39.48-1992.

Printed in the United States of America

To Teresa, *mi vida*

Contents

Author's Note

Like most Americans, I imagine, I had a schoolbook image of Theodore Roosevelt—pince-nez, ferocious grin, broad-brimmed cavalry hat—and a passing familiarity with his resume as Rough Rider, trust buster, environmentalist, big-game hunter. Then, several years ago, while I was teaching at the Columbia Publishing Course, at the Columbia Journalism School, a group of inspired students suggested that someone write a nonfiction book about the attempt on Roosevelt's life that had taken place in 1912, as he was running for a third term as president. I was immediately hooked by the narrative possibilities, and as I delved more deeply into Roosevelt's life and career, I was also fascinated by his consummate intelligence, complex personality, and extraordinary achievements. It was easy to see why, by the time he left the White House, in 1909, he was the most famous and most popular man not just in the United States but on earth.

During my research for what would become *Theodore Roosevelt and the Assassin*, I would catch an occasional glimpse of another character peering out from the story's periphery—J. Pierpont Morgan. In that book, Morgan played only a cameo role, mostly as a (controversial) donor to Roosevelt's 1904 election campaign. But just as Roosevelt forever changed the federal government, Morgan, as America's preeminent financier, presided over an elemental shift in American business, away from family-owned companies and toward huge corporations. As the twentieth century began, Morgan and Roosevelt were the two most powerful men in America, perhaps the world, and the transformations they wrought were essential to creating our modern age. In no small measure, we are all living in a world created by Theodore Roosevelt and Pierpont Morgan.

So I was surprised that the relationship between these momentous figures had never been examined at book length. And when the two had been considered together, usually in passing, they were often depicted as battling colossi, the great trust builder versus the original trustbuster. But their association, I discovered, was far more complex and symbiotic. Despite their many differences, they had much in common—social class, an unstinting Victorian moralism, a drive for power, a need for order, and a genuine (though not purely altruistic) concern for the welfare of the nation. Working this common ground, the premier progressive and the quintessential capitalist were able to unite to accomplish what neither could have achieved alone—including, more than once, averting a national disaster. In the process they also changed the way that government and business worked together.

This is the story of the uneasy but historic collaboration between Theodore Roosevelt and Pierpont Morgan. It is also the story of how government and business evolved from a relationship of laissez-faire to the active regulation that we know today. And it is an account of how, despite all that has changed in the past century, so much remains the same, including a growing divide between rich and poor; the tangled, self-serving bonds uniting politicians and business leaders; and a pervasive feeling that government is working for the special interests rather than for the people. Not least of all, it is the story of how citizens with vastly disparate philosophies and interests managed to come together for the good of their common country.

It is a work of nonfiction. All the characters are real, and no names have been changed. All words in quotation marks were said or written by the person indicated, or at least reported by a witness, such as an aide or a newspaper reporter. On a few occasions, to evoke the late nineteenth or early twentieth century, I have supplied atmospheric details (such as horses neighing) and made a few minor assumptions, which are included in the Notes. Everything else is part of the historical record, down to the clothing the characters wore and the gestures they made.

Many of the events described in these pages were reported by more than one eyewitness, and those accounts sometimes vary meaningfully, especially concerning the time (or even the day) that something happened and the exact words that someone spoke. I have tried to choose my sources with care, and in the Notes I sometimes point out where published accounts disagree. Readers wishing to know more about this pivotal period in our history or these larger-than-life figures may wish to consult the Bibliography, which includes suggestions for further reading.

"This, Then, Is the Place to Stop This Trouble"

Sunday, November 3, 1907

IT WAS 9:00 P.M. WHEN A FIGURE IN A DARK OVERCOAT STEPPED OUT OF a cab at Madison Avenue and Thirty-Sixth Street. The young man was big-boned, but his face was thin and topped by dark, oiled hair parted in the middle. At age thirty-four, Ben Strong was already secretary of Bankers Trust. Though founded just four years earlier, Bankers had grown into one of the nation's largest trust companies, thanks in part to its close ties with Pierpont Morgan. But after the events of the past two weeks, a job at a trust company, even a solvent one like Bankers, hardly seemed something to brag about among Strong's neighbors in Greenwich, Connecticut.

Gripping his briefcase, Strong stepped onto the sidewalk and strode toward the long, low building before him. Designed by Charles McKim in a serene, neoclassical style, it had been completed the year before, with blocks of white marble dressed so perfectly that mortar had not been needed. Mr. Morgan's "library," as it was known, had been conceived to house the fabulous collection of artwork and manuscripts the financier had amassed during his many journeys to Europe. Situated next to Morgan's three-story, ivy-covered townhouse, the library also functioned as a private study. These days, at age seventy, the banker rarely went to the offices of J.P. Morgan & Company, at 23 Wall Street, but worked a couple of hours here every day, whenever he was in New York.

But tonight the library was hardly a place of refuge. On the sidewalk, beyond the iron railing, clustered dozens of men whose notebooks and cheap coats marked them as reporters. They had been planted here for two weeks, ever since Mr. Morgan had rushed back from the Triennial Episcopal Convention in Richmond, where as a lay delegate from the Diocese of New York, he had immersed himself in the business before the Church.

As Strong left the cab, reporters' heads turned in his direction. All evening, some of the most prominent bankers and businessmen in New York, and that meant some of the most prominent in the world, had been dashing in and out of these premises. Coal, steel, and railroad magnate Henry Clay Frick had already arrived, as had Elbert H. Gary, chairman of U.S. Steel. Seeing that the young man wasn't a familiar figure among this august company, the reporters turned away. Strong passed up the low steps, between the pair of carved lionesses, past the marble columns, through the massive bronze doors, and into the sumptuous rotunda.

Pierpont Morgan's library; the back of his townhouse can be seen at left.
LIBRARY OF CONGRESS

He was unprepared for the pandemonium that greeted him. Everywhere, it seemed, men were in motion, gesticulating, pacing the patterned marble floor, oblivious to the antique statuary, the mosaic panels, the frescoed ceilings. To Strong's left the foyer opened onto the West Room, Mr. Morgan's study, with its red silk wall coverings and its wooden ceiling imported from Italy. To his right, in the East Room, tall bookcases housed some of the rarest masterworks of world literature. Directly before him, at the rear of the rotunda, was a smaller door, surmounted by an ancient marble statue of the Christ Child and the Virgin Mary, with the carved inscription *Soli Deo Honor et Gloria*, "Honor and Glory to God Alone." Behind that door, in the office of his beautiful librarian, Belle da Costa Greene, Mr. Morgan would be conferring with a few trusted lieutenants and indulging in back-to-back games of solitaire, his customary diversion in times of trouble. In defiance of his heavy cold and the directives of Dr. Markoe, he was also chain smoking his huge Cuban cigars, though in a nod to medical convention, he had promised to limit himself to just twenty a day.

As Strong paused, he saw three men stride across the rotunda. He recognized Gary, along with two colleagues from U.S. Steel, William J. Filbert and Lewis Cass Ledyard. The heavy wooden door of the librarian's office opened to admit them, then abruptly shut again.

Strong was approached by Harry Davison, the forty-year-old cofounder of Bankers Trust. As Strong's employer, Davison had nominated him for this exceptional and unnerving assignment. Now, for the first time since the crisis began, Strong saw discouragement clouding his mentor's handsome, open features. Davison told him why: Mr. Morgan had concluded that many more millions would be needed to prop up the city's failing trust companies and brokerage houses and, not incidentally, forestall a collapse of the nation's financial system. And it was needed before the markets opened at ten o'clock tomorrow morning.

Strong entered the spacious West Room, where the bankers were milling beneath ancient stained-glass windows, Renaissance paintings of the saints, and a portrait of Pierpont's father, Junius. In the far corner of the room, its door ajar, was the vault where Mr. Morgan kept his priceless manuscripts—letters written by George Washington, texts by Robert

Burns and Lord Byron, manuscripts by Beethoven and Mozart. A log was burning in the huge carved stone fireplace, and on the mantel rested an enamel plaque bearing Mr. Morgan's personal motto: *Pense moult, Parle peu, Écris rien*: "Think much, say little, write nothing."

As the men conferred, an occasional messenger burst in from the Waldorf-Astoria, a few blocks away on Fifth Avenue and Thirty-Third Street, where the boards of the Trust Company of America and the Lincoln Trust were meeting in emergency session. Bank executives continued to arrive in waves; by 9:30, fifty had gathered in the West Room. At 10:45, the door to the librarian's office opened, and Elbert Gary and Henry Frick strode through the rotunda and out of the building. As they climbed into Frick's car, they were mobbed by newsmen. The dapper Gary gave a wan smile and told them, "I can't say anything. I can't talk. I'd like to, but I can't." Later, Oakleigh Thorne, president of the Trust Company of America, emerged and confessed to reporters, "I wish to God I could tell what is going to happen."

As the evening deepened, more bankers appeared at the library, until a hundred men were pacing and smoking in the study, a stunning assemblage that only Pierpont Morgan could have convened. At midnight, Edwin Marsten, president of the Farmers' Loan and Trust Company, was called into the librarian's office. When he returned, after nearly an hour, his expression was grim. There had been an unexpected development, he announced, apart from the crisis in the trust companies. He was not at liberty to disclose its nature, but its resolution would require at least an additional $25 million in funds. Mr. Morgan was prepared to step in, but only if the presidents of the solvent trust companies could raise another $25 million among themselves, to rescue their faltering colleagues. A look of consternation passed from face to face.

Strong settled in a red velvet lounge chair, beside a man with thinning hair and a thick salt-and-pepper mustache: James Stillman, president of National City Bank, the nation's largest. No sooner had Strong seated himself than he dozed off. When he stirred, Stillman asked when he had last been to bed. Thursday, Strong said; this would make his third night in a row without sleep. Stillman suggested that the country wouldn't "smash" if he went home and got some rest. But just then the door to the librarian's office opened again, and the young banker was summoned. Leaving the comfort of his lounge chair, he quit the West Room, crossed the cool marble of the rotunda, and entered the sanctum sanctorum.

— ❦ —

There had been signs of impending trouble throughout 1907. For one thing, the world was starved for cash, which at the time meant gold. In the phenomenal burst of industrialization after the Civil War, American railroads and manufacturers had soaked up huge infusions of foreign capital. But worldwide production of gold had failed to keep pace with demand. Then in April 1906 had come the devastating earthquake in San Francisco, where the rebuilding was consuming tens of millions of dollars. About half the city's fire insurance policies were held by British firms; faced with a sudden shortage of gold, the Bank of England tightened credit to American companies and, to attract more cash, nearly doubled its interest rate, from 3.5 to 6 percent. France and Germany quickly followed London's lead. The City of San Francisco found itself unable to borrow money, and Boston, New York, and the Westinghouse Electric & Manufacturing Company all failed to place large bond issues. The worldwide cash shortage was growing critical.

After the earthquake, the New York Stock Exchange had plunged a billion dollars in value. Through 1907, shares had continued their steady decline, and in August the market had stumbled again. By September, stocks were down 24 percent for the year. But rather than reassuring investors that American capitalism rested on a steady footing, President Roosevelt was only fueling the jitters. Following his inauguration in 1901, he had promised to rein in the big corporations, or "trusts," and to moderate their overweening economic and political clout. During his six years in office, the president had made good on his word, establishing regulatory agencies and bringing dozens of suits under the Sherman Anti-Trust Act. Then in August, a federal court had fined John D. Rockefeller's Standard Oil a stunning $29 million for negotiating preferential rates from the railroads.

As the market continued its slide, many blamed what they saw as the administration's aggressive anti-business stance. In a speech at

Washington's Gridiron Club in January, the president had charged that certain "malefactors of great wealth" were intentionally sowing panic to undermine his reforms, "so that they may enjoy unmolested the fruits of their own evil-doing." To Wall Street, it seemed that the federal government, with excessive regulation and reckless rhetoric, had declared war on capitalism.

The tinder was stacked, and in the end the spark was struck by United Copper, a holding company established by F. Augustus Heinze, a Montana mining baron turned New York banker. During the summer of 1907, a syndicate led by Heinze, his brothers Otto and Arthur, and notorious speculator Charles W. Morse had begun borrowing heavily in an attempt to corner the shares of United Copper. On October 15, when the scheme failed and the company's stock plunged, the syndicate was left owing millions of dollars it could not repay. Worse, the debacle threatened to bring down brokerages and banks, including Knickerbocker Trust, whose president, Charles Barney, was known to have close ties to Morse. The Knickerbocker was one of the nation's largest and most successful trust companies (not to be confused with the monopolistic trusts that Roosevelt railed against), but it was doubtful that its size or reputation could protect it from the frailties of the nation's obsolete banking system.

It had been seventy years since Andrew Jackson had refused to renew the charter of the Bank of the United States, which he called an unconstitutional usurper of the states' sovereignty and a benefit only to the financial elite. In the decades since, the country had done without the stabilizing influence of a national monetary authority, relying instead on a patchwork of nearly twenty-one thousand state and national banks. By law these institutions were required to hold only a small percentage of their deposits as cash, leaving them free to loan the surplus to banks in financial centers such as New York. The New York banks, in turn, invested heavily in stocks and bonds, making the entire system vulnerable to sudden downturns in the market. By 1907, half the bank loans in New York City used securities as collateral.

In this chain of weak links, the trust companies proved the weakest. Established to administer trusts, wills, and estates, which commercial banks were barred from handling, the trust companies had begun taking deposits, making loans, and functioning much like traditional banks, but with less government oversight. In time, the trust companies had grown reckless, paying high interest rates and speculating in stocks, bonds, and real estate. Their minimal reserve requirements, even lower than the banks', also made them susceptible to impulsive runs. As word spread of Charles Barney's involvement with Charles Morse, anxious depositors lined up outside the Knickerbocker's elegant new Fifth Avenue headquarters to demand their money. The panic quickly spread to other institutions, until a dozen of the city's trust companies and banks were on the verge of collapse.

Only one man had the means and reputation to stem the panic. As the nation's foremost financier, J. Pierpont Morgan had revolutionized the railroad industry and led the transformation of American industry from a backwater of family-owned companies to a vast sea of modern corporations such as U.S. Steel, American Telephone & Telegraph, and General Electric. Just a dozen years before, he and his international partners had rescued the federal government from bankruptcy by loaning it $65 million in gold. On Wall Street, Morgan reigned supreme, known as Napoleon or Jove. No one questioned his acumen, and more remarkably, no one doubted his word. The most powerful man in America, he was called, more influential than the president himself.

Recently returned from one of his long European holidays, Morgan had been attending the Episcopal Church conference in Richmond when the crisis broke. He was reluctant to leave the meeting early, for fear of deepening the sense of alarm. But on Saturday, October 19, he'd decided he had no choice. "They are in trouble in New York," he told Bishop William Lawrence. "They do not know what to do, and I don't know what to do, but I am going back."

Meanwhile, President Roosevelt, the man whose policies many blamed for the emergency, was hunting in the bayous outside Stamboul, Louisiana. "We got three bears, six deer, one wild turkey, twelve squirrels, one duck, one opossum, and one wildcat," he told a reporter. "We ate them all, except the wildcat." As Morgan was arriving in New York, the president finally decided he had better return to the capital. Despite his enormous intelligence and political savvy, he still seemed not to grasp the gravity of the situation.

En route to Washington, he stopped in Nashville and gave a speech that included his first public comments about the emergency. But instead of smoothing the troubled waters between him and the business community, he seemed to go out of his way to roil them. Responding to those who were calling the crisis "the Roosevelt Panic," he claimed that his policies were simply meant to punish "dishonesty."

"I doubt," he went on, "if these policies have had any material effect in bringing about the present trouble, but if they have it will not alter in the slightest degree my determination that for the remaining sixteen months of my term these policies shall be preserved unswervingly." Then, as if to underscore the point, he laid a wreath at the grave of Andrew Jackson, sworn enemy of the banking industry. "His memory will remain forever a precious national heritage," he said, "and his public career should be studied and assimilated by every public man who desires to be in good faith the servant of the whole people of the United States." The president arrived in Washington on the afternoon of October 23, appearing tanned and rested. "Do I look as though those Wall Street fellows were really worrying me?" he gloated. "I've got them on the run."

By then, Pierpont Morgan had taken matters in hand. First he established two committees to manage the crisis. One, consisting of himself, James Stillman of National City Bank, and Morgan's friend George Baker, president of First National Bank, would find the funds to bail out the troubled institutions. The second committee would examine the trust companies' books to determine which could be saved from insolvency and which could not. Ben Strong was a member of this group, along with Harry Davison and Morgan partner George Perkins.

At Morgan's urging, Strong and the others pored through the Knickerbocker's books, hoping to uncover enough assets to justify a loan. As he worked in the trust company's back room, Strong would occasionally lift his head and catch a glimpse of the desperate depositors lined up at the tellers' windows. "The consternation of the faces of the people in line, many of them I knew, I shall never forget," he said. But the Knickerbocker was beyond rescue, and at 2:00 p.m. on Tuesday, October 22, the bank closed for good. Police were called to clear the streets outside. Stock prices plummeted to their lowest level in nearly seven years. Morgan telephoned the secretary of the treasury, George Cortelyou, and suggested he come to New York. That evening, as he waited for the secretary's arrival, Morgan admitted to a reporter, "We are doing everything we can as fast as we can, but nothing has yet crystalized."

Late Tuesday night, Morgan, Stillman, Baker, and Perkins left to confer with Cortelyou at the Manhattan Hotel, at the corner of Forty-Second Street and Madison Avenue. At last the administration agreed to step in, with the secretary promising a fund of $6 million in gold, more if needed. And the money would be dispersed, not according to the recommendation of Roosevelt or Cortelyou or any other member of the administration, but at the discretion of Pierpont Morgan. It was a remarkable arrangement reflecting the president's respect for the financier.

At 1:00 a.m., Morgan emerged from his meeting with Cortelyou and announced to the press that a syndicate would be created to lend money to the healthy trust companies. An hour later, Ben Strong was awakened at his Connecticut home by a telephone call. He was to come to New York at once and begin inspecting the books of the Trust Company of America. By midday, he was to be in Mr. Morgan's office to make a preliminary report.

By 1:00 p.m., Strong still hadn't arrived at 23 Wall Street. But Oakleigh Thorne was there, telling Morgan that, with cash reserves of only $1.2 million and long lines of waiting depositors, the Trust Company of America must have a loan that same day. Morgan promised to help, and as Thorne was leaving, Strong finally arrived. Several trust company executives were convened in the front office, but Harry Davison and George Perkins ushered him to a back room, where Baker, Stillman, and Morgan were waiting.

Morgan fixed his gaze on him, and Strong took in the features he had seen before only in the newspapers—the thinning gray hair and drooping mustache; the huge nose, swollen and purple from rhinophyma; the flashing eyes that the photographer Edward Steichen had compared to the headlights of an onrushing locomotive. Morgan offered no pleasantries, and when he spoke, his voice was thick with the cold that refused to leave him. "Have you anyone with you who can make a report to the gentlemen in the next room? They are the presidents of the trust companies. But when

J. Pierpont Morgan.

they came into the office they had to be introduced to one another, and I don't think much can be expected from them!" He had also been appalled to learn that twenty of the directors of the Trust Company of America and the Lincoln Trust weren't even depositors at their own institutions.

Strong had brought pages of figures, but Morgan wasn't interested. He only asked, "Is the Trust Company solvent?"

The young man spoke carefully. Yes, based on his hasty examination, the Trust Company did appear to be solvent. Although the panic had wiped out its surplus cash, its assets seemed intact.

Morgan then asked if J.P. Morgan & Company and the other banks would be justified in loaning TCA the money to see it through the crisis. Strong answered that in his best opinion, yes, such a course of action would be sound.

Morgan turned to Baker and Stillman. "This, then, is the place to stop this trouble," he said. He had never met Strong before this moment, but on the endorsement of Strong's mentor, Harry Davison, he was prepared to stake tens of millions of dollars on his opinion.

At 1:45 p.m., Oakleigh Thorne and a troop of employees filed into 23 Wall Street with bags and boxes stuffed with securities that the Trust Company of America held as collateral on its loans. They dumped the certificates on a table, where Strong and Thorne sorted through them, while Morgan toted up their value with a pad and pencil. There were enough securities to justify a loan of $3 million, which Morgan, Baker, and Stillman agreed to cover.

By three o'clock, the first of the funds arrived at TCA's headquarters, where available cash had dwindled to just $180,000. The Trust Company of America had been saved, at least for the afternoon. But the crisis continued to spread. That same day, Westinghouse Electric & Manufacturing filed for bankruptcy, and the Pittsburgh Stock Exchange, where Westinghouse shares were traded, was forced to suspend trading; it would be three months before it opened again.

That night, Morgan called Baker, Stillman, and various trust company presidents to the offices of Union Trust, where he told them that the Trust Company of America would need another $10 million if it were to survive the following day. The large commercial banks and Morgan & Company were prepared to help, he said, but the solvent trust companies must also contribute. George Baker spoke up, pledging $1 million on behalf of Bankers Trust, but the others hesitated. While they deliberated, Morgan, exhausted from lack of sleep and suffering from his cold, nodded off, still gripping his ever-present cigar.

After half an hour, he abruptly awoke. Turning to Ben Strong, he asked for pencil and paper. "Gentlemen," he said, "the Bankers Trust Company has agreed to take its share. Mr. Marston, how much will the Farmers' Loan and Trust Company subscribe?" Marston also agreed to $1 million.

Morgan made his way around the table. In the end, he extracted pledges of $8.25 million. That was close enough, he allowed: The commercial banks would supply the rest. He then hurried to the Manhattan Hotel to consult again with Secretary Cortelyou, who agreed to make available another $25 million of federal funds, also to be disbursed to the banks and trust companies as Morgan saw fit. The next morning, John D. Rockefeller volunteered to contribute $10 million more.

By then, Morgan's efforts were crowding the front pages of the city's dailies. "Morgan with Bankers Plans to Halt Panic," read the headline in the *New York World*. At 10:00 a.m., as he was driven to his office, strangers cheered him on the street.

But just as one fire appeared to be under control, another flared up, this time on the floor of the stock exchange, where the problem was again a shortage of cash. The trust companies, pressed to meet their obligations, were calling in loans they had made to the brokerage houses. Unable to find buyers for their securities, the brokers couldn't pay. Now hundreds of desperate men filled Morgan's first-floor office and the street outside, begging for his help.

At 1:30 that afternoon, Ransom H. Thomas, president of the New York Stock Exchange, burst into 23 Wall Street. "Mr. Morgan, we will have to close the stock exchange," he blurted.

"What?" Morgan asked sharply. Both men understood that such an action would undermine whatever confidence remained in the nation's financial system.

Thomas repeated that he had no choice but to suspend trading before the three-o'clock end of business.

"It must not close one minute before that hour today!" Morgan roared, jabbing his finger at Thomas's chest.

By two o'clock, Morgan had gathered the presidents of New York's largest banks in his office. If they couldn't raise $25 million straightaway, he told them, fifty brokerage houses would be insolvent by the end of the afternoon. By 2:16, the bankers had committed $23.5 million. When a messenger ran to the stock exchange to deliver the news, frenzied traders tore the coat from his back. Within half an hour, $19 million of the fund had been committed.

Sitting in his office across the street, Morgan heard an ovation. Asking the reason, he was told that it was in his honor.

—◆—

The president, meanwhile, was following the crisis long distance. On Saturday, October 26, in keeping with the tradition established by Abraham Lincoln, he issued a proclamation declaring that a national day of Thanksgiving would be celebrated that year on the last Thursday in November, the 28th. The same afternoon, only after being pressed by Secretary of State Elihu Root, did he address more urgent matters and release a conciliatory statement thanking "those conservative and substantial business men who in the crisis have acted with such wisdom and public spirit. By their action they did invaluable service in checking the panic which, beginning as a matter of speculation, was threatening to destroy the confidence and credit necessary to the conduct of legitimate business."

Sunday, October 27, was the president's forty-ninth birthday. Undeterred by a hard rain, he took a brisk three-hour cross-country walk, without topcoat or umbrella, as his Secret Service detail struggled to keep pace. That evening, he conferred on the financial situation with Secretary Cortelyou. Though the emergency was not yet past, it appeared to be ebbing, and it was obvious who deserved the credit. As the *New York Evening Mail* put it, "There is some debate as to whether it was a 'Roosevelt panic' or not; but the public is pretty well agreed that what followed was a Morgan rally."

Before long, it became clear that the financier had bought only a respite in the crisis. At 4:00 p.m. on Monday, October 28, George B. McClellan Jr., mayor of New York (and son of Abraham Lincoln's general in chief), appeared at Morgan's library. The city was in desperate straits, he said. Its foreign credit had dried up, it had failed to raise a bond issue, and if it couldn't secure $30 million within the next few days, it would be forced into bankruptcy. Morgan and George Perkins met with the mayor for several hours. "We all realized the gravity of the situation," Perkins recalled. "How much fuel would be added to the flame if the credit of the City of New York should be questioned at such a moment?"

The men met again the following afternoon. While they talked, Morgan crossed to his desk and began to write. "With scarcely a hesitation," Perkins reported, "without even stopping to select a word, he covered three long sheets of paper and then after reading it over, he handed it to me and said, 'See what Messrs. Baker and Stillman think of that.'" It was a contract calling for J.P. Morgan & Company to take $30 million worth of New York City's bonds. The mayor signed the document on the spot.

In the days ahead, Morgan and his team worked around the clock to buoy the trust companies and the stock market and to ease frayed nerves. On Friday, November 1, he assembled a delegation of clergymen and asked them to plead for calm when they made their weekend sermons. But that same afternoon, all his efforts appeared to be for nothing, when it was revealed that one of New York's largest brokerage houses, Moore & Schley, was on the verge of insolvency.

The brokerage had borrowed $30 million, offering as collateral the stock of Tennessee Coal, Iron & Railroad, a large steel company based in Birmingham, Alabama. Beginning in 1905, Grant Schley had formed two syndicates and bought a major interest in the company. Then his brokerage had issued loans to the other syndicate members, with the TC&I stock serving as collateral. In turn, Schley had offered the shares to other lenders as collateral for loans they made to his firm. The syndicate had paid $130 per share, but now the stock was worth considerably less, perhaps as little as $60. On Monday, Moore & Schley's loans would be called in.

"It is very serious," Morgan warned. "If Moore and Schley go, there is no telling what the effect on Wall Street will be and on financial institutions of New York, and how many other houses will drop with it, and how many banks might be included in the consequences."

The only possible solution was for Schley and his partners to sell their stake in TC&I before the markets opened on Monday morning. And there was only one buyer large enough to even consider the proposition: United States Steel. Pierpont Morgan and a group of partners had founded the company six years before, buying out Andrew Carnegie and other producers and assembling the world's first billion-dollar corporation. Earlier in 1907, U.S. Steel had lent Tennessee Coal & Iron $1.2 million, accepting $2 million of TC&I stock as collateral. But Elbert Gary, U.S. Steel's chairman, had already declined to buy TC&I at $130 a share. Now, on the morning of Saturday, November 2, Schley indicated that he would entertain an offer for TC&I at $100. Considering the tightness of funds, his attorney, Lewis Cass Ledyard, suggested that U.S. Steel complete the sale by exchanging its gold-backed bonds for TC&I stock, so that no cash would be needed to complete the transaction.

At 2:30 on Saturday afternoon, Morgan convened a meeting of the U.S. Steel Finance Committee, whose members included Henry Frick and Elbert Gary. There was no question that the company had the resources to make the purchase. For the second and third quarters of the year, U.S. Steel had posted record earnings of nearly $90 million, and it was holding $76 million in cash. But Frick and Gary were skeptical. Not only was TC&I known for inefficiency and unprofitability, it was $4 million in debt.

But now Morgan argued that TC&I's huge mineral deposits alone were worth the asking price. With better management and some prudent investment, surely the company could be turned around. Still Frick and Gary resisted. "I have never been more concerned over a situation than I am over this," Morgan told some associates during a break in the discussion. "I think this is the most serious thing we have had to meet in this panic yet, but I cannot urge upon the Steel Corporation to take this property. I hope they will do it, but I do not think I have the right to urge them or force it upon them if I could. They must deal with it as they see fit. I have gone with it as far as I can."

Elbert Gary also worried how the Roosevelt Administration would view the acquisition. Despite his role as chairman of the world's largest corporation, Gary supported the president's efforts to regulate industry. "I think the attitude of the present administration, as frequently stated in your utterances, is exactly what this country needs," he had written the president in March. "If any company in which I am interested is wrong, it must get right. All of us must be measured by the standard of right. The application of this principle, from which as President I think you have never deviated, is building for you a monument which will be permanent and will be the lasting pride of all your friends. It is embodied in the sentiment expressed by you: A square deal for all."

The president had responded, "I wonder if you realize what a friendly and kind and, as I believe, wise, letter you have written. It pleases me very much. Let me see you whenever you come on here. With great regard, Sincerely yours, Theodore Roosevelt."

In the case of TC&I, Gary was concerned that in buying the company, his corporation, which already produced more than half the country's steel, would open itself to prosecution under the Sherman Act. The Finance Committee argued the issue for several hours, but by late afternoon, Morgan had prevailed. Frick and Gary went to Schley's office and offered $90 per share. Schley countered that he and his partners would accept nothing less than $100.

The following day, Sunday, November 3, there was a series of meetings at Morgan's library to consider the fate of the trust companies, some of which remained in peril. The boards of the Trust Company of America and the Lincoln Trust, meanwhile, conferred in adjoining rooms at the Waldorf-Astoria.

At 5:00 p.m., the Finance Committee reconvened at the library and agreed to accept Schley's price of $100 a share, exchanging $30 million in U.S. Steel bonds for $30 million in TC&I stock. But Morgan had a condition: He would rescue TC&I only if the other trust company presidents agreed to help their less stable competitors. As he had said earlier, "I can't go on being everybody's goat. I've got to stop somewhere."

At eight o'clock, the bankers broke for dinner. As Morgan walked across the lawn between the library and his house, reporters shouted out to him, asking the purpose of the conference. He and the others had gathered only to discuss the state of the economy, he assured them.

At nine o'clock, the meeting reconvened and Ben Strong arrived to report on his more thorough examination of the Trust Company of America's books. Other bankers filtered into the opulent premises. Meanwhile, conferring in the librarian's small office at the rear of the building, Morgan, Frick, and Gary finalized the purchase of Tennessee Coal & Iron. But now it was Gary's turn to raise a proviso. "Before we go ahead with this," he said, "we must consult President Roosevelt."

"But what has the President to do with it?" Morgan asked. He had never had much patience for politics or politicians, and throughout the crisis Roosevelt had been most notable by his absence.

"If we do this without consulting the administration," Gary argued, "a bill in equity might stop the sale, and in that case more harm than good would be done. He cannot say that we may or may not purchase, but we ought to know his attitude since he has a general direction of the law department of the United States."

Morgan considered. "Can you go at once?" he asked.

At ten o'clock, Gary telephoned the White House, spoke to Roosevelt's longtime secretary, William Loeb Jr., and arranged a meeting for first thing in the morning, so that any merger could be announced before the market opened and Moore & Schley's loans were called in. Frick and Gary collected their topcoats and hurried from the building. Climbing into Frick's car, they drove to Pennsylvania Station, across the Hudson in New Jersey, where they boarded a specially commissioned train consisting of a locomotive and a single Pullman car. It left at midnight.

At 1:00 a.m., Strong was finally called to the librarian's office. Closing the door behind him, he saw that this room was more intimate, with a lower ceiling, warm paneling, and a parquet floor. Mr. Morgan and the others were seated at a large wooden table. On the tabletop were a pack of playing cards and an ashtray filled with burned-down cigars.

In answer to Morgan's question, Strong said that the more detailed examination of the Trust Company of America's books confirmed their earlier opinion—the company was solvent, with $2 million in assets. Then George Perkins reported that his inspection of the Lincoln Trust books revealed that company was also sound but would need a loan of about a million dollars to pay its depositors.

By three o'clock, Strong had finished his report. Leaving the librarian's office, he crossed the marble rotunda and headed toward the great bronze doors, only to find them locked. The key, he was told, was in Mr. Morgan's vest pocket. The financier was determined that no one leave the building until affairs were settled that night. Strong went back to the cavernous West Room to wait with the others.

Eventually, Morgan emerged. As he and his associates entered, a hush fell over the other men. In the financier's hand was a document. He had prepared an agreement, he told them, detailing how much of the $25 million each of the solvent trust companies would need to advance to bail out their endangered colleagues. He set the paper on the wooden table before him. "There you are, gentlemen," he said.

When no one stepped forward, he reminded them that if this loan were not raised, "the walls of their own edifices might come crumbling down about their ears." He then summarized Strong's report, assuring them that their loan would be safe and reminding the trust companies that it behooved them "to look after their own." Some of the executives argued that their responsibility was to reserve their capital and act in the best interest of their own institutions; besides, they had no authority to proceed without consulting their boards. Morgan countered that the loan amounts were in proportion to each company's size and that he was sure their directors would ratify the decision.

Morgan handed the agreement to an attorney, who read it aloud. Then he approached his friend Ed King, president of Union Trust and chairman of the ad hoc committee of trust company presidents. Putting his hand on King's shoulder, he walked him to the table. "There's the place, King," he said, pointing to the document. "And here's the pen." Taking the gold instrument from Morgan's hand, King signed the agreement. Every one of his colleagues did the same.

At 4:45 a.m., the bronze doors were unlocked. As he prepared to leave, Lewis Cass Ledyard, the attorney who had suggested the solution to the TC&I crisis, stopped to speak to Morgan. "You look tired," Morgan told him. "Go home and get a good night's rest—but be back here at nine o'clock sharp!"

The bankers tumbled into the cold night air. A wind had kicked up, and soft clouds scudded across the sky. Milk and bakery wagons rumbled through the streets. Red-eyed and irritable, the men pulled their overcoats about them as they scurried down the steps and climbed into their waiting automobiles.

When Pierpont Morgan appeared in the courtyard, reporters charged the iron railing. "Nothing to say," Morgan told them. "No statement to give. No, not now. Nothing whatever to say." Then he went inside to get some sleep.

In the nation's capital, the *Washington Evening Star* claimed to have it "on good authority" that, in the midst of all his other activities, Pierpont Morgan had been making "several quiet visits to this city the past few nights" to hold "conferences with President Roosevelt and Secretary of the Treasury Cortelyou." But at eight o'clock that Monday morning, three hours after the weary bankers had left Morgan's library, it was not the financier but his emissaries Henry Frick and Elbert Gary who were seated in the White House anteroom. Following their all-night train journey, they had arrived at the executive mansion in a battered hansom, attracting no undue notice. Now William Loeb, Roosevelt's private secretary, was explaining that the president was having his breakfast and would see no one before ten o'clock.

"But," Gary told him, "this is a serious matter, and I think that if you will tell him just what Mr. Frick and I are here for, he will see us." Loeb was unmoved. Having worked for Mr. Roosevelt for nearly a decade, he was confident in his grasp of the president's wishes. At that moment, James R. Garfield, secretary of the interior (and son of the slain president), happened by. Frick and Gary buttonholed him, and promising to intercede on their behalf, Garfield disappeared down the corridor.

If the president did deign to speak with them, Morgan's men knew, it was far from certain how he would respond. Relations between Roosevelt and Morgan were longstanding and complex, running the gamut from eager collaboration to wary truce to open combat. How would the president interpret Morgan's current offer—as a sincere effort to resolve a national emergency, a brazen quid pro quo, or an underhanded scheme to circumvent the law? Considering his slowness in grasping the severity of the present troubles, would Roosevelt recognize the urgency of the TC&I affair at all? Perhaps Loeb was right; perhaps the president wouldn't care to interrupt his breakfast to receive two emissaries from Wall Street.

As the clock ticked away the minutes to the market opening, Gary and Frick could only sit and wait.

CHAPTER ONE

"I Intend to Be One of the Governing Class"

Saturday, September 14, 1901

THE CROWD OF SEVERAL HUNDRED PRESSED AGAINST THE ROPE LINE. IN front of them, in the center of Delaware Avenue, was stationed a squad of mounted police. One of the horses neighed, breaking the unnatural quiet. On the far curb, officers of the Fourth Signal Corps stood at attention in their full-dress uniforms. Behind the soldiers, set back from the street, rose a handsome Greek Revival home, its high pillars draped with panels of black fabric and a huge American flag.

A column of vehicles was approaching down the wide, leafy avenue. A closed carriage was the first to arrive, escorted by a handful of policemen on horseback. Scarcely before it had squeaked to a stop, a door swung open and a stocky figure burst out, dressed in a frockcoat, striped gray trousers, and a silk top hat: Vice President Roosevelt. Normally, a cheer would have arisen from the throng—"Teddy! Teddy!"—but today no voice broke the somber silence. Two other figures climbed down from the carriage, and the crowd recognized local dignitaries John R. Hazel, judge of the United States District Court, and Ansley Wilcox, progressive attorney, longtime associate of Mr. Roosevelt, and master of this fine old house. Mr. Wilcox and Judge Hazel trailed the vice president across the shaded lawn, up the wooden steps to the wide, vine-covered veranda, and past the Secret Service agents stationed at the front door.

Roosevelt confers with Senator Mark Hanna in Buffalo on the day of his inauguration.
LIBRARY OF CONGRESS

The other vehicles also stopped, and a host of officials stepped down; according to the newspaper reports, every member of the Cabinet was here in Buffalo except Secretary of State John Hay and Secretary of the Treasury Lyman Gage, who had not been able to come from Washington in time. Also in the group were Senator Chauncey Depew, Judge Albert Haight of the New York Court of Appeals, and the three physicians, Drs. Roswell Park, Matthew Mann, and Charles Stockton, who had attended President McKinley in his final days. Last to appear were several carriages and automobiles filled with newspapermen. Denied entrance to the Wilcox home, the men clustered on the sidewalk beside the Signal Corps.

Inside, the vice president entered the front hall and turned to his right. He already knew the house, having stayed there the previous week, after President McKinley had been shot by an anarchist at the Pan-American Exposition. The president had appeared to be gaining strength, and Roosevelt had left on Tuesday, September 10, to rejoin his family on a camping vacation in the Adirondacks. But by early Friday morning, McKinley's condition had worsened. An urgent telegram was dispatched, reaching the vice president on the shore of Lake Tear of the Clouds and launching him on a headlong journey back to Buffalo, via buckboard and special train.

By the time his locomotive pulled into Terrace Station, at 1:30 that afternoon, preparations were already underway for a funeral and an inauguration. The vice president had brought a clean shirt and collar but no formal dress, so Ansley Wilcox, possessed of the same stocky build, lent him a suit of clothes, including a waistcoat, black satin four-in-hand necktie, gloves, and a gold-tipped walking cane; when Wilcox's top hat proved too small, one was requisitioned from a neighbor. Leaving the Wilcox house, Roosevelt had rushed a mile up Delaware Avenue to the home of exposition president John Milburn, where President McKinley had been taken following the shooting. Finding Mrs. McKinley too distraught to receive visitors, and with the president's body undergoing an autopsy in another room, the vice president conferred with the Cabinet for a quarter-hour, then returned to the Wilcox home, which was judged a more appropriate venue for his swearing-in.

Now the vice president stood alone for a moment in the quiet of the Wilcox library. It was an intimate room, Mrs. Wilcox's favorite, with a green-tiled fireplace, floor-to-ceiling bookcases, a pair of gasoliers hanging from the ceiling, and generous windows overlooking the front porch. Roosevelt positioned himself near the large bay window on the room's south side. As the Cabinet members and other witnesses came in, President McKinley's personal secretary, George Cortelyou, arranged them in a broad arc to the right and left. Prominent friends of the Wilcoxes had also been invited, along with their older daughter, twenty-year-old Nina.

It had been decided that only three reporters would be admitted to the proceedings, from the Associated Press, the Publishers Press, and the Laflin Syndicate. But looking about the less-than-full room, the vice president told Loeb to admit the others, with the proviso that no photographs be allowed, lest the cumbersome equipment mar the dignity of the occasion. A minute later, two dozen reporters soundlessly filed in, swelling the number of observers to just over fifty.

The vice president was joined by Secretary of War Elihu Root, his longtime friend and adviser, who as senior member of the Cabinet was supervising the proceedings. Uncertain of the protocol, Root had sent an aide to the local library to study newspaper reports of Chester Arthur's swearing-in after the assassination of James Garfield, twenty years before, almost to the day. Now Roosevelt draped his arm over Root's slender shoulder, and the two conferred for several minutes. From the snatches of hushed conversation, it was understood that they were considering whether it would be more fitting to administer the oath of office before or after signing the corresponding documents, which Judge Hazel's clerk had typed out on ordinary legal cap.

Eventually it was decided that the oath should come first. The vice president stepped into the bay window, which was flooded with sunlight. The library clock struck 3:30. A sparrow was heard singing in a vine outside the front window. The vice president turned and studied it. He tapped his patent leather shoes on the floor.

In a quavering voice, Secretary Root began, "Mr. Vice-President, I—" Then he was overcome with sobs. Roosevelt tugged on the lapel of his own frockcoat, and two large tears rolled down his cheeks.

After two or three minutes, Root was able to continue. "I have been requested by all the members of the Cabinet of the late President who are present in the City of Buffalo, all except two, to request that for reasons of weight affecting the administration of the Government you should proceed to take the constitutional [oath of] office of the President of the United States."

In their tête-à-tête, Root had suggested that the new president declare his intention to uphold the programs of his popular predecessor. Now Roosevelt bowed, cleared his throat, took a step toward Root, and spoke slowly in a voice that wavered at first, then regained its usual force. "I shall take the oath at once in accord with the request of you members of the Cabinet, and in this hour of our deep and terrible national bereavement I wish to state that it shall be my aim to continue absolutely unbroken the policy of President McKinley for the peace, the prosperity and the honor of our beloved country."

Secretary Root joined the other Cabinet members, and Justice Hazel stepped into the bay window, his back to the assembly. Before the judge could begin, Attorney General Philander Knox called out, "Where is the Bible?" That morning Judge Hazel had bought one expressly for the purpose, but on the advice of his clerk, he had decided it would be presumptuous to bring it, since the vice president would surely carry a Bible of his own. But if Roosevelt had brought one on his camping trip, he hadn't thought to pack it before leaving for Buffalo, so now the party began to rummage the library shelves. When a copy couldn't be located, it was resolved to proceed without.

Then Knox announced, "You must swear him with uplifted hand."

Judge Hazel directed, "Theodore Roosevelt, hold up your right hand."

"I do," Roosevelt said, extending his arm above his head.

Speaking in a low voice, Judge Hazel began to read the oath, which his clerk had transcribed onto a sheet of parchment. He paused at the end of each phrase, and the new president repeated in a quiet, earnest tone: "I do solemnly swear . . . that I will faithfully execute . . . the office of President of the United States . . . and will, to the best of my ability . . . preserve, protect, and defend the Constitution of the United States."

"And thus I swear," Roosevelt added. Lowering his hand, he dropped his chin to his chest. Beads of sweat were visible on his forehead. Sobs could be heard in the confined space.

After a few minutes, he raised his eyes.

"Now—?" he inquired.

"Mr. President, please attach your signature," the judge answered, leading him to a small table and handing him a fountain pen. Later, his clerk, George Keating, would place the document in an envelope and post it to Secretary of State Hay in Washington via the regular U.S. Mail.

Turning to the assembly, the new president announced, "I should like to see the members of the Cabinet for a few moments." Then he added, "I should gladly shake hands with you all." Stepping into the hallway, he thanked each witness as he or she passed into the double parlor, where refreshments had been laid out.

Everyone had been moved by the simple, solemn tenor of the occasion. It occurred to their host, Ansley Wilcox, "It takes less in the way of ceremony to make a President in this country, than it does to make a King in England or any monarchy, but the significance of the event is no less great."

Senator Depew told a reporter, "I have witnessed most of the world's pageants in my time, where fleets and armies, music and cannon, wonderful ceremonials and costumes enchanted the onlookers and fired the imagination, but that all seems to me in recollection tawdry and insignificant in the presence of that little company in the library of the Wilcox house in Buffalo."

Out on Delaware Avenue, there was no hint of what was transpiring inside. The short ceremony had ended before the crowd knew it had even begun.

———

Theodore Roosevelt had not been bred for the presidency. Arriving from Holland in the 1640s, his forebear Claes Martenszen van Rosenvelt had devoted himself to farming. Later Roosevelts turned toward trade, and in the 1790s, Claes's descendant James founded the hardware company that would eventually become Roosevelt & Son, specializing in importing plate glass from England. In the next century, Theodore's grandfather Cornelius Van Schaack Roosevelt expanded the family fortune by directing the firm into real estate and banking. By the time Theodore was born, in 1858, the family was among the wealthiest in New York. Though Theodore Sr. still made the daily trip to the offices of Roosevelt & Son, it was understood that his passion lay in philanthropy, not commerce. Among the charities he had a hand in founding were the Children's Aid Society, the New York Children's Orthopaedic Hospital, and the Newsboys' Lodging House, where the young Theodore would sometimes tag along on his father's weekly visits. Theodore Sr. also pledged $1,000 toward the founding of the Metropolitan Museum of Art, and the charter for the American Museum of Natural History was signed in the parlor of the family home on East Twentieth Street. Known as "Great-heart," after the benevolent character in *The Pilgrim's Progress*, the elder Roosevelt was revered throughout the city for his generosity.

Among the other well-heeled, public-minded men in Theodore Sr.'s circle was a financier, six years his junior, named J. Pierpont Morgan. Morgan was also a charter member of the Metropolitan Museum and a trustee of the American Museum of Natural History. Both men belonged to the Union League Club, which had been founded during the Civil War to advance patriotic and civic causes, and to the Republican Reform Club, which had assumed the quixotic mission of eradicating corruption from the city's government. Lifelong Republicans, both endorsed the

G.O.P.'s reform candidate for president, Rutherford B. Hayes, in the bitter, brokered election of 1876, and Morgan's firm contributed $5,000 to the cause. In November of the following year, Theodore Sr. was among the nearly one hundred governors, senators, railroad presidents, and business leaders invited to Delmonico's restaurant for a gala dinner in honor of Pierpont's father, Junius Morgan, to recognize his decades of service to the nation's financial industry.

After his inauguration, Hayes horrified party regulars by calling for the awarding of government posts on the basis of merit rather than patronage. As a particular target for reform he singled out the New York Custom House, which by generating more revenue than all other American ports combined, presented unparalleled opportunity for graft. In October 1877, in recognition of the elder Roosevelt's reputation for probity, and in gratitude for his help in winning the nomination, Hayes named Theodore Sr. as collector of customs in New York City. Though Roosevelt had no interest in this or any other political appointment, he felt duty bound to accept, and he used the occasion as an opportunity to argue against the spoils system and on behalf of civil service reform. But after a vicious, two-month confirmation battle in the U.S. Senate, the nomination was scuttled by anti-reform senators led by New York's notorious Roscoe Conkling, whose own bid for the presidency Roosevelt had scotched with a blistering speech at the Republican convention.

By then Theodore Jr. was a sophomore at Harvard. Growing up, "Teedie" had been a delicate child, slight, pale, and "sickly," as he described himself, "nervous and timid" and prone to fevers, intestinal upsets, and debilitating asthma. When he was twelve, with his father's encouragement, he had begun to build himself up with weightlifting and boxing, and by the time he entered college, his efforts had had perceptible effect; his asthma had also abated, though sporadic attacks would continue into adulthood. Like his brother and two sisters, Theodore had been schooled mostly by private tutors, and he'd shown an intense appetite for learning, particularly in history and natural history. He may have chosen Harvard partly because of the school's preeminence in science, and he seriously considered making that his career, an ambition his father supported as long as Theodore was willing to work diligently and live within the bounds of the relatively modest remuneration.

Theodore's mother, Martha Bulloch Roosevelt, "Mittie," was born to a prominent family in Roswell, Georgia, and growing up Teedie had been captivated by her stories of antebellum life in Bulloch Hall. During the Civil War, Mittie's brothers served the Confederate cause, and though she was married and living in New York by then, she remained a southern sympathizer, even making clandestine shipments of medicine, clothing, and cash to the rebels. Rather than see her husband take up arms against her family, she prevailed on Theodore Sr. to pay for a substitute to take his place in the Army (as did Pierpont Morgan and many other affluent young men). But the senior Roosevelt aided the Union in other ways, such as establishing an allotment system whereby soldiers could send their pay home to their families. The work called for him to be away for the better part of a year, visiting camps to persuade skeptical troops to enroll in the program. But despite these efforts, he never quite threw off the shame of not having served in uniform; to Theodore, his father's avoidance of the draft would be a lasting disgrace.

Still, the boy was exceptionally close to his father. Strong, handsome, fun-loving, unpretentious despite his wealth, the elder Roosevelt was to Theodore "the best man I ever knew." "But," his son confessed, he was also "the only man of whom I was ever really afraid. . . . With great love and patience, and the most understanding sympathy and consideration, he combined insistence on discipline." Theodore gave his father cause to spank him only once, when he was four years old and bit his older sister Bamie on the arm. Running in from the backyard, Teedie hid beneath the kitchen table. When his father crawled under, Teedie darted for the stairs but was apprehended halfway up. "The punishment that ensued fit the crime," he recalled, "and I hope—and believe—that it did me good."

By the time Theodore left for college, his father had nothing but pride for his son. "As I saw the last of the train bearing you away," he wrote him, "I realized what a luxury it was to have a boy in whom I could place perfect trust and confidence." He also advised, "Take care of your morals first, your health next, and, finally, your studies." Theodore turned often to his father for advice. From Harvard he wrote, "I do not think there is a fellow in college who has a family that love him as much as you all do me, and I am sure there is no one who has a father who is also his best and most intimate friend, as you are mine."

Then on February 9, 1878, Theodore Sr., just forty-six, lost his months-long fight with bowel cancer. Theodore was devastated, calling it "the blackest day of my life." "He was everything to me," he wrote in his diary, "the one I loved dearest on earth." Like the rest of the family, Theodore believed that the strain of politics had contributed to his father's death, since his decline had coincided with the bitter public fight over the customs nomination. In his last letter to his son, Theodore Sr. had written: "The 'Machine politicians' have shown their colors. . . . I feel sorry for the country, however, as it shows the power of partisan politicians who think of nothing higher than their own interests. I fear for your future. We cannot stand so corrupt a government for any great length of time." For the rest of Theodore's life, his father would remain his principal influence and the yardstick by which he measured himself.

Two years later, Theodore graduated from Harvard magna cum laude. That fall, on October 27th, his twenty-second birthday, he married Alice Hathaway Lee, daughter of a wealthy Boston family and cousin to one of his college friends. About their first meeting, two years earlier at her family's home in Chestnut Hill, west of Boston, Theodore wrote, "I loved her as soon as I saw her sweet, fair, young face." Alice was only seventeen then, but by that Thanksgiving, he had determined he would marry her. It hadn't been an easy courtship; after proposing the following June, he'd campaigned for eight agonizing months before finally winning her acceptance.

Alice may have been one reason that Theodore had begun to rethink a career in natural history. At Harvard he had discovered, to his dismay, that the field was becoming highly specialized, and that the faculty considered biology, as he put it, "purely a science of the laboratory and the microscope." During his courtship of Alice, he began to doubt the advisability of the three years of European study that a scientific career would require, and he may have wondered whether his affluent, vivacious fiancée would be satisfied with a naturalist for a husband. In college he'd also been drawn to history and politics (beginning work on his first book, *The*

Naval War of 1812), and after graduation he enrolled in Columbia Law School, with the idea of launching a career in public service. His aim, he told a friend, was to "help the cause of better government in New York City," though he admitted, "I don't exactly know how."

But at Columbia, Roosevelt found himself repelled by what he called "legalism," the ingrained aspects of the law that favored the rich and powerful and seemed to run counter to justice. Thanks to a $125,000 inheritance from his father, and the $8,000 annual income it would generate (at a time when the average American family earned less than $400 a year), he realized, "I could afford to make earning money the secondary instead of the primary object of my career." Quitting law school, he took a shocking step that even his reform-minded father had never considered: In the fall of 1880, he joined the local Republican Association and prepared to enter electoral politics.

Other Roosevelts had served as city aldermen and state senators. Theodore's bohemian uncle Robert Roosevelt was a reforming Democratic congressman who had helped to bring down the infamous Boss Tweed. His own father had accepted the nomination as collector of customs. But no Roosevelt had ever made a career of politics, and the prevailing sentiment among his class was that no gentleman ever would. Although his immediate family supported the decision, Theodore found that "the men in the clubs of social pretension and the men of cultivated taste and easy life" considered politics a "low" calling, dominated by "saloon-keepers, horse-car conductors, and the like," who would be "rough and brutal and unpleasant." To these detractors, Roosevelt responded "that if this were so, it merely meant that the people I knew did not belong to the governing class, and that the other people did—and that I intended to be one of the governing class."

Through his work with the City Commission of Charities and Corrections, Theodore Sr. had gotten to know Jake Hess, leader of the Twenty-First District Republicans. At the club's headquarters, located in a dingy hall above a saloon, the regulars were skeptical at first of the young, dandified Roosevelt. But in time they were impressed by his energy, intelligence, and flair for words. In the fall of 1881, Hess's lieutenant Joe Murray, eager to capitalize on the clamor for reform and the glamour of the Roosevelt name, sponsored Theodore for assemblyman from the Twenty-First, which as Manhattan's wealthiest district, was considered a safe seat for Republicans in the generally Democratic city. On October 28, eleven days before the election and one day after his twenty-third birthday, Theodore was nominated on the first ballot, by a vote of 16 to 9.

His Democratic opponent was Dr. William W. Strew, machine hack, former adversary of Theodore Sr., and onetime superintendent of Blackwell's Lunatic Asylum in the city, until he was fired for incompetence. As the campaign began, the professional politicians canvassed the shops and saloons on Sixth Avenue, while candidate Roosevelt was sent to solicit the silk-stocking set along Fifth. His father's reputation had helped to win him the nomination, and now his father's friends—among them prominent attorneys Joseph Choate and Elihu Root and former U.S. attorney general William Evarts—footed his campaign expenses. The *New York Times* endorsed him, as did the *Tribune,* which judged him a "gentleman every way worthy of his parentage," with "very definite ideas of honorable and useful politics," who would "go to Albany to serve the public interest." He was "owned by no man," Theodore assured voters; "untrammeled and unpledged," he would "obey no boss and serve no clique."

On Election Day, he won by 3,502 votes to 1,974, nearly double the margin of his predecessor. He and Alice packed for Albany, where during the assembly session they rented rooms at the Delavan House, one of Albany's best hotels, and took the train to New York or Boston to spend weekends with family. In the capital, as the youngest member ever to serve in the legislature, Roosevelt launched a tornadic assault on corrupt officials and what he called "the wealthy criminal class." In his first term, battling state political boss Conkling, he shocked members of both parties by urging an investigation of New York Supreme Court justice Theodore Westbrook, who had facilitated robber baron Jay Gould's corrupt takeover of the Manhattan Elevated Railway. One day during the Westbrook controversy, Theodore was invited to lunch by a "member of a prominent law firm, an old family friend." While allowing that Theodore had "done well," the friend (according to some reports, his uncle James A. Roosevelt) suggested that it was "time to leave politics and identify . . .

with the right kind of people, the people who would always in the long run control others and obtain the real rewards which were worth having." When Theodore asked if that meant he should "yield to the ring in politics, the friend answered somewhat impatiently that [he] was entirely mistaken . . . about there being merely a political ring, of the kind of which the papers were fond of talking; that the 'ring,' if it could be called such—that is, the inner circle—included certain big business men, and the politicians, lawyers, and judges who were in alliance with and to a certain extent dependent upon them, and that the successful man had to win his success by the backing of the same forces, whether in law, business, or politics." It was an epiphany for the young politician, "the first glimpse I had of that combination between business and politics which I was in after years so often to oppose."

The campaign to impeach Westbrook was squelched by legislators under the sway of the powerful Gould, but the "Cyclone Assemblyman" had made an impression. In 1882, he ran for another one-year term, and this time his father's old acquaintance Pierpont Morgan was listed in a newspaper advertisement along with the other notables supporting his candidacy. "The undersigned, members of both parties," read the notice in the *New York Sun*, "earnestly recommend to citizens in the twenty-first assembly district to cast their vote for Theodore Roosevelt, Esq., as Assemblyman. Mr. Roosevelt's record in the last Assembly establishes the fact that he can at all times be depended on for fearless, honest, and independent action, and for the protection of the best public interests." Like Roosevelt, Morgan saw the need for reform, and in October, both were among the dozens of prominent men who were invited to the Manhattan home of businessman D. Willis James to urge honest, capable government and to endorse City Comptroller Allan Campbell for mayor.

Despite their efforts, Campbell lost to his Tammany opponent that fall. But Roosevelt was returned to Albany by a margin of more than two to one, even as the state (and his own Twenty-First District) elected a Democrat for governor—Grover Cleveland, the anti-corruption mayor of Buffalo. Though in only his sophomore year in the assembly, the hyperactive Roosevelt was voted minority leader, and during that session he collaborated with Cleveland to pass a landmark civil service law, the first

Roosevelt during his tenure as the "Cyclone Assemblyman" from Manhattan's Twenty-First District. LIBRARY OF CONGRESS

enacted by any state, which introduced a system of competitive examinations for government positions. After union president Samuel Gompers conducted him on a shocking tour of the tenement houses on New York's Lower East Side, Roosevelt also introduced a bill meant to improve the wages and working conditions of the city's impoverished cigar makers, who lived and labored in squalid, overcrowded apartments. Though he managed to force the bill through the legislature and persuaded Governor Cleveland to sign it, the law was eventually deemed unconstitutional by the State Court of Appeals, which considered it an unwarranted interference in landlords' use of their premises.

In the fall of 1883, Roosevelt was elected to a third term. While Alice, who was pregnant with their first child, remained in New York City, he once again prepared for legislative combat. With Republicans now in the majority, he expected to be chosen as speaker and was bitterly disappointed to be thwarted by the bosses of his own party. Even so, over three exhilarating terms, Roosevelt leveraged his superhuman energy and bulldog persistence to block scores of corrupt bills and to enact some important progressive reforms. During his time in the legislature, he wrote, "I worked on a very simple philosophy of government. It was that personal character and initiative are the prime requirements in political and social life."

On February 12, 1884, while at work in Albany, Roosevelt received a telegram. Back in Manhattan, Alice had given birth to a baby girl. But several hours later came another wire, with the news that both Alice and his mother, Mittie Bulloch Roosevelt, were desperately ill. Hurrying to New York and the family's elegant townhouse on West Fifty-Seventh Street, Roosevelt barely reached his mother's bedside before she died of typhoid, at 3:00 a.m. on Valentine's Day. Then, at two o'clock that afternoon, as Alice lay in Theodore's arms, she succumbed to kidney failure. It was an incomprehensible blow, even more devastating than the death of his father. In his diary he made a great black *x*. "The light has gone out of my life," he wrote.

He named the baby Alice. Then, leaving her in the care of his unmarried older sister, Anna, known as Bamie, he returned to Albany and lost himself in work for the remainder of the legislative term. In June, he was attending the Republican National Convention in Chicago, fighting for the nomination of the flinty U.S. senator from Vermont, George F. Edmunds. But on the fourth ballot the party chose the flamboyant James G. Blaine, who, as Speaker of the House and a senator from Maine, had been notorious for his unwholesome relations with the railroads and his shameless trading of votes and offices. The nomination "made me perfectly heartsick," Theodore wrote his Harvard classmate William Roscoe Thayer. To Bamie he admitted, "Of all the men presented to the convention as presidential candidates, I consider Blaine as by far the most objectionable, because his personal honesty, as well as faithfulness as a public servant, are both open to question."

Many other reform-minded Republicans refused to work for Blaine's election, and some longtime party members, including Pierpont Morgan, chose to support the Democratic candidate, Grover Cleveland, whom Roosevelt had successfully collaborated with in Albany. Despite the revelation that Cleveland had fathered a child out of wedlock, the *New York World* endorsed him, citing four reasons: "(1) He is an honest man. (2) He is an honest man. (3) He is an honest man. (4) He is an honest man." But Roosevelt, along with his close friend Henry Cabot Lodge, stood by their party and Blaine.

After Roosevelt's frequent and voluble calls for clean government, he was at pains to explain himself. To Bamie, he wrote that he felt compelled to support his party's candidate as "the free choice of the great majority of the Republican voters of the northern states." To a reporter for the *New York Times*, he stressed his autonomy: "It has always been my luck in politics, and I suppose it always will be, to offend some wing of the party—generally the machine, but sometimes the independents. I should think little of myself should I permit the independents to dictate to me any more than the machine." But perhaps his justification to the *Boston Herald* best captures the mixture of party loyalty and political expediency that influenced the decision: "I am by inheritance and by education a Republican; whatever good I have been able to accomplish in public life has been accomplished through the Republican party. I have acted with it in the past, and wish to act with it in the future." Even so, in supporting Blaine, he had alienated his fellow reformers, and now he found himself with few friends among the Republicans.

During the campaign, Roosevelt made several speeches on Blaine's behalf. But afterward, he struck out for fresh pastures. In September 1883, after spending two weeks hunting buffalo in the badlands of the Dakota Territory, he had bought a cattle ranch near what would become the town of Medora. After Cleveland's election, he boarded a train, determined to leave New York and all its memories and to embrace the rugged, restorative life of the cowboy. He wrote a friend, "I shall probably never be in politics again."

Theodore Roosevelt's career in public office may have been uncertain, but there was never any doubt that Pierpont Morgan would be a banker. His forebear Miles Morgan had arrived from Wales in 1636, becoming one of the first settlers around Springfield, Massachusetts. Miles did well in farming, and his descendant Joseph Morgan did even better, relocating to Hartford, Connecticut, and investing in hotels, railroads, canals, and cofounding the Aetna Fire Insurance Company. By the time of his death, in 1847, Joseph had amassed an estate of more than $1 million. His son Junius clerked for a merchant in Boston, worked in banking in New York and dry goods in Hartford, then relocated to Boston and became a partner in a thriving import business. In 1853, George Peabody, the preeminent American financier in Britain, offered him a partnership in his London banking house, and the following October, Junius, his wife, Juliet Pierpont Morgan, and their five children sailed for England. By then, their elder son, John Pierpont Morgan, had grown into a handsome seventeen-year-old, with dark hair, hazel eyes, a self-assured aspect, and a mischievous smile.

Like Theodore Roosevelt, Pierpont had been a sickly child, suffering from convulsions, rashes, headaches, fevers, inflammatory rheumatism, influenza, mood swings, earaches, sore throats, stiff necks, acne, and corns. Though he would mature into an imposing figure, over six feet tall, he would never throw off his childhood sense of infirmity, and throughout his life he would be prone to an array of ailments, including depression and nervous exhaustion.

Attending a succession of schools in Connecticut and Boston, Pierpont had made an impression with his rambunctiousness and his refusal

Pierpont Morgan, at about seventeen years of age.
THE PIERPONT MORGAN LIBRARY, NEW YORK

to be cowed by authority. Though he didn't prove a scholar, he did show a flair for mathematics and an early passion for business. In his father's firm, he copied correspondence and learned to keep accounts, and in an essay at Boston's English High School, he announced his ambition to find "a good situation in a store or office," for which he recognized the importance of "good character . . . as no one will want a clerk who is not strictly correct and gentlemanly in his conduct and attentive to his business." But he also gave notice that he planned "to act and think in all cases for myself."

Despite a bout of rheumatic fever that kept him out of Boston English for a full year, Pierpont graduated with his class in spring 1854, a few months before the family's move to London. He was keen to begin work, but Junius insisted that he study French and German in preparation for a career in international banking. So Pierpont enrolled first in a boarding school in Switzerland and then in the prestigious university at Göttingen, Germany. In July 1857, when Pierpont was twenty, Junius finally dispatched him to New York, where he worked as an unpaid apprentice at one of America's leading investment houses—Duncan, Sherman. Beside his other duties, Pierpont would handle orders and payments for his father's firm and report back to London on clients, competitors, and market conditions.

The economy was flourishing in the 1850s, as the expanding railroads began to knit the country into one vast market. Thanks partly to the frenzied trading in railroad shares, New York had become the center of American finance and was on its way to surpassing London as the commercial capital of the world. Fed by speculation, the securities market had boomed as well. Then in October 1857, a weakening of the grain market and a tightening of credit helped to fuel a financial crisis. Stocks plunged, railroads declared bankruptcy, and banks were shuttered, marking the start of an international depression. Junius had correctly read the warning signs, and though severely pressed, Peabody & Company managed to show a slight profit for the year. "You are commencing your business career at an eventful time," Junius wrote his son from London. "Let what you now witness make an impression not to be eradicated. In making haste to be rich how many fall, *slow & sure* should be the motto of every young man."

It was one of scores of cautionary letters, dating back to Pierpont's school days. Just as Theodore Roosevelt Sr. would counsel his son to look first after his morals, Junius strove to impress on Pierpont the importance of hard work, frugality, and above all, uncompromising integrity. "Never under any circumstances do an act which could be called in question if known to the whole world," he admonished. "Remember that there is an Eye above that is ever upon you & that for *every act—word & deed* you will one day be called to give account." In another letter he warned, "Do not let the desire of success or of accumulating induce you ever to do a single action which will cause you regret. Self approbation and a feeling that God approves will bring far greater happiness than all the wealth the world can give." Even Pierpont's digestion was not beneath parental scrutiny: "You are altogether too rapid in disposing of your meals, and then there is the great irregularity in the matter I so often spoke to you of when in New York. You may depend upon it you can have no health if you go on in this way."

Rather than becoming browbeaten or rebellious in this torrent of unsolicited advice, Pierpont internalized his father's stern perfectionism. Even as an unpaid apprentice, he began to show the brusqueness for which he would later be renowned; when the perceived failings of colleagues at Duncan, Sherman piqued his temper, his employers were compelled to remind him that "suavity and gentle bearing toward those with whom we deal goes also a long way towards making up the capital which ensures success." But Pierpont reserved his most stringent standards for himself. "When I have responsibility laid upon me," he would write his father, "I cannot throw it upon anyone else however competent the party may be. I am never satisfied until I either do everything myself or personally supervise every thing done even to an entry in the books. This I cannot help—my habit since I have been in business has been so & I cannot learn to do otherwise."

Like the young Roosevelt, Pierpont idolized his father, and his implacable drive to succeed stemmed partly from a need to impress him. For more than three decades, separated much of the year by an ocean, Pierpont and Junius would communicate principally through letters and cables. Still, the intensity of their bond would transcend physical distance.

In August 1860, as the presidential election loomed and the country edged toward civil war, Pierpont became engaged to Amelia "Memie" Sturges, the petite, dark-haired daughter of a wealthy New York businessman. During their fourteen-month engagement, Memie was plagued by a series of respiratory complaints, until by the day of the wedding, in early October, she had grown so weak that she gripped Pierpont's arm not just in affection but for support. The couple left on their European honeymoon, as planned, but in Paris, Memie was diagnosed with a particularly virulent strain of tuberculosis. They repaired first to Algiers, then to a villa outside Nice, where Memie's mother, Mary Sturges, was summoned from New York. At 8:30 on the morning of February 17, 1862, Mary was sitting with the unconscious Memie, when the patient's breathing became labored. Mrs. Sturges called for Pierpont, who raced into the sickroom just as Memie took her final breath. "Poor Pierpont knelt by her in an agony of grief," Mrs. Sturges wrote, "calling upon her only to speak to him once more." They had been married four months. Pierpont was just shy of his twenty-fifth birthday.

That September, back in New York, Pierpont joined with his cousin and close friend James J. Goodwin to form the banking firm J. Pierpont Morgan & Co. As Theodore Roosevelt had done after the death of Alice, Pierpont tried to fill every moment with work. Though his health had improved during his courtship of Memie, he was now revisited by headaches and periods of depression. Like Roosevelt, Morgan would demonstrate throughout his life a craving for power and control, but instead of being energized by his responsibilities, Pierpont would find them enervating.

Junius counseled him to be bullish on America. Once, as they were sailing home from abroad, Junius took him aside and said, "Remember, my son, that any man who is a bear on the future of this country will go broke. There may be times when things are dark and cloudy in America. ... In such times and at all times remember that the great growth of that vast country will take care of all."

Even so, Junius was more than once alarmed by some of his son's riskier speculations. In 1861, Pierpont had financed a controversial but lucrative arrangement to buy obsolete carbines from the Union army, rifle their barrels and enlarge their breeches, then sell the retooled weapons back to the government at a profit that some considered unseemly in time of war. In 1863, he'd participated in a shrewd manipulation of the gold market that netted him $66,000 but infuriated his father. To Pierpont's partner, Jim Goodwin, Junius fumed that he was "disappointed & pained to learn that P. continues his speculations on such a scale notwithstanding my repeated admonitions. . . . Is it not surprising that persons having such a snug good business—giving them without risk or trouble all the profit they ought to desire are willing thus to jeopardise every thing for the purpose of speculating to make a little more[?]" The following year, believing that his son was in need of a stabilizing influence, Junius arranged for the twenty-seven-year-old to join with Charles H. Dabney, Pierpont's former colleague from Duncan, Sherman, to form Dabney, Morgan & Co.

Also in 1864, as the third anniversary of Memie's death approached, Pierpont started a romance with Frances "Fanny" Louisa Tracy. Five years younger than Pierpont, with brown hair and blue eyes, Fanny was the daughter of successful New York lawyer Charles Tracy, who attended Morgan's church, St. George's Episcopal, located on Stuyvesant Square. Pierpont proposed in March 1865, and the couple were married on May 31, then left for an extended European honeymoon. But it wasn't long after their wedding that Pierpont and Fanny discovered fundamental differences in temperament and interests. Although they would have four children together, they would come to lead largely separate lives, as he worked long hours, socialized at exclusive clubs, and traveled to Europe either alone or with one of his daughters, and she, also prone to depression, retreated into a private world with her children as her principal companions. In time, Pierpont's name would be linked to a succession of mistresses.

The Morgans' business prospered in the years after the Civil War, with Junius in London and Pierpont in New York playing an increasingly prominent role in attracting European capital to finance America's burgeoning railroads. As his stature on Wall Street grew, Pierpont became known for his honesty, shrewdness, and preemptory style. His "brusqueness of manners have made him personally unpopular with a great many,"

Jim Goodwin wrote Junius. "*All* admit his great executive abilities—but *and I say it in all kindness*—many . . . object to his impulsiveness and manners, and *I* have not sufficient force to control him."

Among those who had difficulty getting along with Pierpont was his partner Charles Dabney. In early 1871, Dabney decided to leave the firm, and the thirty-three-year-old Morgan announced that he planned to retire permanently from business, for reasons of health. Instead, Junius arranged a new partnership with Anthony J. Drexel, whose father, Francis, had founded Drexel & Company in 1837 and built it into one of the leading banks in Philadelphia. Pierpont would manage the new firm, which would be headquartered in New York and called Drexel, Morgan & Co. But first, along with Fanny and the rest of the family, he would take a year's sabbatical in Europe.

In 1873, Drexel, Morgan moved into an elegant new building at 23 Wall Street, at the intersection of Broad, across from the stock exchange and the U.S. Subtreasury. Known as "the Corner," the six-story white marble structure boasted walnut and mahogany interiors, steam heat, two elevators, and a central staircase that was among the grandest in New York. Later, after Pierpont financed the launch of the Edison Electric Illuminating Company, the building would also be among the first lit entirely by electricity. Before long, the Corner would become the most storied business address in the world.

Also in 1873, Pierpont scored his first important coup for the new firm, when Drexel, Morgan was selected to participate in a $300-million refinancing of the government's Civil War debt. In London, Junius was furious on hearing that Pierpont had signed the agreement without his final authorization. But by now, at the age of thirty-five, Pierpont had begun to work with his father on a more equal footing. And the deal proved a turning point for the House of Morgan: Later that year, when Jay Cooke & Co., the longtime leader in federal bonds, was forced into bankruptcy, Drexel, Morgan suddenly found itself the chief player in that lucrative and prestigious market.

Cooke's bankruptcy sparked the great financial crisis known as the Panic of 1873. Four years earlier, he had underwritten $100 million worth of bonds for the Northern Pacific Railroad. Then in September

The Drexel Building, at the corner of Wall and Broad Streets. LIBRARY OF CONGRESS

1873, when the overextended line defaulted, he was unable to honor his commitments. Shocked at the failure of such a major bank, investors withdrew their money from the stock market, shares plummeted, and the exchange took the unprecedented step of suspending trading for ten days. In the ensuing six-year depression, half the nation's railroads failed, hundreds of banks and tens of thousands of businesses closed, uncounted farmers and small businessmen were ruined, and workers faced unemployment or reduced wages. Violence flared in cities including New York and Chicago and in the coalfields of Pennsylvania. In July 1877, after their wages were cut, rail workers in West Virginia initiated the Great Railroad Strike, which quickly spread nationwide; before it was quelled weeks later by militiamen and federal troops, the strike had exacted more than a hundred lives and millions of dollars in property damage, from Pittsburgh to San Francisco. Meanwhile, taking advantage of the economic turmoil, Andrew Carnegie and John D. Rockefeller bought out distressed competitors and bolstered their enormous monopolies in steel and oil.

The depression also proved profitable for Pierpont Morgan. He had taken to heart his father's unrelenting pleas for prudence, and as the economy showed signs of strain in early 1873, he had begun to call in loans, stockpile cash, and sell all except the most bankable bonds. Owing to his prudence, Drexel, Morgan showed a profit of more than $1 million for the year that the crisis began. If he had any lingering question about the advisability of caution, the Panic of 1873 eliminated all doubt. Henceforth he would deal only with the most creditworthy companies and handle the soundest securities. It would be his creed for the rest of his career.

By 1879, the country was finally pulling out of the depression. The stock market was recovering, and following a crop failure in Europe, farm prices began to improve. That year, Pierpont's business took another leap forward, when he was chosen to lead an international syndicate making the largest public stock offering to date, of shares of the New York Central Railroad. The second-largest railway in the nation (after the Pennsylvania), the New York Central was the last great line still owned by a single family. But after the death of its founder, Cornelius Vanderbilt, his son William Henry decided to sell much of his stake in the company. To avoid flooding the market, it was crucial that the stock—as many as 250,000 shares—be sold discreetly. Working through his father in London, Pierpont quietly placed much of the offering abroad. For his pains he earned $3 million in commissions. And when the news broke, Wall

Street was stunned that a transaction of such magnitude could have been accomplished with so little publicity.

As the economy recovered, railway building surged. By far the largest industry in the United States, the railroads were beset by overbuilding, enormous debt, high fixed costs, and withering competition, and they often resorted to underhanded stock manipulations and patently unfair shipping rates. Yet the lines' sheer scope, combined with their tremendous demand for capital, created an opportunity for financiers like Pierpont Morgan. In the interest of protecting their clients (the railroads' investors), bankers began to demand a central role in running the companies, including filling seats on the board of directors, hiring managers, and negotiating with other lines to ease competition. Their favored method of exacting control was the voting trust, in which shareholders agreed to transfer their stock and the corresponding voting rights, usually for a term of several years, to a few trustees handpicked by the banker.

On assuming control of a railroad, Morgan would trim its crushing debt by trading some of its bonds for new shares of preferred stock, which, owing to his reputation for both rectitude and aptitude, would sell briskly. Wherever possible, he would also negotiate with the owners of nearby lines to set shipping rates and to divide customers' business between them. In 1885, Morgan's prestige was bolstered again when he brokered an agreement between the New York Central and the Pennsylvania, resolving a rate war that threatened the future of both companies. In London, the seventy-two-year-old Junius bestowed the ultimate praise, writing Pierpont that he couldn't have handled the affair any better himself.

Pierpont proved so adept at rescuing failing lines and bringing order out of the chaotic, inefficient, and often corrupt industry that his name became synonymous with such restructurings. For Drexel, Morgan, each of the complex reorganizations could generate millions of dollars in fees and commissions. For the business community, "Morganization" represented nothing less than the salvation of the country's railroads. After Pierpont's rescue of the Reading, his father wrote to congratulate him on "a success of which you may well be proud, and of which *I* am proud for you."

The pacts between competing lines were legal at the time, and they certainly made the railroads more efficient and profitable, but they limited competition and raised prices. In 1887, Congress responded with the Interstate Commerce Act, which outlawed price-fixing and discrimination in shipping rates and established a commission to set fees that were "just and reasonable." But with limited means of enforcement and an unsympathetic Supreme Court (which from 1887 to 1905 ruled in favor of the railroads in fifteen of sixteen cases brought by the ICC), the law did little to alter the industry's methods. To the dismay of the public and the wrath of progressive politicians such as Theodore Roosevelt, Pierpont Morgan assumed unparalleled control over the nation's railroads, including major lines such as the New York Central, the Northern Pacific, the Reading, and the Erie. Eventually, he would amass a degree of personal power unprecedented in American business.

As Junius aged, Pierpont's reputation climbed, and the United States grew into the world's foremost industrial force, the balance of power within the House of Morgan inevitably shifted from London to New York. Although Pierpont's personal fortune would never match that of the Vanderbilts or the Rockefellers, he was earning close to a million dollars a year, and his and his father's wealth, taken together, had reached $30 million. As his personal worth grew, Pierpont began to live accordingly. In 1872, he purchased a country estate called Cragston, set on the Hudson River just south of West Point. In 1881, he bought a brownstone mansion at 219 Madison Avenue, on the corner of Thirty-Sixth Street. After an extensive modernization, the house became the first private home in the city fully equipped with electric light (and, to the aggravation of the neighbors, its own generating plant).

In 1882, Pierpont purchased his first yacht, the legendary *Corsair*. At 185 feet, the vessel (along with her twin, the *Stranger*) was the largest and most opulent pleasure craft ever constructed in America. In fine weather, while the rest of the family lived at Cragston, Pierpont would often sleep aboard, moored in the Hudson River near Twenty-Third Street. The *Corsair* also provided a venue for private entertaining and confidential business conferences. (The agreement between the New York Central and the Pennsylvania Railroad was brokered on the *Corsair*, as the ship cruised the Hudson River, and was dubbed "the *Corsair* Compact.") In 1890, Pierpont commissioned the even grander *Corsair II*, measuring 241 feet from bow to stern.

Now fifty-three, he still suffered from headaches and depression. His weight had grown to over two hundred pounds, and his lifelong rosacea had blossomed into rhinophyma, transforming his nose into a swollen purple protuberance. Yet when he stepped aboard the *Corsair*, he seemed able to set aside his cares and complaints, especially during excursions with several friends who called themselves the Corsair Club. Seeking further relief for body and mind, he took extended annual vacations in Europe, where he indulged his passion for collecting artwork, manuscripts, and rare books.

Pierpont's mother, Juliet, had died suddenly in February 1884, after suffering a seizure. Devoting less time to business, Junius had begun to pass much of every year in Monte Carlo. One afternoon in the spring of 1890, as he took a carriage ride outside the city, a train panicked the horses and the driver lost control. Junius was thrown from the vehicle and into a stone wall. Though he lingered for several days, he never regained consciousness, and he died on April 8, just short of his seventy-seventh birthday. The bulk of his estate, valued at $23 million, was left to his only surviving son. For the rest of his life, Pierpont would revere his father's memory, hanging portraits of him in his downtown office and his library and making large philanthropic contributions in Junius's name.

In 1895, Pierpont achieved an eminence that even his father had never attained, when he came to the rescue of the federal treasury. Since 1873, the United States had managed its currency on the gold standard, meaning that every dollar was freely convertible into an equivalent amount of that metal. If the government required more funding, it would be unable to simply print more money but would need to purchase more gold for the treasury, through borrowing if necessary. To bankers like Pierpont Morgan, the gold standard was financial bedrock, crucial to preserving the value of the dollar and reassuring foreign investors that their American holdings were on firm ground. But farmers, small business owners, and other borrowers preferred dollars backed by silver as well as gold, since expanding the monetary supply would loosen credit and allow them to repay their loans with cheaper money. And so the gold standard became a financial and regional litmus test, with wealthy, urban, largely eastern interests advocating "sound money" and less affluent, rural, generally southern and western factions arguing just as vehemently for bimetallism.

In 1890, Congress had passed the Sherman Silver Purchase Act, which required the federal government to buy more silver and to dramatically increase the amount of money in circulation. But investors, as predicted, lost confidence in the dollar, hoarded gold, and began to sell off their American bonds. Then, three years later, the bankruptcies of two major corporations, the Philadelphia & Reading Railroad and the National Cordage Company, wreaked panic in the stock market and triggered yet another depression. President Grover Cleveland convinced Congress to repeal the Silver Purchase Act, but legislators refused to authorize the sale of more gold bonds. With gold leaving the Treasury at an alarming rate, and with no authority to borrow more, the government found itself within just a few million dollars of defaulting on its debts. The country was facing, in Morgan's words, "the brink of the abyss of financial chaos."

On February 4, 1895, he hurried to Washington to see President Cleveland. Reluctant to rely on the private sector to resolve the crisis, the president at first declined to meet with him. But Morgan refused to leave the city, announcing, "I have come down to see the president, and I am going to stay here until I see him." Cleveland relented, but the following day Morgan sat wordlessly during the four-and-a-half-hour conference, as other bankers and advisors exhausted all apparent options. Finally, the president asked, "What suggestions have you to make, Mr. Morgan?" Then the financier laid out a plan as ingenious as it was audacious: He would assemble an international syndicate and loan the government up to $100 million in gold—not in bullion but in coins, which under a forgotten Civil War statute, required no authorization from Congress. The president agreed immediately, and within days, the details were arranged and the contracts signed. With Morgan's imprimatur, the bond issue, in the end amounting to $65 million, sold out in London in two hours; in New York it was bought up in twenty-two minutes.

After the government bailout, Morgan was recognized as one of the preeminent bankers not just in the United States but in the world. Though his remuneration for the rescue was a modest $300,000 in interest and fees, he had realized that the cost of not acting would have been astronomically high. (As he tersely wired a partner during the crisis, "We all have large interests dependent upon maintenance sound currency U.S.") Under his father's tutelage, he had come to think in the long term. Like his father, he believed it his duty to act in the public interest, and he took pride in contributing to the nation's prosperity, both in good times and in crisis. And he understood that in serving his country he also served himself, since his diverse enterprises could not thrive if the country did not. To his mind, the interests of J.P. Morgan & Co. (as the firm had been renamed that year) were identical to those of the nation. Not everyone agreed, of course—especially with the corollary that what was in the best interest of Pierpont Morgan was always in the best interest of the United States. To most Americans, Morgan's unquestioned dominance of Wall Street, the nation's railroads, and, increasingly its industrial corporations, would prove a source not of consolation but of consternation.

December 1886 found Theodore Roosevelt in London, not on business but an affair of the heart. In September of the year before, while visiting New York from his Dakota ranch, he had run into Edith Carow in the front hall of his sister Bamie's townhouse. As a girl Edith had been close to the Roosevelt children. She and Theodore had shared a passion for reading and natural history, and in time they had become sweethearts. But one afternoon in August 1878, while Edith was visiting the Roosevelt estate in Oyster Bay, Long Island, the couple had slipped away to the summerhouse, where they had quarreled. Neither ever divulged the nature of the argument, but family members believed that Theodore had proposed and been rebuffed. The romance abruptly ended, and not long afterward he had met Alice Lee. But now, following this chance meeting, Theodore and Edith renewed their relationship; by November 1885, a (for the time) shockingly brief twenty-one months after Alice's death, they were secretly engaged.

The following year, the Republican Party surprised Roosevelt by inviting him to run for mayor of New York. Although it was understood that the G.O.P. had little hope of prevailing that fall, he accepted the nomination as the cost of resuming his political career. Edith by then had gone to live with her sister and widowed mother in Europe, where Mrs. Carow's pension would go further, and now the couple planned a quiet wedding in London. Roosevelt was so certain of the electoral results that even before Election Day he booked passage to England for him and Bamie, under the assumed names of Mr. and Miss Merrifield. In the end, the balloting was even more lopsided than he'd feared, and he finished third in the three-way race, behind the Democrat Abram Hewitt and United Labor Party candidate Henry George. A month later, on December 2, he and Edith were married in St. George's Church, Mayfair.

After honeymooning in England and on the Continent, the newly-weds returned to the rambling shingled house that Theodore had built in Oyster Bay, Long Island, on land purchased from his uncle James. Originally planned for him and Alice, the 155-acre estate, at first called Leeholm but renamed Sagamore Hill, would be the only home that he and Edith would ever own. Together they would have a daughter and four boys, and over the course of their resilient and loving marriage, Theodore would prove the quintessential family man, savoring long walks with Edith and bouts of roughhousing with their noisy brood. "I then believed, and now believe," he would write in his autobiography, "that the greatest privilege and greatest duty for any man is to be happily married, and that no other form of success or service, for either man or woman, can be wisely accepted as a substitute or alternative."

As the newlyweds settled into Sagamore Hill, Roosevelt's ranching days were all but over. A severe drought in the summer of 1886, followed by historic blizzards that winter, had devastated cattle herds throughout the Dakota Territory. By the time he finally sold his ranch, Theodore's cowboy adventure had cost him $40,000, nearly a third of his inheritance, and now he and Edith were starting their marriage in straitened circumstances. To support them, he resumed his literary career, publishing biographies of Missouri senator Thomas Hart Benton and Founding Father

Gouverneur Morris and a memoir of his own years in the badlands, then beginning a multivolume history, *The Winning of the West*. Eventually, his published works would number nearly forty.

In 1888, Roosevelt volunteered to campaign for Benjamin Harrison and was dispatched on a whistle-stop tour of Minnesota and Michigan. After Harrison's inauguration, Roosevelt's old friend and mentor Henry Cabot Lodge prevailed on the new president to appoint Theodore to the three-member U.S. Civil Service Commission. Charged with enforcing the Pendleton Act, which replaced the spoils system with competitive examinations for civil servants, the commission had been a backwater since its resurrection in 1883. But over the course of his six-year leadership, Roosevelt was so tenacious in purging corruption, especially in the postal service, that he and the agency gained national attention. Sometimes the president seemed to regret the appointment, grousing that his commissioner "wanted to put an end to all the evil in the world between sunrise and sunset."

In 1895, New York's reforming mayor William L. Strong named Roosevelt to the city's board of police commissioners, where he attracted more controversy, and more national publicity, with his efforts to remake the notoriously corrupt department, which reportedly took in bribes of $10 million annually. Roosevelt began by ousting superintendent Thomas F. Byrnes, who had managed to set aside a personal fortune of $350,000 while drawing a salary of $2,000 a year. Then in June 1895, to deprive the police of a major source of illicit revenue, Roosevelt began to enforce the blue laws prohibiting the sale of alcohol on Sunday. The crackdown earned him more national headlines, but it proved so unpopular, particularly among the vast immigrant population, that Roosevelt found himself the most despised politician in New York. The contempt proved contagious, and that November, every Republican candidate in the city was defeated at the polls. During the campaign Roosevelt had stumped out west for William McKinley, and now he petitioned the incoming president to be appointed secretary of the navy. Although McKinley found him too impulsive for that position, he reluctantly agreed to appoint him assistant secretary, and in April 1897, the Roosevelts packed again for Washington.

For Pierpont Morgan, the choice for president in 1896 had been as obvious as the difference between gold and silver. Thanks in part to Morgan's government bailout the previous year, the United States had remained on the gold standard. But in the run-up to the Republican convention, McKinley, former governor of Ohio, had straddled the gold-versus-silver issue. Morgan was infuriated by the equivocating, and in an evening meeting on the *Corsair* with McKinley's principal adviser, wealthy businessman Mark Hanna, he extracted a promise that the candidate would come out squarely on the side of gold. In exchange, Morgan agreed to endorse the Ohioan and to raise funds for his campaign. At the convention, espousing a platform of "sound money," McKinley was nominated on the first ballot.

His Democratic opponent, former Nebraska congressman William Jennings Bryan, had built his reputation on opposing the gold standard, and during the campaign he argued eloquently for the free coinage of silver, memorably warning the money interests, "You shall not press down upon the brow of labor this crown of thorns; you shall not crucify mankind upon a cross of gold." That year the country was still suffering through the depression, and blaming incumbent president Grover Cleveland for the economic troubles, voters turned heavily toward the Republicans. Although Bryan dominated in the South and West, McKinley prevailed by more than 600,000 in the popular vote and nearly 100 in the electoral college. The day after the election, Morgan telegraphed his partner Walter Burns, reveling in the party's "glorious victory." Burns wired back, "We congratulate you most heartily & we feel you have contributed largely to the result." In the end, the McKinley campaign had received millions from business interests and the wealthy. Conservatives had won this round, but the crucial underlying issue, how to reconcile the interests of ordinary people with those of big business, would linger, propelling the progressive movement and the career of the man who would become its principal advocate, Theodore Roosevelt.

Barely a year after McKinley's inauguration, the United States was at war. Cubans had been chafing under Spanish rule for decades, and in

1895, exiled revolutionary José Martí had returned to the island to lead the fight for independence. Most Americans sympathized with the rebels, especially after newspapers published accounts of brutal Spanish reprisals, and pressure mounted on McKinley to intervene. American investors in Cuba, with interests in everything from sugar plantations to manganese mines, also pressed for intervention, as did expansionists, who saw an opportunity to seize Spanish colonies in the Caribbean and Pacific. Although new territories might open more markets to American exports, Pierpont Morgan and most of his Wall Street colleagues argued against war and the resulting loss of political and economic stability. But one of the most strident hawks was Theodore Roosevelt, who in his position as assistant secretary of the navy, spent his days preparing the U.S. fleet for action (sometimes without the knowledge of his superiors). "I rather hope that the fight will come soon," he wrote. "The clamor of the peace faction has convinced me that this country needs a war."

In January 1898, President McKinley imprudently ordered the USS *Maine* to Cuba to protect American interests. On the night of February 15, while anchored in Havana Harbor, the ship exploded and sank, taking the lives of 266 sailors. An American board of inquiry determined that the vessel had been sunk by a mine, although a more likely explanation was the accidental explosion of one of its munitions chambers. After the disaster, the call for retaliation became irresistible. On April 20, Congress passed a joint resolution declaring Cuba independent and demanding that Spain withdraw its army and navy from the island. The following day, Spain severed diplomatic relations with the United States, and on the 22nd the American Navy began a blockade. Three days later, Congress made an official declaration of war.

As Roosevelt prepared the Navy for battle, Pierpont Morgan had his eye on another pending calamity. When a contact in Washington alerted him that war was about to be declared, Morgan boarded a hansom in Manhattan and rode from store to store, buying up every box he could find of his favorite Cuban cigars, before the supply was interrupted. But Roosevelt's Navy Department was less accommodating: Commandeering Morgan's beloved *Corsair II*, it converted the yacht into a gunboat, the USS *Gloucester*, which was deployed in the blockade of Santiago Harbor.

The reimbursement was $225,000; within a month Morgan had commissioned a replacement, the *Corsair III*.

Roosevelt, meanwhile, had no intention of sitting out the war in Washington. Resigning from the Navy, he co-organized the First U.S. Volunteer Cavalry Regiment, better known as the Rough Riders, consisting mostly of bona fide cowboys from out west. Offered command, Roosevelt demurred in favor of his friend Army surgeon Leonard Wood, but after the regiment landed in Cuba and Wood was promoted out of the unit, Roosevelt assumed the colonelcy. On July 1, which he would forever after call "the great day of my life," he donned his bespoke Brooks Brothers uniform and led his troopers up the slopes of San Juan Heights through withering fire. The regiment sustained eighty-eight casualties, including fifteen killed, and Roosevelt himself was grazed in the left elbow. But by day's end, the Spanish had been routed, the Rough Riders had helped to secure the principal land victory of the war, and their colonel was a certified hero.

When his troop transport docked at Montauk, on the eastern tip of Long Island, New York's Republican bosses were waiting with an invitation that he run for governor—not out of any newfound affection for the rogue reformer but because he appeared to be the only Republican with a chance of winning that year. In October, Roosevelt began a ferocious barnstorming tour, and on November 8, he narrowly bested Augustus Van Wyck, son of another old New York family and ex-justice of the state Supreme Court. As a member of the Republican campaign committee, Pierpont Morgan had contributed $10,000 toward Roosevelt's election. But once in office, the forty-year-old "boy governor" once again showed his independence from party bosses and business interests. Leveraging his personal popularity and his warm relations with the press, he circumvented the machine politicians and shepherded through the legislature several bills attacking what he called "the combination of business with politics and with the judiciary which has done so much to enthrone privilege in the economic world."

Among them were laws to improve conditions in sweatshops and factories; taxes on public franchises such as street railways; enhancements to the educational system; measures to protect wilderness areas; and a new civil service law. As a proposed tax on mortgages was debated in the legislature, an exception was requested for Morgan's New York Central Railroad, but Roosevelt refused, despite the financier's substantial contribution to his campaign. "The exemption was of course put in at the request of Pierpont Morgan," the governor wrote a friend. "Now I like Pierpont Morgan, and his partner [Robert] Bacon is my classmate and close friend, but of course I cannot consider that in connection with this bill." Without the governor's support, the exemption died.

There was no question that Roosevelt would be reelected, and he was already being mentioned as a presidential candidate for 1904, when McKinley would be ending his second term. But after the vice president, Garret Hobart, died of a heart ailment in November 1899, New York Republicans agitated for Roosevelt to join the ticket the following year—not in hopes of advancing his career but to shunt him to a largely ceremonial position where he could do little harm. As New York's Republican boss Thomas Platt privately admitted, "I want to get rid of the bastard. I don't want him raising hell in my state any longer. I want to bury him."

Roosevelt waffled but in the end allowed himself to be drafted at the nominating convention in Philadelphia. That summer, while McKinley honored the tradition that prevented sitting presidents from actively campaigning for reelection, his running mate made a whirlwind tour through twenty-three states. The country was in an ebullient mood, with a booming economy and an easy victory in the war with Spain, and McKinley was reelected in a landslide, again over William Jennings Bryan.

Barely a week after the election, the Morgans opened their Madison Avenue home for the wedding of their eldest (and Pierpont's favorite) daughter, Louisa, who was marrying New York attorney Herbert Satterlee. The vice president–elect and Mrs. Roosevelt were among the six hundred guests who received invitations. Then on December 29, Roosevelt threw a dinner in Morgan's honor at New York's Union League Club, where both men were members. "You see," Theodore jotted in the invitation to his old friend Secretary of War Elihu Root, "it represents an effort on my part to become a conservative man, in touch with the influential classes, and I think I deserve encouragement. Hitherto I have given dinners only to professional politicians or more or less wild-eyed reformers. Now I am hard at work endeavoring to assume the Vice Presidential poise."

Nine months later, William McKinley would be dead from an assassin's bullet and Root would be wiping away tears in the library of the Wilcox home in Buffalo, as he administered to Theodore Roosevelt the oath of office of the president of the United States.

CHAPTER TWO

"I Am Afraid of Mr. Roosevelt"

ON THE MORNING OF SATURDAY, SEPTEMBER 14, 1901, AS THEODORE
Roosevelt was making his breakneck dash toward Buffalo, Pierpont Morgan arrived at 23 Wall Street at his accustomed hour. Soon afterward a
work crew appeared on the sidewalk, and unpacking bulky crates, bales of
cloth, and a sewing machine, they began to fashion long black panels and
hang them from the white marble facade. The Corner was the first building on Wall Street to be swathed in crepe, just hours after the president's
death, and a rumor began to circulate that Mr. Morgan had been notified
of the president's passing well before the general public. When asked for
a comment on the assassination, Morgan told a reporter for the *New York
World*, "President McKinley was a much-beloved man, and his death is
a great sorrow to the nation. While it was a great shock to all, I do not
think business interests will be affected. Our Government is sound and
prepared for great emergencies." The day before, after news had spread of
the president's worsening condition, the market had closed sharply lower.
Today, the usual Saturday trading had been suspended.

By the next morning, the entire financial district was shrouded in
black. And Wall Street had reason to grieve. From the day William
McKinley had taken his seat as a congressman from Ohio, in 1877, he
had been a faithful friend of business. In 1890, as chairman of the House
Ways and Means Committee, he had sponsored the so-called McKinley
Tariff, which had raised the duty on many imported goods. By protecting
domestic manufacturers from cheap foreign merchandise, the tax had
encouraged the tremendous expansion of American industry that had

begun after the Civil War, and businessmen pointed to the thousands of jobs created as a result. But while the tariff was applauded along Fifth Avenue, the reception was less enthusiastic on the Lower East Side and in farmhouses across the country. For one thing, with modern manufacturing practices reducing production costs, American companies seemed to need less protection from overseas competitors. Also, the tariff was expensive for consumers, raising prices, depending on the category of good, anywhere from 5 to 75 percent. And not just on imports—with less competition from overseas, American manufacturers could increase prices on domestic products as well. In the absence of an income tax, the federal government relied on the tariff for more than 40 percent of its revenue, but little of the manufacturers' extra profits reached the treasury, and even less ended up in workers' pay. Farm families, still the majority of Americans, fared the worst, since most of their crops weren't threatened by imports, but every time they purchased a plow blade or a yard of wool, they paid a premium.

McKinley had been elected in 1896 with the help of bankers and manufacturers, who valued his support of both the tariff and the gold standard. But then their steadfast ally had been succeeded by that ex-cowboy Theodore Roosevelt. At his swearing-in, Roosevelt had pledged to continue the policies of his predecessor, but could he be trusted? Pierpont Morgan, as an inveterate Republican, an acquaintance of Theodore Sr., and a longtime advocate of clean politics, had contributed to Roosevelt's campaigns going back to his days in the New York Assembly. Now he confessed to a journalist, "I am afraid of Mr. Roosevelt, because I don't know what he'll do." When the remark reached the new president, he shot back, "Mr. Morgan is afraid of me because he does know what I'll do."

And it was true. By the time he reached the White House, Roosevelt had given fair warning of his intentions toward business. During his years in the assembly, he had battled the corporations' corruptive influence on government, as when he had tried to force the impeachment of Judge Westbrook because of his too-cozy relationship with Jay Gould. Roosevelt had also tried to mediate between the competing interests of laborers and employers, as when he had sponsored the bill to improve the working and living conditions of New York City's thousands of cigar makers. Even so, he had to admit that during his years in the legislature he and his fellow reformers were "by no means as thoroughly awake as we ought to have been to the need of controlling big business and to the damage done by the combination of politics with big business."

By the time he'd left the Civil Service Commission, in 1895, he had come to understand that rooting out corruption was not enough, that "an even greater fight must be waged to improve economic conditions, and to secure social and industrial justice, justice as between individuals and justice as between classes." The long-standing policy of laissez-faire, he now realized, too often meant "freedom for the strong to wrong the weak." And so as governor, he had begun the problematic process of regulating the trusts, through laws to improve working conditions and to tax the state's street railways and other public franchises.

Now that Roosevelt was president, what was his plan for the corporations? In 1890, with virtual unanimity, Congress had passed the Sherman Anti-Trust Act, which declared illegal "every contract, combination in the form of trust or otherwise, or conspiracy, in restraint of trade or commerce," and made it a felony to "monopolize, or attempt to monopolize, or combine or conspire with any other person or persons, to monopolize any part of the trade or commerce among the several States." But its wording, though emphatic, proved vague, failing for instance to even define *monopoly* or *trust*, and the measure had little practical effect. Five years later, the Supreme Court eviscerated the law by ruling, in the case of *United States v. E. C. Knight Co.*, that although the American Sugar Refining Company produced 98 percent of all the refined sugar in the United States, it was not in violation of the Sherman Act because it controlled manufacturing, which was "only incidentally and indirectly" related to trade. After that, the rate of industrial conglomeration only quickened. In 1895, forty-three American companies had gone out of existence because of mergers, and the value of all combinations (as measured by capitalization, or the sum of a corporation's stock, long-term debt, and retained earnings) was $41 million. In 1899, 1,208 firms were swallowed up by mergers, and were valued at $2.26 billion.

To Pierpont Morgan and his associates, this consolidation was a mark of progress, an indication that American business was moving away from destructive competition and toward the economies of scale that would help it to surpass foreign rivals and to better the lives of all Americans. Moreover, the change was inevitable. As historian (and one-time president of the Union Pacific Railroad) Charles Francis Adams Jr. had argued before a legislative committee in the 1870s, "The principle of consolidation . . . is a necessity—a natural law of growth. . . . The modern world does its work through vast aggregations of men and capital. . . . This is a sort of latter-day manifest destiny."

Yet most Americans agreed with Theodore Roosevelt that the corporations should be regulated and that, since they operated across state borders, the task must fall to the federal government. The new president took a radical view of executive authority, believing it to be "limited only by specific restrictions and prohibitions appearing in the Constitution or imposed by the Congress under its Constitutional powers." Leveraging this power, he meant to reengineer the federal government so that he, not the Congress, would be its mainspring. And his first target would be the trusts.

But not all trusts. Like most Americans, he saw that the corporations had already become a permanent feature of the business landscape, and he welcomed the increased productivity, higher standard of living, and international competitiveness they brought. "Those who would seek to restore the days of unlimited and uncontrolled competition," he wrote, "and who believe that a panacea for our industrial and economic ills is to be found in the mere breaking up of all big corporations, simply because they are big," wanted "to dam the Mississippi, to stop its flow outright. The effort would be certain to result in failure and disaster." Instead he sought to build "levees along the Mississippi, not seeking to dam the stream, but to control it."

If a corporation prospered by inventing new products or developing more efficient processes, by treating its workers fairly, and by dealing equitably with its competitors and the public, that corporation was "behaving well." The companies he would take aim against had "sinned," by engaging in unfair competition, by limiting production and then extorting high prices from customers, by adulterating their products or making false claims for them, by abusing workers, by seeking to achieve an illegal monopoly, "or in any shape or way offending against the moral law either in connection with the public or with its employees or with its rivals."

In October, barely two weeks into the new administration, Morgan sent two of his partners to the White House to have a word with the president. One of the envoys was Robert Bacon, a classmate of Roosevelt's from Harvard. Athletic and handsome, with curly blond hair and an easy smile, Bacon had been president of the glee club, captain of the football team, heavyweight boxing champion, and sometime sparring partner of Roosevelt (who liked to say that he might have landed a punch, if only his arms had been longer—or Bacon's shorter). After college, Bacon had gone into business in Boston, and in 1894 had been tapped for a partnership at J.P. Morgan & Company. In February of the following year, when Morgan had sped to Washington to rescue the federal government from default, he had chosen his new partner to accompany him. And in 1900, when Morgan had tried to win the tax exemption for the New York Central Railroad, he had dispatched Bob Bacon to Albany to cajole then governor Roosevelt. By the time Morgan sent him to see President Roosevelt in October 1901, Bacon had become the financier's most trusted partner. (Roosevelt also had a high opinion of Bacon, later naming him assistant secretary and then secretary of state.)

Traveling with Bacon was George W. Perkins. At age fifteen, Perkins had started as an office boy at New York Life Insurance Company's Chicago office, where his father, George Sr., was a manager. The boy worked his way up

Robert Bacon, partner of Pierpont Morgan and lifelong friend of Theodore Roosevelt. LIBRARY OF CONGRESS

George Perkins, Pierpont Morgan's "secretary of state." LIBRARY OF CONGRESS

through clerk, agent, and regional manager, before being transferred, at age thirty, to the head office as a vice president. In New York, he revolutionized the sales force of four thousand men and propelled New York Life from a distant third among its competitors to the largest insurer in the nation. Taking an ever-larger role in management, he was universally recognized as the driving force behind the company's success.

In 1900, through a trustee of New York Life, the dapper, charming Perkins wrangled a private meeting with Governor Roosevelt and persuaded him to withdraw his support for a bill that would have limited the size of life insurance companies operating in the state. Roosevelt was sufficiently impressed that soon afterward he appointed Perkins chairman of the Palisades Interstate Park Commission, charged with conserving the dramatic basalt cliffs rising on the Hudson River's western shore. At the Republican National Convention in June of that year, Perkins supported Roosevelt for vice president.

Perkins had already come to Pierpont Morgan's attention through some pioneering work he had done for New York Life in the area of international securities. Then in November 1900, he was appointed a director of National City Bank. When Morgan asked the bank's president (and New York Life trustee), James Stillman, what he thought of Perkins, Stillman was full of praise. So Morgan had Bob Bacon, also a director at National City Bank, bring him by the Corner and introduce him.

They met in December 1900. Bacon had suggested that Perkins solicit a contribution toward the $125,000 he hoped to raise for the Park Commission, but as the visitor began his pitch, Morgan cut him off.

"All right, put me down for $25,000." Taken aback, Perkins asked about other men he might approach for a contribution. But Morgan told him, "I will give you the whole $125,000 if you will do something for me."

"Do something for you. What?"

"Take that desk over there." He pointed through the glass partition to the partners' room.

"I have a pretty good desk up at New York Life," Perkins answered.

"No," Morgan said. "I mean come into the firm."

Perkins asked for some time to think about it. "Certainly," Morgan told him. "Let me know tomorrow if you can."

That evening Perkins conferred with friends—including President McKinley, whom he had met years before in Ohio—and decided that, despite the fortune a partnership would bring, his ties to New York Life were just too strong (though he did use the offer to extract a raise from the company, to $75,000). But a couple of months later, Morgan invited Perkins to his home for breakfast and made a more nuanced appeal. Knowing Perkins's interest in the problem of reconciling the needs of corporations with those of workers and the broader society, Morgan presented the partnership as an opportunity to do important work that would benefit the nation. This time Perkins was swayed, and on February 27, 1901, he signed an agreement making him the eleventh partner in the House of Morgan, with $250,000 a year plus a share of the profits. In Perkins's decade at the firm, only Bob Bacon and one other partner, Charles Steele, would work as closely with Morgan. Though Perkins would play a key role in forming great industrial combinations such as United States Steel and International Harvester, he would specialize in what today we would call public relations, explaining and justifying J.P. Morgan & Company to the public, the press, and the government. As the company's principal liaison with Washington, including President Roosevelt, he would become known as Morgan's "secretary of state." (Still, as a condition of his acceptance, he insisted on maintaining his relationship with New York Life, working there part time at a reduced salary.)

During their meeting with the new president in October 1901, Perkins and Bacon urged Roosevelt to "go slow" on the trusts and not to turn a "searchlight" on them by legally requiring them to issue earnings statements. Besides, they pointed out, some corporations, including some controlled by Morgan, had already begun to release the documents voluntarily. Although the message was delivered by two friends, whom the president considered men "of the highest character ... genuine forces for good as well as men of strength and weight," he was irritated that they wanted him to "accept the publication of what some particular company chooses to publish, as a favor, instead of demanding what we think ought to be published from all corporations as a right." The emissaries spoke half-heartedly, he thought, like attorneys forced to argue a bad case by "so strong and dominant a character as Pierpont Morgan."

The following month, as Roosevelt drafted his first annual message to Congress (which in those days was presented in written form, not delivered as a speech, as the State of the Union Address is given today), he included long sections decrying the ills of the trusts and outlining the measures he proposed to rein them in. But by the time he completed the message, in early December, many of the incendiary passages had been pared at the behest of advisers, including Attorney General Philander Knox and Mark Hanna, now a U.S. senator and chairman of the Republican National Committee. In the final version, Roosevelt congratulated American business on its success and applauded its contribution to the nation's welfare. But he also argued that the "tremendous and highly complex industrial development" in recent decades had created "very serious social problems" and "real and grave evils," requiring that the corporations be "supervised and within reasonable limits controlled."

Specifically, he said, the trusts must be forced to open their records to government inspection; the federal government must regulate interstate business; a Cabinet-level position of secretary of commerce and industries should be created; and for businesses dealing directly or indirectly with the federal government, women and children must be prohibited from night work, excessive hours, and dangerous conditions. Apparently Wall Street had expected worse: After the president's message was released, the stock market climbed, until a mid-afternoon drop in Amalgamated Copper erased the gains. Various financiers were quoted in the press applauding the president's reasonable stance, but Pierpont Morgan was not among them.

It wasn't that Morgan believed in an unregulated marketplace any more than Roosevelt did. The financier had spent his life trying to impose order on the business community, advancing efficiency, stability, and decency, and rooting out chicanery, "wasteful" competition, and any uncertainty that might cause investors to tighten their purses. Like Roosevelt—and his father, Junius—Morgan viewed commerce through the prism of Victorian morality, which refracted all the confused striving and grasping into tidy bands of virtue and evil. Like Roosevelt, he believed that individuals and corporations sometimes behaved sinfully, and that they must be compelled to act honorably.

But whereas Roosevelt considered the president the natural authority to cull the sinners from the corporate saints, Morgan saw the government's role as simply supportive, such as maintaining the gold standard and the tariff and preserving the stable political and financial climate needed for business to thrive. Only other business professionals, certainly not politicians, had the expertise to police the corporations. And, he believed, businessmen possessed the moral compass. Indeed, if the politicians were such honest and able managers of the nation's finances, why had he been compelled to rescue the government from bankruptcy in 1895? Like Roosevelt, Morgan had unbounded faith in his own ability and rectitude—and he believed that he, not the president, was the best arbiter of his colleagues' conduct.

Driven by his penchant for order and efficiency, Morgan had played a central role in the conglomeration of American business, first with the railways and later with the creation of industrial corporations such as Westinghouse and American Telephone & Telegraph. In March 1901, he had announced the creation of the world's largest corporation, United States Steel.

By the time Roosevelt assumed office, steel had surpassed the railways as the nation's largest industry. And with dazzling growth had come the sort of problems plaguing the railroads, including overcapacity, speculation, and brutal competition. The titan of steel was Andrew Carnegie, the Scots immigrant who dominated the market through superior products, ruthless efficiency, and ferocious cost control, including curbs on workers' salaries. Yet in 1898, Morgan had taken the Scotsman head on, by financing the creation of Federal Steel, a holding company that had merged Illinois Steel with several other companies to become second only to Carnegie's firm. The merger was the brainchild of Elbert Gary, a onetime judge and the lead attorney for Illinois Steel, who was named the corporation's president. Over the next couple of years, Federal acquired more companies, building market share and setting the stage for the type of disruptive battle that Morgan despised. But when Gary suggested they buy Carnegie out, Morgan dismissed the idea, saying that even he could never raise the funds for a merger on such a scale.

Then on December 12, 1900, Morgan attended a banquet in New York in honor of Charles Schwab, the thirty-eight-year-old president of Carnegie Steel. In his after-dinner speech, Schwab evoked a visionary prospect for American steel, suggesting that, with more consolidation and integration, the industry could achieve even greater efficiency and come to dominate the world market. Morgan, who had been seated next to Schwab, was captivated by the young man's image of an orderly, profitable future. Not long afterward, he met with Schwab and Bob Bacon in the study of the Morgan home on Madison Avenue. Before they broke up, at 3:00 a.m., he had agreed to purchase Carnegie Steel.

By this point, Carnegie had decided to devote more time to his philanthropies, and the year before he had accepted an option of $1 million for the sale of his company, but the promoters had failed to raise the money to execute the option. He had likely approved Schwab's speech on the brilliant future of American steel, perhaps even with the idea of enticing Morgan into a buyout. But was Carnegie really prepared to step away from his life's work? Cannily, Schwab chose a round of golf to tell him of Morgan's interest. Carnegie mulled the idea overnight and the next day gave Schwab a handwritten note with his price—$480 million, including stock and bonds in the new company. Later that day, when Schwab handed Morgan the slip of paper, the financier glanced at it and told him, "I accept this price." In one blow, Carnegie had added $240 million to his personal fortune, making him the richest man in the world.

For Morgan, the merger was his most ambitious venture to date. In early March, he announced that the new company, United States Steel, would be capitalized with $1.1 billion in stock and $304 million in bonds, at a time when the federal budget ran to about $600 million. No corporation had ever been valued so highly, and in the face of such a sum, the *New York Tribune* confessed bewilderment: "A billion dollars of capital! The human mind staggers when it tries to think what it means. It cannot grasp it." The *Wall Street Journal* was prompted to wonder whether the merger might represent "the high tide of industrial capitalism." With typical acerbic wit, author Henry Adams suggested, "Pierpont Morgan is apparently trying to swallow the sun."

Folding in dozens of other companies in addition to Carnegie's— from iron mines to shipping fleets to manufacturers of finished products such as tubes and wire—Morgan's new corporation would produce more than half the nation's steel. In light of the Supreme Court's ruling in *United States v. E. C. Knight Co.*, this didn't appear to constitute restraint of trade. Even so, Elbert Gary went out of his way to stress the purity of their motives. "It is probable there will be such ownership or control as to *secure perfect and permanent harmony* in the larger lines of this industry," he admitted in his press release. "It is not intended, however, to obtain control of any line of business or to create any monopoly or trust, or in any way *antagonize* any principle or *policy of the law.*"

With J.P. Morgan & Company backing the sale, demand for U.S. Steel shares was brisk, despite complaints that the stock had been watered, that is, assigned a much higher value than the company's actual assets. Half a million shares were traded in the first two days, a million in the next week. And U.S. Steel proved phenomenally profitable at first, posting earnings of $60 million for the last nine months of 1901 and $90 million for 1902. The syndicate underwriting the sale also did extraordinarily well, taking commissions of $50 million, including a $10-million management fee for J.P. Morgan & Company. To run the new corporation, Morgan appointed Charles Schwab as president and Elbert Gary as chairman of the Executive Committee. Bob Bacon and George Perkins were made members of the Finance Committee, and Perkins played a leading role in organizing the new company. In 1902, he would introduce the nation's largest and most inclusive employee stock ownership and bonus plan, intended to encourage loyalty and reduce turnover. (And to reduce the appeal of unionizers. In summer 1901, the company had crushed a strike brought by the Amalgamated Association of Iron, Steel and Tin Workers, after the United Mine Workers and the American Federation of Labor failed to join the walkout.)

In February 1902, as Morgan was still consolidating U.S. Steel, tensions between him and Theodore Roosevelt bubbled into the open, not because of the gargantuan corporation but over a railroad holding company known as Northern Securities. Formed only the previous November, Northern Securities had grown out of Morgan's longstanding involvement with the Northern Pacific, a major but troubled railway running from Minnesota to Washington State. Morgan had helped to finance construction of the railroad in 1880, had rescued it from bankruptcy in 1883 and 1893, and had reorganized the line in 1896. The year before, he had tried to merge it with its major competitor, James J. Hill's Great Northern Railway, but after the combination had been blocked by the Minnesota Supreme Court, he and Hill had settled for a gentleman's agreement to minimize direct competition.

That was where matters stood in early May 1901, when, while vacationing in Europe, Morgan received a cable from Bob Bacon warning that the Northern Pacific had become the target of a hostile stock takeover. The instigator was Edward H. Harriman, chairman of the rival Union Pacific. Because that line, the Northern Pacific, and the Great Northern were without a terminal in the all-important hub of Chicago, Harriman and Hill had been competing to buy a midwestern railroad called the Chicago, Burlington & Quincy. In March 1901, Morgan and Hill managed to take control of the railroad. Now Harriman determined to acquire the CB&Q through the audacious backdoor maneuver of buying a controlling interest in the Northern Pacific itself.

With financing from the investment bank of Kuhn, Loeb and James Stillman's National City Bank, Harriman took advantage of Morgan's absence to quietly buy up shares of Northern Pacific. Fueled in part by the recent incorporation of U.S. Steel, the stock market was booming, and at first Bacon attributed the increased demand for NP shares to the robust market activity. But Hill became suspicious and confronted a Kuhn, Loeb partner, who brazenly invited him to join the takeover attempt. Instead, Hill alerted Bacon, who cabled Morgan over the weekend and got his authorization to purchase 150,000 additional shares of Northern Pacific.

On Monday morning, Morgan and Hill began to buy Northern Pacific stock in both New York and London. With the new demand, NP shares rose so sharply that traders started to short it—that is, to borrow shares and sell them now at the inflated price, in the belief that they could purchase them later at a lower price to fulfill their commitments. But in three days, Northern Pacific stock shot from 127½ to 1,000, and it became clear that the shorts had sold more stock in the company than had even been issued. Unless they could find shares to buy, the speculators faced bankruptcy—and the market faced a full-blown panic. But by then Morgan and Hill had acquired more than the needed majority of NP stock, and, along with Loeb, Kuhn, they agreed to part with some of their shares, at the bargain price of $150, to allow the shorts to cover and to prevent a crash (which, of course, would have proved calamitous for Morgan and associates as well). Even so, many investors were ruined in the affair, which has been called "perhaps the most controversial takeover fight in American history"; to Morgan detractors it served as an example of his egocentric despotism, while to his supporters the blame rested squarely on Harriman's raiding. As a peace offering, Morgan appointed Harriman to the board of Northern Pacific, and in November, NP merged with the Great Northern and the CB&Q to create Northern Securities. The new company issued $400 million in stock, making the company so large that Morgan "did not believe in a night or week anybody would ever be able to get control of it."

To Morgan, Northern Securities represented the culmination of decades of work consolidating the nation's railroads, putting them on a stronger financial footing, and eliminating "wasteful" competition. But operating ten thousand miles of track and enjoying a near monopoly in the Northwest, the railroad provoked widespread fear and outrage. Samuel R. Van Sant, Republican governor of Minnesota, declared it "a startling menace to the commercial welfare," and William D. Washburn, former U.S. senator from Minnesota, called it "commercial slavery," warning that "freebooters and plungers . . . are playing with great railroad properties in utter disregard of the railroads themselves and the people in the sections of the country which they traverse." Worse, there were rumors that Morgan planned to extend his rail monopoly nationwide.

On January 7, 1902, Minnesota's attorney general petitioned the U.S. Supreme Court for permission to file a complaint against Northern Securities as an illegal monopoly. But late on the afternoon of February 19, before the Court ruled, Attorney General Philander Knox announced that the administration was preparing a federal suit. "Some time ago," the statement read, "the President requested an opinion as to the legality of this merger, and I have recently given him one to the effect that, in my judgment, it violates the provision of the Sherman Act of 1890, whereupon he directed that suitable action should be taken to have the question judicially determined."

That evening, Pierpont Morgan was at home, hosting a dinner party for some business associates. The men had assembled in the elegant dining room, with its red walls, oak wainscoting, and stained-glass skylight, when Morgan was called to the telephone. Returning to the table, he was visibly shaken. That was an acquaintance at a newspaper, he told his guests, calling to inform him of the attorney general's announcement. As much as the news itself, Morgan was livid over the means of delivery. The president should have warned him, he said, and given him a chance to amend the trust, or even to disband it, to satisfy the objections. Although he and Roosevelt had their differences, he had always considered him a gentleman. He had known the man's father. He and Theodore were members of the same clubs. It was only a year ago, after his election as vice president, that Roosevelt had hosted the dinner in Morgan's honor.

But there was nothing honorable about this ambush. And it defied common sense. Given fair warning, Morgan said, he could have stepped in to shore up the market. Although Knox had waited until after the closing bell to make his announcement, tomorrow stocks were sure to fall. The whole business was another example of the terrible damage that politicians did when they involved themselves in affairs they didn't understand. As Morgan's partner in Northern Securities James Hill put it, "It really seems hard that we should be compelled to fight for our lives against the political adventurers who have never done anything but pose and draw a salary."

The next day the stock market did stumble badly. "It has been a long time, indeed, since the speculative community had suffered such a sudden and severe shock as it did this morning," reported the *Washington Times.* "In fact, Wall Street showed rather positive symptoms of actually losing its head over this news. As was to be expected, the Street took an entirely personal view of the matter, and expressions of resentment were coupled with those of surprise, and in unmeasured terms." Added the *New York Tribune*'s financial columnist Cuthbert Mills, "Wall Street has been reminded that the cautious and slow moving McKinley is no longer at the head of affairs," and "his successor is apt to give you something abruptly unpleasant over night."

The Northern Securities Company promptly released its own statement: "We do not propose to be made scapegoats of by President Roosevelt, Attorney-General Knox or anyone else. . . . There are many other instances of existing mergers which have been entirely overlooked by the President. But they will all have to join us in this fight. We won't stand the brunt alone." An unnamed officer of the corporation told a reporter, "We think President Roosevelt acted most unjustly toward us and in a most surprising way toward the Supreme Court of the United States. . . . It was just like President Roosevelt's nerve." The president hadn't waited for the Supreme Court to rule in *Minnesota v. Northern Securities Co.* because to him that case was beside the point: He wasn't interested in whether a state could sue in federal court to break up a monopoly; he wanted to establish once and for all that the federal government had the right to do so.

Morgan concluded the time had come to pay a personal call on the president. He had been invited to the White House for a state dinner in honor of Prince Henry of Prussia, who was visiting the United States to launch a schooner commissioned by his older brother, Kaiser Wilhelm. After the

Northern Securities announcement, Morgan considered boycotting the event, but now he decided to attend after all.

Morgan's train arrived on Saturday, February 22, during the worst snowstorm of the season. He made his way to the Arlington Hotel, the city's most luxurious, situated just across Lafayette Square from the White House. That evening, he and a dozen other financial and political luminaries, including William Rockefeller, Elihu Root, Mark Hanna, and Lewis Cass Ledyard, dined at the elegant Italianate mansion of Chauncey Depew, just around the corner from the Arlington, at Connecticut Avenue and H Street. As a lawyer for Cornelius Vanderbilt, Depew had helped to organize the New York Central, then had served as the railroad's president and chairman of the board. (In the summer of 1885, when Morgan had concluded the *Corsair* Compact, making peace between the New York Central and the Pennsylvania, Depew had negotiated on behalf of the NYCRR.) Depew had also been involved in Republican politics since the Civil War. In 1898, he'd been given the honor of nominating Theodore Roosevelt for governor at the state convention in Saratoga. The following year, at the age of sixty-five, he had been elected U.S. senator from New York.

During the dinner at Depew's home, the atmosphere wasn't festive but "black," reported Henry Adams, with Morgan sulking "like a child" over Northern Securities. Then, at ten o'clock, the mood turned even darker, when President Roosevelt telephoned to invite the group to the White House. It was still snowing, and the men piled into a convoy of cabs and motorcars to travel the few blocks to the mansion. Upstairs, as they chatted with the president, all studiously avoided the subject foremost on everyone's mind. An hour later, when they were leaving, a reporter asked Depew if they had discussed Northern Securities. "No," the senator said, "not a word of it. . . . It was a social call." But, the newsman wrote, "There is a strong belief in well informed circles here that some one of these men will have an interview with one or more government officials about the railway combinations before returning to New York." In case his readers didn't catch his meaning, he went on, "George W. Perkins, who saw the President Friday in regard to this matter, is identified with the banking house of J.P. Morgan & Co."

The following morning, Morgan was back at the White House, along with Chauncey Depew and Mark Hanna. Hanna had come late to public office, having been appointed to fill a vacancy in the U.S. Senate only in 1897, at the age of fifty-nine. But, like Depew, he'd been active in the Republican Party for three decades, even as he'd made a fortune as a partner in his father-in-law's coal and iron business. Recognizing William McKinley's political potential while McKinley was still a freshman in Congress, Hanna had become his close friend and adviser and had orchestrated his successful presidential campaigns in 1896 and 1900. In 1898, Hanna was elected to a full term as senator from Ohio.

One area where Hanna and McKinley differed was the subject of Theodore Roosevelt. Finding New York's young governor brash and unpredictable, Hanna had objected to putting him on the ticket in 1900. "Don't you realize," he had railed at the convention in Philadelphia, "that there's only one life between that madman and the White House?" Then, after Thomas Platt had engineered Roosevelt's nomination, Hanna had written McKinley, reminding him, "Your *duty* to the Country is to *live* for four more years from next March." After assuming the presidency, Roosevelt courted Hanna, and the senator would later play a key role in one of TR's signal achievements, the purchase of the Panama Canal. In 1903, Pierpont Morgan and others would implore him to challenge Roosevelt for the Republican nomination, but by then, in failing health, Hanna would choose to run for reelection to the Senate.

Now, arriving at the White House on the snowy morning of Sunday, February 23, 1902, Hanna, Depew, and Morgan passed under the high pediment of the North Portico, then entered the olive-drab vestibule, where Chester Arthur had installed Louis Comfort Tiffany's spectacular, red-white-and-blue stained-glass screen to keep drafts from the building's central corridor. Ascending a long, narrow staircase, they came to the second-floor landing, where a clerk was stationed behind a desk. Directly beyond was the Cabinet Room, with the long mahogany table where, according to the newspapers, the president had finally broached the Northern Securities lawsuit with his Cabinet a few days before. Turning to the left, the visitors ascended some low steps to a waiting room dominated by an Eastlake table and chairs and, at the far end, a huge fan-shaped window.

A wide white door opened, and the visitors were admitted to the president's office. Crossing the tastefully patterned carpet, they skirted a great mantel surmounted by an enormous mirror. Directly ahead, set between two large windows, was the president's desk, a big, intricately carved affair that had been constructed from the timbers of the British warship H.M.S. *Resolute* and presented to Rutherford Hayes by Queen Victoria.

Waiting with the president was Attorney General Knox. As a successful corporate lawyer in Pittsburgh, Philander Knox had counted Andrew Carnegie among his clients, and he had handled the sale of Carnegie Steel to Pierpont Morgan. In 1901 President McKinley, a friend since college days, had appointed Knox attorney general. Roosevelt had asked him to stay on, as he had the other members of McKinley's Cabinet, and in the months since, the unassuming attorney general and the boisterous president had forged an unlikely friendship. Roosevelt called Knox his "playmate."

Attorney General Philander Knox, whom Roosevelt called his "playmate." LIBRARY OF CONGRESS

As the visitors took their seats in the upholstered armchairs, Morgan, with customary directness, told the president he should have been given advance warning of the action against Northern Securities.

"That is just what we did not want to do," Roosevelt answered. To the contrary, he had hoped by his actions to "prevent violent fluctuations and disaster in the market," which would have resulted from a drawn-out period of uncertainty while the attorney general prepared his case. (Most likely, Roosevelt was also keen to avoid a public-relations counter-attack in the press and a discordant debate in his own Cabinet. Secretary of War Elihu Root, his longtime friend and mentor, was said to be particularly wounded to have been left in the dark.)

Morgan changed tack. "If we have done anything wrong," he told the president, "send your man to my man and they can fix it up." By Roosevelt's man, he presumably meant the attorney general; by his own, most likely George Perkins, his "secretary of state."

"That can't be done," the president countered. The government had announced its intention to file suit, and there would be no changing course now.

"We don't want to fix it up," Knox put in, "we want to stop it."

Morgan understood that the president meant to set a precedent with the suit. "Are you going to attack my other interests," he asked, "the Steel Trust and the others?"

"Certainly not," the president said, "unless we find out that in any case they have done something that we regard as wrong."

Morgan warned there would be disastrous consequences if the president interfered in the nation's financial affairs, but Roosevelt told him, "I am neither a bull nor a bear in Morgan stock. I am President of the United States, and am sworn to execute the law. I would proceed against you or any of your combinations as quick as I would against a striker— but not because I am opposed to either capital or labor, except as either of them may be violators of the laws of the country."

When the visitors had left, Roosevelt could scarcely contain his ire. "That is a most illuminating illustration of the Wall Street point of view," he told Knox. "Mr. Morgan could not help regarding me as a big rival operator, who either intended to ruin all his interests or else could be induced to come to an agreement to ruin none." But the president was determined that he, not Pierpont Morgan, would decide which trusts were in the public interest and which were not.

The meeting left Morgan even more infuriated than it had Roosevelt. Returning to his room at the Arlington Hotel, he wrote the president an indignant letter, which one of his attorneys intercepted before it could be sent. The next day, Morgan was sitting in the front row when the Supreme Court read its opinion in Minnesota's anti-monopoly lawsuit against Northern Securities. As expected, the Court declined to take up the case, for lack of jurisdiction, and referred it back to the court in Minnesota. But it was understood that Roosevelt had preempted the state tribunal in any event. That evening, Morgan attended the dinner for Prince Henry at the White House, and on Wednesday, the 26th, he was back in New York, hosting a luncheon at Sherry's Restaurant for the prince and more than a hundred of the city's business leaders. Toward the end of the event, as master of ceremonies, Morgan proposed four toasts. The first, with no apparent irony, was offered in honor of Theodore Roosevelt.

Despite his contretemps with the president, Morgan had cause for celebration. It wouldn't become public until mid-April, but a few days before the luncheon for Prince Henry, Morgan had concluded an agreement with Germany's two largest shipping companies, effectively dividing up the busy North Atlantic trade routes. The ten-year pact, involving the Hamburg-Amerika and North German Lloyd lines, called for the companies to cooperate on assigning routes and establishing rates and to collaborate on various joint ventures, including the acquisition of other steamship companies.

But the agreement with the Germans wasn't the half of it. In December 1900, Morgan had begun to combine several transatlantic shippers, among them the two largest American concerns, International Navigation Company and Atlantic Transport Company, and four British companies, including Frederick Leyland & Company, the busiest freight line in the North Atlantic, and White Star, the country's most luxurious passenger line. When complete, in October 1902, the new corporation would be capitalized at $170 million and would operate 136 cargo and passenger ships. But even while the negotiations were in progress, rumors of the Anglo-American combination had reached Kaiser Wilhelm, who had been bolstering Germany's navy and merchant marine to challenge Britain's mastery of the sea. Sending an emissary to New York, the Kaiser had managed to negotiate the German companies' inclusion in Morgan's trust, contributing 329 more ships to the venture but retaining greater independence than the British lines had done.

The new company, christened International Mercantile Marine, represented corporate consolidation on an unprecedented intercontinental scale. To Morgan, it was the logical extension of the dozens of railway combinations he had engineered over decades. Like the railroads, the shipping industry was capital intensive and ruthlessly competitive. American exports were thriving, and steamship companies were posting record profits. Yet only 10 percent of the country's overseas trade was shipped on American-flagged vessels. If several shipping lines could be combined under U.S. control, improving efficiency and eliminating competition, the industry could become more profitable still, even as it reduced America's reliance on foreign lines.

A bill before the Senate promised to make the steamship business even more attractive. For years, Congress had debated raising the subsidy paid to American shipping companies, to give the lines an advantage over foreign carriers, which were also subsidized by their governments. Roosevelt had called for an increase in his message to Congress, and George Perkins had gone to Washington to confer with the president on the possibility. Mark Hanna and Chauncey Depew, members of the Senate's Committee on Commerce, both supported the legislation. With the backing of eastern senators, the bill passed that chamber on March 17—but then stalled in the House, where it was amended to make foreign-built ships ineligible for the higher subsidies. Since the majority of vessels in Morgan's company had been constructed abroad, this made the issue moot from his point of view. Meeting again with George Perkins, the president said he was loath to sign the bill as revised.

On April 16, 1902, the subsidy was shelved by both houses of Congress. By then, the outlook for the shipping industry had darkened considerably since Morgan had begun assembling the International Mercantile Marine at the end of 1900. With business flourishing, steamship lines had rushed to build more vessels, but over the past year demand for shipping had fallen, due to factors ranging from an economic depression in Europe to a failure of the American corn crop. In 1901, profits for both cargo and passenger carriers were half of what they had been the year before. Under the agreement with his foreign partners, Morgan still had time to withdraw from the combination. But rather than sacrifice the considerable effort and the almost $4 million already invested, he decided to proceed. On April 19, associates in London released news of the merger to the press.

Perhaps thinking of the pending Northern Securities suit, George Perkins took pains to emphasize the constituent companies' relative independence. "The proposed company will be essentially like the United States Steel Corporation," he told reporters, "in that it will bring together under a central control several independent companies, which will in no wise lose their identities. The different ships will sail under the same flags, and will receive the same subsidies as at present." In June, Perkins spoke to the president and various Cabinet members, looking for reassurance that IMM wouldn't be prosecuted under the Sherman Law. But he needn't have worried about the administration's reaction. Secretary of State John Hay and Secretary of War Elihu Root were among the Cabinet members expressing enthusiasm, as did the president himself. To Roosevelt, the shipping trust was one of the "good" ones, serving the national interest by encouraging exports, keeping the profits for shipping those goods in the United States, and employing more American shipbuilders and sailors. The press and the public were also eager to expand the nation's merchant marine. At last, the country had found a trust it could rally behind.

A decidedly dimmer view prevailed in Great Britain. "John Bull does not like these foreign raids upon the world's shipping," reported the *New York Tribune*, "nor these continuous displays of American megalomania in organizations and combinations affecting European industries and interests, but he does not know how he can prevent the operations of the tremendous money power, especially when directed by master minds in finance."

It also rankled that, while the British lines were acquired outright, the German companies would be folded in as partners. Despite Perkins's guarantee, the British worried about losing control over the fleets on which their empire depended. And they resented the power of the American moneymen, as personified by Pierpont Morgan. "The [London] *Daily News* says that when matters have gone a little further," the *New York Sun* reported, "a man in England will be able to sail in a Morgan liner to the United States, cross them on a Morgan railway, and travel again by Morgan shipping to Australia or the China seas. Mr. Morgan is the modern Puck, who will one day set a girdle about the earth, and will take a profit from it, which is more than Oberon's imp could manage." On the streets of London, peddlers were offering a "License to Stay on Earth," signed *J. Pierpont Morgan.*

Morgan passed that spring and summer in Europe, devoting much of his time to appeasing the British. Eventually, Whitehall conceded that they had no legal means of stopping the merger, and in September, the government gave its blessing, having won several concessions: British ships entering the trust would retain their own flags and sailors; half the combination's new tonnage would be constructed in Britain; in case of national emergency, the Admiralty would maintain its power to commandeer British ships; and American freight would not be carried in the trust's ships at a discounted rate.

By October, when IMM's papers of incorporation were finally filed, England was feeling more sanguine about the combination. Vice Admiral Lord Charles Beresford professed to be "satisfied that it will be a very good thing. . . . I have come to the conclusion that the interests of our both countries are the same, and that the prosperity of England means the prosperity of America, and that of America means prosperity in England. . . . We need to be waked up, and this is one of the things which will help to awaken us." Even so, as an incentive to keep the Cunard Line out of Morgan's combination, the British government agreed to increase its subsidy to the company, including a low-interest loan and an annual payment toward the construction of a pair of passenger ships that would be the grandest ever built, the *Mauritania* and the *Lusitania.* To compete with Cunard, Morgan's White Star Line, though it could ill afford the expense, felt compelled to build three huge new ships of its own, the *Britannic,* the *Olympic,* and the *Titanic.*

Even with the acquiescence of the British and the support of the Americans, International Mercantile Marine would wreck on the shoals of changing business conditions. In the year after the merger, only the White Star Line was profitable. Partly because of the loose organizational structure that George Perkins had touted to the press, the combined company was never able to find the hoped-for efficiencies in its operations. IMM bonds sold poorly, and its stock price dropped. Morgan had made his reputation on dry land, with railroad reorganizations, but it seemed, in the words of the *Wall Street Journal,* "The ocean was too big for the old man." In the end, the House of Morgan would post a loss of $2 to $3 million on the venture. And on the foggy night of April 14, 1912, the North Atlantic would demonstrate the malevolence of which it was capable, claiming the White Star's luxury liner *Titanic,* as it made its maiden voyage from Southampton to New York. Several prominent business leaders died in the disaster, including John Jacob Astor IV and Benjamin Guggenheim. Pierpont Morgan had reportedly reserved a private suite but then canceled it, deciding to extend his stay in the South of France.

In September 1902, as Morgan was signing his agreement with the British government, Theodore Roosevelt was completing his first year in office. Launching an extraordinary, activist presidency, he had stolen a march on the business community, especially its most visible and powerful exemplar, Pierpont Morgan. Morgan had supported Roosevelt for two decades, ever since "the Cyclone Assemblyman" had opened his fight against corruption in the New York legislature. But in the interim, their dealings had been fraught. During his brief tenure as governor, as he had tried to balance the needs of business with those of workers and consumers, Roosevelt had alienated the commercial interests that had helped to elect him. Then, just as he seemed to be safely sidetracked into the vice presidency, he had succeeded to the most powerful office in the land. And, though he had neither financial expertise nor electoral mandate, he had engaged the nation's business leaders with the same abandon he'd shown against the Spanish on San Juan Heights. On occasion, the president could prove an ally, Morgan had to admit, as when he had come out in favor of the shipping subsidy bill. But at other times he was erratic and wanton, as in his ambush of Northern Securities. It would be two years until the Supreme Court ruled in that case. Before that, the great trust builder and the would-be trustbuster would confront a national crisis threatening to claim hundreds of lives and to overturn the social and political order.

CHAPTER THREE

"No Power or Duty"

Saturday, September 24, 1902

"I FEEL BETTER THAN I LOOK," THEODORE ROOSEVELT ASSURED THE policemen and railroad workers gathered around him. He was seated in a caned wheelchair, both legs elevated, with his left foot sporting a bedroom slipper. As he was trundled out the baggage entrance of Washington's Sixth Street Station, the crowd across the street raised a cheer. He smiled and lifted his hat.

Mrs. Roosevelt was waiting in a carriage. After receiving the telephone call, she and a maid had boarded the 10:22 Congressional Limited from Jersey City, arriving in Washington at 3:40 in the afternoon. At six o'clock, the first lady was back at the station to meet the presidential special from Indianapolis. A wicker chair was carried out to the platform for her, and during the half-hour wait she spoke softly with Surgeon General Presley Rixey; another physician, John Urie; Secretary of the Navy William Moody; and Secretary of the Interior Ethan Allen Hitchcock.

The president's train steamed in, and she caught a glimpse of him seated at a window, propped on pillows, his hands clasped behind his head. The moment the locomotive hissed to a stop, she climbed aboard. Then, several minutes later, satisfied of his well-being, she emerged with his personal secretary, George Cortelyou, and went to the carriage to wait. Before long, Drs. Rixey and Urie, joined by George Lung, a physician who had been traveling with the president, lifted him down the steps, settled him in the wheelchair, and conducted him to the end of the platform and the conclusion of his truncated but eventful journey.

A month before, the president had left Oyster Bay, where he, Edith, and the children were planning to spend the summer, to begin a tour of New England on behalf of Republican candidates in the midterm elections. After making some forty stops throughout Connecticut, Massachusetts, Rhode Island, New Hampshire, Vermont, and Maine, he was appearing in Pittsfield on Wednesday, September 3, on the final leg of his journey. He addressed a crowd of several thousand at a city park, then stopped briefly at the home of eighty-five-year-old ex-senator Henry L. Dawes. At 9:30 a.m. the president's landau, pulled by four gray horses and accompanied by several other carriages and a cavalry escort, was traveling on South Street, toward the country club, where a crowd was waiting. Riding with the president in the open carriage were George Cortelyou, Massachusetts governor W. Murray Crane, and William Craig, chief of the Secret Service detail, who happened to be a favorite of the Roosevelt children. They were running late, and the driver, D. J. Pratt of nearby Dalton, moved smartly down Howard's Hill, skirting the tracks of the Pittsfield and Lenox Street Railway.

At the foot of the slope, the tracks veered to the left. Pratt pulled the carriage to the right to cross them, but he didn't see trolley no. 29 coming up fast behind him. Craig spun in his seat and cried, "O, my God!" The streetcar struck the carriage in the right-front hub, knocking it thirty feet and hurling the passengers to the ground. Craig fell under the trolley's wheels and was killed instantly. The others were pitched onto a mound of dirt that had collected beside the roadway.

The president's lip was cut, his forehead and right cheek were bruised, and a painful lump was rising on his left shin, midway between knee and ankle. His glasses were thrown from his face; his frockcoat was torn at the elbow. Collecting himself, he began to see to the other passengers. Only Governor Crane appeared uninjured. Pratt had a fractured skull, and Cortelyou was bleeding from the nose and forehead. Rushing to his secretary's side, the president stanched the blood with a handkerchief. Then he dropped to one knee beside Craig's mangled body. "Too bad, too bad," he murmured. "Poor Craig. How my children will feel." He turned on the motorman and, in a shaking voice, spat out, "If your car got out of control, if it got away from you, why, then, that is one thing. But if it is anything else, this is a damnable outrage!" The man, Euclid Madden, was arrested and charged with manslaughter.

Craig's body was carried to a nearby home, and Pratt was taken to the House of Mercy. The president's head was bandaged, and, finding seats in the other carriages, he, Governor Crane, and George Cortelyou continued on their journey. The rest of the day's speeches were canceled, and by 8:30 that evening the presidential yacht, the *Sylph*, had crossed Long Island Sound and slipped into Oyster Bay.

The president was adamant that his injuries not curtail his schedule, and two days later, on the morning of September 5, he began a five-day swing through Virginia, West Virginia, Tennessee, and North Carolina. Then on the 19th, after a brief rest, he began a more ambitious tour that was to take him from Ohio as far west as South Dakota. Traveling with him were George Cortelyou, his assistant secretary William Loeb, several Secret Service agents, throat specialist James Richardson, and Dr. Lung. Although the bruises on the president's face had healed, his leg grew more swollen and painful. After only a few days, Dr. Lung, perhaps recalling the blood poisoning that had killed President McKinley after his physicians had pronounced him out of danger, urged him to cancel the tour. Finally, on September 23, following a luncheon for war veterans in Indianapolis, the president was in such pain that he agreed to be taken to St. Vincent's Hospital in that city. A local surgeon, John Oliver, numbed the leg with ethyl chloride. Then, as the president made small talk with doctors, and betrayed the occasional grimace, a needle was inserted into the abscess and two ounces of clear fluid were drawn off. The procedure lasted only five minutes, but to avoid complications the physicians prescribed ten days of bed rest. At 7:50 that evening, the presidential special departed, not for points west but back to Washington.

The president wasn't returning to the White House, where a long-overdue remodeling had begun in June. The repairs were scheduled to be finished by October 1, but doctors had cautioned the family to stay away for at least another month, to give the unwholesome dampness from the new plaster time to dry. For the interim, a temporary White House had been rented at 22 Lafayette Square, across the way from the Executive Mansion. Located in one of the city's most fashionable neighborhoods, near the homes of Secretary of State John Hay and senators Chauncey Depew and Mark Hanna, the house had belonged to late representative (and coal, iron, and railroad magnate) William Lawrence Scott of Pennsylvania and was now owned by his daughter, prominent socialite Mary Scott Townsend. Mrs. Townsend had made extensive renovations in 1895, transforming it into what a newspaper judged "one of the most handsomely appointed houses in the city," but not long afterward she and her husband, Richard H. Townsend, had relocated to the even more elegant Dupont Circle.

The government had taken a four-month lease on the Lafayette Square house. Though it was rented furnished, some items were carried over from the Executive Mansion, including the large mahogany Cabinet table, now erected in the dining room, which would also serve as the president's office. The main parlor had been converted into a reception room for visitors, and the second parlor would serve as an office for George Cortelyou.

Four years younger than the president, Cortelyou was also descended from an old New Amsterdam family. After training as a stenographer and a lawyer, he had worked his way up through the Customs Service and the Post Office, until 1895, when President Cleveland, acting on the recommendation of Postmaster General Wilson Bissell, had hired him as a stenographer. Five years later, McKinley had promoted him to secretary, and on taking office Roosevelt had asked him to stay on. In time, Cortelyou would become one of Roosevelt's most trusted advisers, serving as secretary of commerce and labor, postmaster general, secretary of the treasury, and chairman of the Republican National Committee. During his tenure as the president's secretary, he would introduce a number of innovations in the White House, including briefings for newsmen, the distribution of press releases, and the opening of the building's first pressroom.

On the second floor of the Townsend house, one large bedroom facing the square was furnished as a sitting room, while the other two

George Cortelyou in his office at the White House. LIBRARY OF CONGRESS

were kept as overnight accommodations. The president had spent only a few nights there in June, before joining the family in Oyster Bay. Prior to this afternoon, Mrs. Roosevelt had never seen the house at all. As soon as she satisfied herself that Theodore was comfortable, she would return to Long Island and the children. The president was to have joined them, but now it seemed he would be staying in Washington.

The change in plans was partly to avoid further travel on his injured leg. But there was also urgent work waiting in the capital, a crisis that had helped to prompt his campaigning that fall. In May, nearly 150,000 coal miners in eastern Pennsylvania had gone on strike, in one of the largest labor walkouts in the nation's history. The country was looking to the party in power to end the trouble, and if the Republicans couldn't resolve the dispute by Election Day, it could cost them their majority in Congress.

But more than votes were at stake. Over the past half century, America's demand for coal had increased nearly forty-fold, until by 1900 the country depended on the fuel for about 70 percent of its energy needs. America ran on coal, to heat its homes, cook its food, and feed its factories and railroads. As Ralph Waldo Emerson wrote, "Every basket [of coal] is power and civilization. For coal is a portable climate. It carries the heat of the tropics to Labrador and the polar circle; . . . and with its comfort brings its industrial power." A coal famine would idle factories and put employees out of work. And if the strike weren't resolved by winter, poor families in northeastern cities would begin to freeze to death in their tenements, where the kitchen stove was generally the only source of heat. When that happened, it was already predicted, the country would be shaken by the worst social upheaval in its history.

By the turn of the century, Pennsylvania was mining more than eighty million tons of coal a year, almost twice as much as the next ten coal-producing states combined. But conditions were hard for the largely immigrant miners, who lived in squalid company housing, were forced to buy their food and other supplies from company stores, and often found themselves trapped in permanent debt to their employers. Boys as young as eight worked sixty hours a week at the breakers, where they perched above a wooden frame and picked out impurities such as slate while the coal rushed beneath them on a conveyor belt. The air was thick with coal dust, their fingers were bloodied on the sharp stones, and if a hand or foot became caught in the conveyor, they could lose a limb or be crushed to death.

Conditions were even worse deep underground, where men and boys faced brutal, hazardous conditions. Typically working in an assigned "room," the miner and his helper would stand in groundwater, surrounded by rats, breathing coal dust, and enveloped in an unearthly darkness broken only by the light from their headlamps. Using hand picks, they would dig an undercut at the bottom of the vertical coal seam, then drill holes, fill them with blasting powder, and detonate it. Several tons of coal would be loosed, which they would then load into mine cars using shovels.

The opportunities for disaster were legion, including ignitions of methane or coal dust, cave-ins, floods, and asphyxiation from gases such as carbon dioxide and carbon monoxide. The country had seen more than a hundred coal mine disasters in the past twenty-five years, and across the nation more than fifteen hundred coal miners lost their lives annually. The worst catastrophe to date occurred on the morning of May 1, 1900, in Scofield, Utah, when at least two hundred workers were killed in an explosion at the Winter Quarters Mine.

Desperate to improve wages and working conditions and to gain recognition of their unions, miners called dozens of strikes every year. In December 1874, after their pay was reduced during a nationwide depression, ten thousand Pennsylvania miners walked out in a violent, five-month strike that culminated with twenty men, accused as members of the Irish secret society called the Molly Maguires, being hanged for murder. The strike was crushed, the miners' wages cut, their union demolished. Then in 1897, in the midst of another economic downturn, wages were cut to near-starvation level and a walkout was called by the seven-year-old United Mine Workers of America. During a demonstration in Latimer, Pennsylvania, sheriff's deputies shot nineteen unarmed miners to death and wounded scores of others; although the lawmen were tried for murder, all were acquitted. But in the aftermath of the strike, many mine owners reluctantly signed a contract with the UMW, and membership skyrocketed from ten thousand to more than a hundred thousand.

One of the union's charter members was a young miner from Braidwood, Illinois, named John Mitchell. The son of Irish immigrants, Mitchell had lost his mother at age three. When he was six, his father, a coal miner, was killed by a runaway team of horses. To support his stepmother and siblings, Mitchell went to work early as a breaker boy but managed to attend night school and later to study law and economics. Rising through various leadership positions at the UMW, he was named the union's president in 1898, at the age of twenty-eight.

In August 1900, Mitchell asked further concessions from owners. When they rebuffed him, he offered to submit the union's demands to binding arbitration. When they still refused to negotiate, Mitchell declared a strike, which started on September 17. This time the six-week walkout ended in victory for the union, after Pierpont Morgan and Mark Hanna convinced the mine presidents that labor trouble could undermine the McKinley-Roosevelt ticket and result in the election of the populist William Jennings Bryan. And so the miners won their first

John Mitchell, president of the United Mine Workers of America. LIBRARY OF CONGRESS

pay increase in twenty years, a 10-percent raise that brought their average wage to $560 annually.

But the mine owners had refused to recognize the UMW, and the strike had done nothing to curtail child labor or improve living and working conditions. On March 18, 1902, the miners authorized a new strike, demanding another 10-percent raise, an eight-hour workday, a fairer system for weighing coal (since the miners were paid by the ton), and recognition of their union. Rather than calling an immediate walk-out, Mitchell offered to submit the dispute to arbitration by a committee of three clergymen. The operators refused, with their spokesman, George Baer, reminding the workers, "Anthracite mining is a business, and not a religious, sentimental, or academic proposition." Roosevelt enlisted Mark Hanna again, and the senator telegraphed Pierpont Morgan asking him to prod the mine owners to another concession. But, still prickling at their earlier defeat, determined not to be used again as political pawns, and filled with antipathy for Mitchell, this time the owners would not bargain. Finally, on May 12, after a meeting with the mine presidents produced no movement, Mitchell called the strike.

As spring turned to summer, the operators still refused to negotiate, calculating that a coal famine and anticipated bloodshed at the mines would force the president to call in federal troops and break the strike, as Grover Cleveland had done during the Pullman walkout in 1894. But the soft-spoken, dignified Mitchell preached only reason and nonviolence. "The worst enemy the organization has is the miner who violates the law," he warned his members. "If this strike cannot be won by honorable means, I say a thousand times it is better to lose it. . . . If you resort to unlawful means, the strike will be broken."

Mitchell's adversary, George Baer, was also born in coal country, in Somerset County, Pennsylvania, but the son of a comfortable farmer, not an impoverished miner. After attending local academies and Franklin and Marshall College, he edited a newspaper, studied law, and during the Civil War, served as commander of a volunteer company that fought at Antietam, Fredericksburg, and Chancellorsville. Afterward he became a prominent lawyer in Reading, Pennsylvania, where his clients included the powerful Philadelphia & Reading Railroad. Like the other railways in the area, the Reading owned a coal mine. Across the region, 80 percent of the coal was dug by the railways that carried it to market—and nearly all those lines were under the control of Pierpont Morgan. In 1901, Morgan named Baer president of the Philadelphia & Reading Railroad and the Philadelphia & Reading Coal and Iron Company, one of the mines now being struck.

As de facto leader of the mine presidents, the sixty-year-old Baer was more combative than Mitchell, and less sensitive to how his pronouncements would appear in print. Most of the miners were recent

Catholic immigrants from Eastern Europe, recruited en masse to keep wages low. "[These men] don't suffer," Baer claimed. "Why, they can't even speak English." When a citizen from Wilkes-Barre wrote arguing that the owners had a moral responsibility to negotiate with the workers, Baer loftily assured him, "The rights and interests of the laboring man will be protected and cared for—not by the labor agitators—but by the Christian men to whom God in his infinite wisdom has given the control of the property interests of the country." Since the Molly Maguire troubles of the 1870s, public sentiment typically ran against strikers, especially if they were immigrants, but after Baer's claim to divine right was published, popular opinion surged in favor of the miners. As the *New York Times* put it, "A good many people think they superintend the earth, but not many have the egregious vanity to describe themselves as its managing directors."

The fifty-five million tons of coal that were dug every year in northeast Pennsylvania was of a type called anthracite, the hardest, cleanest-burning, but rarest variety. Worldwide, anthracite accounts for just 1 percent of coal deposits, and in the United States virtually all of it is found in this five-hundred-square-mile area, where it was produced, some three hundred million years ago, by the same tectonic forces that created the Appalachian Mountains. As the west coasts of what is now Europe and Africa collided with the east coast of present-day North America, forming the supercontinent called Pangea, the Appalachians rose up in a fifteen-hundred-mile ridge stretching from today's Newfoundland to Alabama. Subjected to intense geologic pressure, the underground remains of decayed plants were converted, over millions of years, into the carbon-rich rock we call coal. Since the eastern, leading edge of the fault was subjected to more heat and pressure than the western, trailing edge, the coal located there metamorphosed into the particularly pure form known as anthracite.

Although anthracite releases less smoke than bituminous, or "soft" coal, it is more difficult to ignite. Accordingly, anthracite was slow to catch on when it was first marketed in the 1790s. But eventually eastern city dwellers were sold on its advantages, and in 1825 the hundred-mile Schuylkill Canal was opened to take the coal from northeastern Pennsylvania to Philadelphia. Other canals followed, and when they couldn't keep up with demand, some of the nation's first railroads were built to carry the fuel (although these early locomotives burned wood, since their fireboxes hadn't yet been designed to burn anthracite). In time these "coal roads," such as the Reading, would come to own the mines they served.

By 1902, northeastern cities such as New York (which were close enough to the coalfields to make the shipping of anthracite affordable), had adapted their factory boilers and home stoves for hard coal, and even where the equipment could accept sooty bituminous, its use was often prohibited by law. But now, with anthracite stockpiles dwindling and its price spiraling upward like smoke from a chimney, industries and street railways began to burn bituminous, risking damage to their equipment and citations from the Health Department. In June, just one month into the strike, the hulking silhouette of the Brooklyn Bridge disappeared in a manmade haze, and growing numbers of New Yorkers began to seek treatment for respiratory distress.

In Pennsylvania, union engineers, firemen, and pump men had remained at their stations, keeping the mines ready for the workers' return. But on June 2, they were called out as well, leaving the pits to fill with groundwater and lethal gases. As both sides dug in for a siege, thirty thousand miners abandoned the region, many to return to Europe. But some twenty thousand nonunion men continued working, and as spring turned to summer there were sporadic and conflicting reports of violence in the coalfields, where strikers were pitted against substitutes and private police hired by the mine owners.

One of the worst incidents occurred on the evening of July 30, in Shenandoah, Pennsylvania, when a group of picketing miners severely beat two strikebreakers. A sheriff's deputy who had been escorting the nonunion men barricaded himself in the railroad station, which was surrounded by a mob that swelled to five thousand union members. When a townsman tried to aid the officer, he was beaten to death. Municipal policemen came to the deputy's assistance, but the union men pressed the attack, and the police fired into the crowd. Some in the mob returned fire. Although no one else was killed, sixty were wounded before the officers managed to escape.

President Roosevelt itched to intervene in the strike, but Attorney General Knox explained that under the Constitution the executive could act only at the request of Pennsylvania officials or in the case of a direct attack on federal authority. When Roosevelt asked whether he might prosecute the mines as an illegal trust under the Sherman Act, Knox informed him that as president he had "no power or duty in the matter."

Growing increasingly alarmed, the New York Board of Trade and Transportation called on the president to take the radical step of appointing an arbitration panel. It wasn't the first time during the strike that such a proposal had been offered, but it would be a course without modern precedent. Beginning in 1878, a few states had passed laws allowing governors to appoint commissions to mediate labor disputes, and starting in 1888 Congress had created various mechanisms for arbitrating between workers and owners. But the federal measures had proved ineffectual, and in the couple of recent cases where the president had become directly involved in a labor dispute—the Great Railroad Strike of 1877, during the Hayes Administration, and the Pullman Strike of 1894, when Cleveland was president—it had been to break the strike, not to mediate.

On August 20, John Mitchell announced that the miners, bolstered by an adequate relief fund, would "fight to the bitter end. . . . We favor arbitration," he claimed. "Since the operators, however, will not budge, the fight resolves itself into a prolonged struggle. The weakest will lose. The mine workers are well fixed financially. We shall not give in." The operators were equally unyielding, and as the calendar slid inexorably toward fall, the president searched in vain for a pretext to act. Faced with a bitter, seemingly intractable dispute between what has been called "the nation's biggest union and its most powerful industrial combination over its most vital commodity," Roosevelt was at a loss. "I do not know that I have ever had a more puzzling or a more important problem to deal with," he confided to his sister Bamie.

Pressure for action was mounting, and increasingly eyes turned to Pierpont Morgan. The year before, Morgan and John Mitchell had found themselves unlikely allies in the U.S. Steel strike, when Mitchell had persuaded T. J. Shaffer, president of the Amalgamated Association of Iron, Steel and Tin Workers, to accept Morgan's compromise settlement.

But the union board balked, and the strike proved a disaster for workers. Then in February 1902, before leaving on his annual tour of Europe, Morgan had met with Mitchell. The union leader had gone to New York hoping to see E. B. Thomas, president of the Erie Coal Company, and after Thomas had refused the interview, Mark Hanna had prevailed on Morgan to meet with Mitchell instead. According to Mitchell's account, Morgan had privately assured him that he would "do what was right when the opportunity for action came," promising that "if the railroad presidents were wrong he would not sustain them; if the miners were wrong he would not help them."

During his European travels, the financier followed news of the strike. But whereas Roosevelt was searching for a pretext to intervene, Morgan seemed desperate for an excuse to stay clear. Mitchell and the miners trusted in Morgan's integrity and evenhandedness, and they hoped he would step in. In June, a few days after Morgan announced that he did not plan to involve himself, strikers in Wilkes-Barre hanged his effigy, stoned it, and buried it in a shallow grave. Then on August 20, Morgan arrived in New York, amid speculation that he had come back to end the walkout. Pouring aboard his ship, the luxurious White Star liner *Oceanic*, reporters peppered him with questions. "I don't know anything about the coal strike," he bantered. "How should I settle it? I don't know a thing about the situation."

Yet on the day of his homecoming he met with several of the mine presidents. The operators weren't keen for Morgan to interfere, and although he exercised ultimate control of the mines and railroads, his power was not absolute. He had appointed George Baer and the other executives, but (like the presidents of the companies constituting United States Steel) they retained considerable independence. As Ralph Easley, director of the National Civic Federation, an organization founded to mediate disputes between labor and industry, explained to John Mitchell, "[Morgan] has a lot of unruly presidents on his hands who are willing to resign any minute if he undertakes to coerce them. He has not got a lot of men standing around to put in their place."

Other prominent men pressed Morgan to involve himself, including Easley, Mark Hanna, and Senator Chauncey Depew. As financier Russell

Sage told a newsman, "His influence is so great that all that it is necessary for him to do is to speak, declare his mind on the subject, and if it favors a termination of the strike it would not be long before the miners would resume work. . . . Circumstances have placed Mr. Morgan in his present position, a position where the public welfare makes it obligatory on him to act. Considering the circumstances I think it is not right for him to remain reticent."

Still Morgan equivocated and a few days after his return made this tortured statement to newsmen: "I have not said I would not interfere, or that I will interfere. This is not the time to talk on such a subject. When the proper time comes to make a statement I will make one, if it is necessary to make it. I do not say, however, that it will be necessary at any time to make a statement on the subject. When there is anything to say the reporters can have it."

On August 26, more than three months into the strike, George Baer was still insisting, "The issues do not admit of arbitration, and arbitration, therefore, no matter from what source it emanates, cannot be considered. Nothing has occurred or can occur which will change the policy of the operators. We are simply waiting until the miners come back." But an unnamed mining official confided to a reporter, "I wouldn't be surprised if the question of arbitration would be taken up immediately. Mr. Morgan wants the strike ended. He does not want to excite public clamor, and the public look to him to end the trouble." Rumors flew that a settlement would soon be announced.

But a month later, the only change had been in the scarcity of coal. "Price has become of little consequence," reported the *New York Tribune*, since "hard coal cannot be had for love or money." In the New York suburb of Mount Vernon, a mob attacked a train carrying soft coal while it was stopped in a freight yard, until the train crew managed to fend the thieves off with picks and shovels. In the city, vendors began offering, for a nickel, stickpins mounted with a bit of "rare mineral"—anthracite. Since May the price of anthracite had quadrupled, to twenty dollars a ton, or fifty cents a bushel. Prices for the alternatives—bituminous, oil, and even wood—climbed as well. And the cost of all fuels was certain to go higher once the cool weather set in, assuming any were available at all. Along with the price of coal, the cost of other necessities had already risen, from bread and milk to laundry and rents. The poor, living on ten dollars a week, combed the streets for bits of wood to feed their cook stoves.

In a letter to his old friend Henry Cabot Lodge, the president expressed his frustration: "Unfortunately, the strength of my public position before the country is also its weakness. I am genuinely independent of the big monied men in all matters where I think the interests of the public are concerned. . . . But where I do not grant any favors to these big monied men . . . , it is out of the question for me to expect them to grant favors to me in return. . . . I am at my wits' ends how to proceed."

In late September, the president underwent a second surgery on his leg. He had begun to run a slight fever, raising fears that the wound had become infected. Orthopedist Newton M. Shaffer was called from New York for a consultation, and it was determined that the inflammation had reached the bone. At two o'clock on the afternoon of the 28th, in the temporary White House, cocaine was applied to the wound as an anesthetic, and Dr. Rixey, assisted by Dr. Shaffer and four other physicians, made an incision and scraped the tibia of dead tissue. Then the wound was sponged and dressed but not sutured, to promote drainage. The doctors said they expected no further complications and prescribed absolute rest. After the procedure, in a sunny disposition and attended by two male nurses, the president was wheeled to the window of his bedroom, where he spent the rest of the afternoon reading with his leg elevated.

Meanwhile, the strike dragged on, and the miners and operators waged a battle for public opinion. On the evening of September 28, in Philadelphia, John Mitchell released a long statement reiterating the miners' demands and refuting some comments George Baer had made concerning wages, working conditions, and causes of the violence. Toward the end, in a more conciliatory tone, Mitchell added: "We have entered and are conducting this struggle without malice and without bitterness; we believe that our antagonists are acting upon misrepresentation rather than in bad faith; we regard them not as enemies, but as opponents, and we strike in patience until they shall accede to our demands or submit to impartial arbitration the differences between us." Then he ended with an emotional plea: "Involved in this fight are questions weightier than any question of dollars and cents. The present miner has had his day; he has been oppressed and ground down, but there is another generation coming up; a generation of little children, prematurely doomed to the whirl of the mill and the noise and blackness of the breaker. It is for these little children we are fighting. . . . In the grimy and bruised hand of the miner was the little white hand of a child—a child like the children of the rich—and in the heart of the miner was the soul-rooted determination to starve to the last crust of bread and fight out the long, dreary battle to win a life for the child and secure for it a place in the world in keeping with advancing civilization." Sympathies among the public and the press continued strongly in favor of the union.

The following day, Mitchell and four of his lieutenants met at a Philadelphia hotel with a representative of the owners, who told them there would be no negotiation until the miners returned to work. On the morning of the 30th, the president met in his sickroom with a few of his most trusted Cabinet officers, and the attorney general reiterated the president's lack of constitutional authority. Yet demands continued to mount for him to do something. Jacob Riis, the Danish-American journalist who years before had helped to open Roosevelt's eyes to the misery of the poor, wrote to warn him, "The arrogance of the money power will bring a revolution." The American Federation of Catholic Societies and the Methodist Preachers' Meeting petitioned the president to appoint an arbitration committee. Seth Low, Republican mayor of New York, telegrammed him, pleading: "The welfare of a large section of the country imperatively demands the immediate resumption of anthracite coal mining. In the name of the city of New York, I desire to protest through you against the continuance of the existing situation, which, if prolonged involves, at the very least, the certainty of great suffering and heavy loss to the inhabitants of this city, in common with many others." On September 30, W. Murray Crane, the Republican governor of Massachusetts, who had been riding in the president's carriage at the time of the accident, went to Washington to make a personal appeal. The situation was growing desperate in his state, he told the president. "Unless you end this strike, the workers in the North will begin tearing down buildings for fuel. They will not stand being frozen to death." By early October, the retail price of anthracite had risen to thirty-eight dollars a ton, or nearly two cents a pound. Even with "the greatest economy," the *New York World* reported, a poor family required twenty-four pounds of coal a day to prepare meals and heat water. At that rate, the needy were spending more than a third of their income on fuel.

Roosevelt decided he must act. Taking the greatest risk of his young presidency, he sent a terse telegram to six presidents of the struck mining companies: "I should greatly like to see you on Friday next, October 3, at 11 o'clock A.M., here in Washington, in regard to the failure of the coal supply, which has become a matter of vital concern to the whole nation. I have sent a similar dispatch to Mr. John Mitchell, President of the United Mine Workers of America."

In the end, he said, it was Low's message and especially Crane's visit that finally pushed him to action, constitutional responsibility or no. He knew that Crane was no alarmist, and he had heeded the governor's prediction of the "untold misery" the coal famine would extract and "the certainty of riots which might develop into social war."

Also crucial to Roosevelt's decision was the idea that coal was "a necessity of life." As he wrote Bamie, "Under ordinary conditions a strike is not a subject for interference by the President," and therefore "there would be no warrant in interfering under similar conditions in a strike of iron workers," since "iron is not a necessity. But I could no more see misery and death come to the great masses of the people in our large cities and sit by idly" than if someone had poisoned the New York City water supply. The coal famine, he decided, was the moral equivalent of "the invasion of a hostile army of overwhelming force."

Five of the mine presidents telegraphed their acceptance: George Baer of the Philadelphia & Reading; William H. Truesdale of the Delaware, Lackawanna & Western; E. B. Thomas of the Erie; Thomas P. Fowler of the New York, Ontario & Western; and John Markle of the large independent coal operator G. B. Markle & Company. Robert M. Olyphant, of the Delaware & Hudson, begged off on account of his advanced age but agreed to send his vice president, David Willcox. John

Mitchell was "elated" to receive the president's invitation and telegraphed his acceptance within minutes. It was unclear what could be gained from the summit, since the union leader reiterated that the strikers would not return to work without significant concessions and the operators insisted that they would attend the conference not to bargain but only to clarify their position. Even so, hope surged. "Solution of Strike Seems Near at Hand" prophesied the *World*, while the *Tribune* reported a "general impression . . . that the strike will end within a week."

Pierpont Morgan also expressed relief that the government was finally stepping in, telling a reporter, "The plan to have these gentlemen meet the President and confer about the situation is a most admirable one." But some observers openly wondered why Morgan, the ultimate authority behind the coal mines, had been left out of the meeting. And some thought they detected "signs of lukewarmness toward the political welfare and general success of the Roosevelt administration" on Morgan's part, suggesting that "the President and Mr. Morgan have been traveling in opposite directions ever since the inauguration of the suit against Northern Securities Company." Did Morgan genuinely support a settlement of the strike, or was he secretly pleased to see the president inch out on such a long and precarious limb?

At four o'clock on the afternoon of Thursday, October 2, a private train left Jersey City's Pennsylvania Station, carrying five of the mine operators. After stopping in Philadelphia to collect George Baer, the men traveled on to Washington, where they spent the night in their two Pullman cars, parked on a siding, while a pair of private detectives kept watch outside.

Also on Thursday afternoon, John Mitchell, along with UMW district presidents Thomas Duffy, Jon Fahey, and Thomas Nicholls, left Buffalo, not aboard a special train but on a regularly scheduled departure. Reaching Washington's Baltimore & Ohio terminal at 1:00 a.m., the union men made their way to the corner of Pennsylvania Avenue and 4½ Street, where they checked into the small Hotel Fritz Reuter, renowned for its excellent German restaurant, which featured a *table d'hôte* for fifty cents. (Such was the reputation of Reuter's kitchen that on his stay in Washington that spring, Prince Henry of Prussia had gone there to dine.)

The next morning at his hotel Mitchell conferred over a long breakfast with Samuel Gompers, who many years before, as president of the Cigar Makers' Union, had helped to spark then assemblyman Theodore Roosevelt's social conscience by taking him on an inspection of New York City's filthy, overcrowded tenements. Gompers had persisted in his union work, and in 1886 had been elected founding president of the American Federation of Labor, of which the UMW would become a member.

At 10:30 Mitchell and his three deputies left for the temporary White House. The day was fair and mild, and they walked to the corner of Pennsylvania Avenue and 7th Street, where they boarded a northbound streetcar. They disembarked just off Lafayette Square, and as they rounded the corner, a few minutes before eleven o'clock, they found the park filled with spectators crowding the sidewalks, grass, and benches. As he passed through the throng, dressed in a long frockcoat, white shirt, black tie, and black fedora (in place of the more traditional tall silk hat), Mitchell's dark features were set and his gaze preoccupied. He and his companions mounted the house's front steps, passed the police guards, and were shown into the front parlor that served as George Cortelyou's office.

Baer and the other mine operators arrived a few minutes later, in two hired landaus. The owners' representatives had taken a leisurely breakfast in their Pullmans, then adjourned to one of the cars' drawing rooms, where they had read newspapers, chatted, smoked cigars, and occasionally stepped outside to stretch their legs on the station platform. They sported smart business suits, including short sack coats with high lapels, and as they stepped down from their carriages, their faces reflected a cool self-confidence. They were shown into Cortelyou's office along with the union men.

Presently the secretary led the visitors upstairs. As they entered the generous, handsome room that served as the president's parlor, they saw that Attorney General Knox and Commissioner of Labor Carroll D. Wright were already with him. Also there were his assistant secretaries

79

William Loeb and Benjamin Barnes, poised to take a transcript of what was said.

Wrapped in a dressing gown, the president was seated in his wheelchair with his left leg stretched out before him, his foot resting on a cushion. As Cortelyou introduced the visitors, the president thanked them for coming. He apologized for his informal attire and for not rising to greet them. "Be seated, gentlemen," he said, and they found places in the semicircle of chairs that had been set out.

In the president's hand was a sheet of stationery. He had carefully considered what he wished to tell them, he explained, and thought it better that he read his comments to avoid any misunderstanding. The room was silent as he began in a serious tone, filled with feeling:

"I wish to call your attention to the fact that there are three parties affected by the situation in the anthracite trade—the operators, the miners and the general public. I speak for neither the operators nor the miners, but for the general public. The questions at issue which led to the situation affect immediately the parties concerned—the operators and the miners; but the situation itself vitally affects the public.

"As long as there seemed to be a reasonable hope that these matters could be adjusted between the parties it did not seem proper to me to intervene in any way. I disclaim any right or duty to intervene in this way upon legal grounds, or upon any official relation that I bear to the situation; but the urgency and the terrible nature of the catastrophe impending over a large portion of our people in the shape of a winter fuel famine impel me, after much anxious thought, to believe that my duty requires me to use whatever influence I personally can bring to end a situation which has become literally intolerable.

"I wish to emphasize the character of the situation and to say that its gravity is such that I am constrained urgently to insist that each one of you realize the heavy burden of responsibility upon him. We are upon the threshold of winter with an already existing coal famine, the future terrors of which we can hardly yet appreciate. The evil possibilities are so far-reaching, so appalling, that it seems to me that you are not only justified in sinking, but required to sink, for the time being, any tenacity as to your respective claims in the matter at issue between you. In my judgment the situation imperatively requires that you meet upon the common plane of the necessities of the public.

"With all the earnestness there is in me I ask that there be an immediate resumption of operations in the coal mines in some such way as will, without a day's unnecessary delay, meet the crying needs of the people. I do not invite a discussion of your respective claims and positions. I appeal to your patriotism, to the spirit that sinks personal considerations and makes individual sacrifices for the general good."

When he finished, John Mitchell stood and said, "Mr. President, I am much impressed with what you say. I am much impressed with the gravity of the situation. We feel that we are not responsible for this terrible state of affairs. We are willing to meet the gentlemen representing the coal operators to try to adjust our differences among ourselves. If we cannot adjust them that way, Mr. President, we are willing that you shall name a tribunal who shall determine the issues that have resulted in the strike, and if the gentlemen representing the operators will accept the award or decision of such a tribunal the miners will willingly accept it, even if it is against their claims."

The president was taken off guard by Mitchell's swift response. "Before considering what ought to be done," he said, "I think it only just to both of you, both sides, and desirable from my standpoint, that you should have time to consider what I have stated as to the reasons for my getting you together, and I shall trespass so far upon your good nature as to ask that this interview cease now, and that you come back at three o'clock. I should like you to think over what I have stated, not to decide now, but give it careful thought and return at three o'clock."

George Cortelyou showed the delegations back downstairs, where he gave each man a copy of the president's opening statement. It was 11:19. The conference had lasted twelve minutes.

———

John Mitchell and his deputies returned to the Reuter Hotel, where they conferred again with Samuel Gompers. The mine presidents went back to their Pullman cars, locked the doors, drew the wooden blinds, and restationed their security guards. A stenographer was called, and each man repaired to his private compartment to draft a response to the president's statement. After a while, Baer entered the station, went to a telephone booth, and made a long-distance call—to Pierpont Morgan, it was said. Then the operators reconvened over lunch, which their chefs cooked over wood and soft coal, since no anthracite was available, even for the presidents of the companies that mined it. At 2:45, four of the executives boarded a carriage to return to the temporary White House. The others followed ten minutes behind, after the lone stenographer had finished typing their statements.

When the meeting recommenced in the upstairs sitting room, fifteen minutes behind schedule, George Baer began with a question. "Mr. President, do we understand you correctly that we will be expected to answer the proposition submitted by Mr. Mitchell this morning?"

"It will be a pleasure to me to hear any answer that you are willing to make," Roosevelt told him.

"I have prepared an answer," Baer said. He stood, and making no acknowledgment of John Mitchell, lest that be mistaken for recognition of the union, he began to read. Sidestepping the proposed arbitration, he offered "a statement of what is going on in the coal regions." With his Van Dyke beard bobbing and his narrow face shining with indignation, he protested that the fifteen to twenty thousand men still working the mines were "abused, assaulted, injured and maltreated by the United Mine Workers. They can only work under the protection of armed guards. Thousands of other workmen are deterred from working by the intimidation, violence and crimes inaugurated by the United Mine Workers, over whom John Mitchell, whom you invited us to meet, is chief. I need not picture the daily outrages committed by the members of this organization. The 'domestic tranquility' which the Constitution declares is the chief object of government does not exist in the coal regions. There is a terrible reign of lawlessness and crime there. Only the lives and property of the members of the secret, oath-bound order, which declared that the locals should 'have full power to suspend operations at collieries' until the non-union men joined their order, are safe. Every effort is made to prevent the mining of coal, and, when mined, Mitchell's men dynamite bridges and tracks, mob non-union men, and by all manner of violence try to prevent its shipment to relieve the public. . . ."

During this recitation of alleged outrages, George Cortelyou glanced at John Mitchell and saw him struggling to contain himself. The president shot the union man a sympathetic look.

Baer went on: "The duty of the hour is not to waste time negotiating with the fermenters of this anarchy and insolent defiance of law, but to do as was done in the War of the Rebellion—restore the majesty of law, the only guardian of a free people, and to reestablish order and peace at any cost. The Government is a contemptible failure," he said, if it cannot protect lives and property from "violators of law and the instigators of violence and crime. Just now it is more important to teach ignorant men dwelling among us . . . that at whatever cost and inconvenience to the public Pennsylvania will use the whole power of government" to protect the nonunion men, their families, and the right to work. "Under these conditions we decline to accept Mr. Mitchell's considerate offer to let us work on terms he names. He has no right to come from Illinois to dictate terms on the acceptance of which anarchy and crime shall cease in Pennsylvania. He must stop his people from killing, maiming and abusing Pennsylvania citizens and from destroying property. He must stop it because it is unlawful and not because of any bargain with us." He ended by suggesting that if any of the workers had grievances, they should take them up with the local Court of Common Pleas.

Cortelyou studied Roosevelt's face. Though the president hadn't interrupted Baer's tirade, he was plainly furious at the insolence and intransigence. He called on John Mitchell to speak next.

In a measured tone, Mitchell began, "At the conference this morning, we, the accredited representatives of the Anthracite Coal Mine Workers, were much impressed with the views you expressed, and the danger to the welfare of our country from a prolongation of the coal strike that you so clearly pointed out. Conscious of the responsibility resting upon us, conscious of our duty to society, conscious of our obligations to the one hundred fifty thousand mine workers whom we have the honor to represent, we have, after most careful consideration, and with the hope of relieving the situation and diverting the sufferings and hardships which would inevitably follow in the wake of a coal famine, decided to propose a resumption of coal mining upon the lines hereinafter suggested." They weren't making this offer out of weakness, he pointed out, because they had the means to carry on the strike indefinitely. "But, confident of our ability to demonstrate to any impartial tribunal the equity of our demands for higher wages and improved environment," they would return to the mines immediately if the matter were referred to a tribunal of the president's choosing, whose conclusions would be binding on both parties, with the only other condition being that any pay raise awarded would be retroactive to the day that work resumed.

Then, as the afternoon shadows lengthened in the park across the street, each operator followed in turn, denouncing anarchy and violence, demanding protections for men who were willing to work, and calling on the president to send in federal troops if the state militia could not ensure the peace. John Markle began to read his statement: "I have listened with deep interest to the remarks that you made us before a few minutes after eleven o'clock this morning, and do thoroughly appreciate the seriousness of the situation in the anthracite coal fields of Pennsylvania. As you disclaim any right or duty in this way to intervene in your official capacity, but are using your personal influence, and as you admit this matter is beyond the merits of the issue between the coal presidents and operators on one side and the miners on the other—"

"I did not say that!" the president erupted, thrusting his right hand toward the speaker.

"But you did, Mr. President," Markle said, then added, "At least we so understood you."

"I did not say it, and nothing that I did say could possibly bear that construction," the president seethed. He had Cortelyou read that portion of the morning's transcript, where the president had rather said, "I do not invite a discussion of your respective claims and positions."

Corrected but undeterred, Markle proceeded to lecture the president on the responsibilities of his office. "I fully indorse these remarks from you," he read, "and as an American citizen and a citizen of the Commonwealth of Pennsylvania I now ask you to perform the duties vested in you as the President of the United States, to at once squelch the anarchistic condition of affairs existing in the anthracite coal regions by the strong arm of the military at your command. . . . Will you do it?" he challenged.

When his turn came, William Truesdale demanded that the federal government, through the courts, "institute proceedings against the illegal organization known as the United Mine Workers' Association, its well-known officers, agents and members, to enjoin and restrain permanently it and them from continuing this organization and requiring them to desist immediately from conspiring, conniving, aiding, or abetting the outlawry and intolerable conditions in the anthracite regions for which they and they alone are responsible."

David Willcox went further, calling the UMW "the most extensive combination and monopoly which the country has ever known." Although he didn't place the railroads and coal mines in that category, he found the union that dug the coal "a combination or conspiracy not only at common law, but also in restraint of trade and commerce among the several States, and also an attempt to monopolize the labor necessary in supplying coal found in one State to the markets of other States, and thus to monopolize this part of the commerce among the several States."

From the moment the operators began speaking, it was clear that nothing but disappointment would come from the president's bold gamble. At length he turned to John Mitchell and asked whether his men would agree to return to work and to file individual claims in the county Court of Common Pleas, as the operators had proposed. The union leader, to no one's surprise, answered that he would not.

The president asked if he had any further comment to make, and Mitchell, straining to maintain his calm, said, "The charge by the gentlemen that twenty murders have been committed in the anthracite coal regions during the present strike is untrue. If they will name the men and will show that they have committed the murders, I will resign my position. That is a fair proposition, Mr. President, a fair example of how our organization and our people are maligned. The truth of the matter is, as far as I know, there have been seven deaths, unfortunately. No one regrets them more than I do. Three of them were committed by the Coal and Iron police and no one else has been charged with them. . . . I want to say, Mr. President, that I feel very keenly the attacks made upon me and my people, but I came here with the intention of doing nothing and saying nothing that would affect reconciliation."

Then the president posed a question to the mine executives, though he already knew the answer. Would they accept the UMW's proposal that he name a commission to settle the strike? To a man, the operators replied in the negative. They had, they told him, nothing to add beyond what they had read in their statements.

It was after five o'clock when the conference adjourned. Although it had lasted two hours, it had made no more headway than the brief session that morning. If anything, the prolonged recitation of the owners' grievances seemed to have hardened attitudes on both sides and shifted the possibility of a settlement even further out of reach.

As they stepped outside into the cooling October air, the mine presidents would make no comment to reporters, but John Mitchell, with typical understatement, told them, "There has been no settlement." Later, in a press release, he left no doubt as to the union's course: "As a consequence of the refusal of the operators to either grant concessions or defer to impartial arbitration the coal strike will go on. I am firmly convinced that the miners will win, although we deeply regret the refusal of the railroad presidents to defer to the wishes of the nation's Chief Executive."

Roosevelt couldn't let the mine presidents' effrontery pass unremarked. "Mitchell behaved with great dignity and moderation," he wrote Governor Crane. "The operators, on the contrary, showed extraordinary stupidity and bad temper, did everything in their power to goad and irritate Mitchell, becoming fairly abusive in their language to him, and were insolent to me." Of Baer, he said, "If it wasn't for the high office I hold, I would have taken him by the seat of the breeches and the nape of the neck and chucked him out of that window." The president had been in pain throughout the afternoon session, and afterward Surgeon General Rixey and Dr. Lung examined his leg and redressed the wound. Fearing his patient had overexerted himself, Dr. Lung checked in on him again at eight o'clock that evening.

The president sent Elihu Root to the Arlington Hotel to consult with the mine operators, but despite Root's repeated explanations that there was no constitutional basis for such an action, the owners would only restate their demand for federal troops to protect nonunion workers. The coal executives had planned to leave the city at 7:00 p.m., but the session didn't adjourn until two in the morning, and it was after three by the time their private train left the B&O Depot. John Mitchell didn't depart until 12:15 the following afternoon; he had hoped to go earlier in the day but had missed the previous train.

Before the conferees had even left town, the president wrote Mark Hanna, "Well, I have tried and failed. I feel downhearted over the result both because of the great misery made for the mass of our people, and because the attitude of the operators will beyond a doubt double the burden on us who stand between them and socialistic action. . . . What my next move will be I cannot yet say. . . . A coal famine in the winter is an awful ugly thing, and I fear we shall see terrible suffering and grave disaster."

The country shared Roosevelt's sense of foreboding. While some condemned him for overstepping his authority, most Americans applauded his efforts at mediation. And though some citizens agreed with the mine owners that the paramount consideration was the preservation of order, most appreciated the union's willingness to arbitrate and condemned the operators' intransigence and disregard for the president.

Besides the suffering that would be brought on by a winter coal famine, Roosevelt worried over the violence the strike would engender—not just in the coalfields but in cities across the North. Already there were rumors of a general strike, which would impact every American family. And as cold weather set in, "men who have been maddened by want and suffering" would begin to riot. Then he would have no choice but to call out the army to restore order, which would result in even greater loss of life. Before calm was restored, the country could well find itself in the throes of class warfare. The nation was facing its most urgent crisis since the Civil War, the president decided, and the coal famine must be broken at all costs.

The day after the failed summit, Pierpont Morgan announced that he would buy fifty thousand tons of coal in Wales, load it on the ships of his

International Mercantile Marine, and transport it with all speed to New York, where it would be distributed free of charge to the poor (as he had once done during the depression of 1893). The coal was estimated to be worth at least half a million dollars, most likely to be paid out of Morgan's personal account. Was the financier, some wondered aloud, trying to shame the operators for their hard-headedness and goad them into negotiating with the union? Throughout his career, Morgan had consistently tried to inject order and stability in the economic system, and his actions now appeared to be yet another example of those efforts. Moreover, the strike had become an embarrassment to the House of Morgan, and public resentment surrounding it could threaten his many other interests.

On October 6, faced with continuing reports of violence at the mines, Governor Stone ordered all ten thousand troops of the Pennsylvania National Guard into coal country. That same day, Labor Commissioner Carroll Wright traveled to Philadelphia and met with John Mitchell, carrying an offer from the president: If the miners would return to work, he would appoint a commission to investigate their grievances and would promise to use all his influence to resolve the workers' complaints. The proposal was a step the president felt obliged to make, but he wasn't surprised when Mitchell respectfully declined, since the panel's recommendations would not be binding on the coal companies. Two days later, a convention of miners voted to maintain the strike. In New York, wooden boxes and barrels were broken down and distributed to the poor for fuel, and when the *World*'s printing plant ran out of coal, old chairs and tables were burned to keep the boilers churning and the presses rolling.

On October 9, New York governor Benjamin Odell and Pennsylvania senators Boies Penrose and Matthew Quay met in New York City with five of the coal operators, but they made no more headway than the president had managed. The next day, Penrose conferred with Pierpont Morgan at the Fifth Avenue Hotel, to stress the danger to the Republican ticket if the strike were not resolved before the election. As the financier was leaving the building, a reporter stopped him. "Mr. Morgan, some of the morning newspapers accuse you of blocking the negotiations looking to a settlement of the strike yesterday." Morgan seemed stunned by the inference. Taking the cigar from his mouth, he said in an earnest voice, "It is not true. Don't you know it is not true?" Later that afternoon, he called George Baer to the Corner. Publicly Morgan was still disclaiming any right to involve himself, but there was little doubt that he had summoned Baer to press him to resolve the walkout.

On October 9, Elihu Root wrote Morgan and asked his help in persuading the mine presidents to accept an arbitration panel appointed by the president—or even by Morgan if necessary. The miners would return to work while the commission was deliberating, and both sides would agree to be bound by the committee's findings for five years. This was substantially the same proposal that Mitchell had offered and the owners had refused at their meeting with the president, but the new iteration included a fig leaf for the operators: Since the commission would hear testimony from each company and its workers individually, technically the owners would not be negotiating with the UMW. No one was surprised when nothing came of this proposal either.

The following day, the president walked on crutches for the first time since his accident, to board a carriage for his daily outing with the first lady. Although labor progress was less apparent than the orthopedic variety, Roosevelt continued to work behind the scenes, using every means at his disposal. On the one hand, he made plans to appoint his arbitration panel even without the operators' agreement, on the hope that both sides could be brought to accept its findings after the fact. Toward this end, he approached ex-president Grover Cleveland, who agreed to act as chairman.

At the same time, he prepared a more drastic course, though he admitted it "would form an evil precedent": If all efforts at mediation failed, he would call in federal troops to seize the mines and work the coal. He met secretly with retired general John Schofield, veteran of both the Civil War and the Pullman Strike, who agreed to accept the assignment and to answer to no civil or military authority other than the president. In a bow to the Constitution, Roosevelt conferred with Senator Quay, who privately assured him that Governor Stone could be persuaded to request federal intervention whenever the president indicated. The Constitution didn't give the president authority to seize private property, even with the governor's approval, but Roosevelt determined to proceed as though the nation were in "a state of war. . . . I do not know whether I would have had any precedents," he allowed, "save perhaps those of General Butler at New Orleans [in 1862]," but it was "imperative to act, precedent or no precedent." Besides those directly involved—Quay, Cleveland, and Schofield—he confided his plans only to the two most trusted members of his Cabinet, Philander Knox and Elihu Root.

The torpedo was primed and loaded, but before it was fired, Root suggested a less dire alternative. What if he—acting confidentially and as a private citizen, not as secretary of war—made one last effort to persuade Pierpont Morgan to intervene? Roosevelt seized on the idea, and on the afternoon of October 10, citizen Root made a lengthy telephone call to New York, setting an appointment for the following day.

Arriving early in the morning, Root went first to a polling place at Madison Avenue and Seventy-First Street and registered to vote in the upcoming midterms. Then he took a cab to the Union League Club at Fifth Avenue and Thirty-Ninth Street, where he was intercepted by reporters. When a newsman repeated a rumor that Root had come to New York to meet with Pierpont Morgan, the secretary of war explained that he was there to register for the fall election.

For the rest of the day, reporters dogged Root's every movement. After breakfast he took a cab to the Thirty-Fifth Street Pier, where a launch was waiting, and a little after ten o'clock he climbed aboard the *Corsair*, moored in the Hudson River. As he and Morgan began their discussion, Root found the financier "alive to the seriousness of the situation"—and undoubtedly his interest only deepened on hearing of the president's plan to seize the coal mines. Over the morning and early afternoon, the "private citizen" and the representative of industry managed to find some common ground. Root located some ivory notepaper, bearing a pair of crossed nautical pennants in the upper left-hand corner and, in the upper right, the motto *On board the Corsair*, and he began to commit their understanding to paper.

He started in pen, but before the end of the first sentence changed to pencil. Writing quickly, he crossed out and rewrote as he went, his haste

Secretary of War Elihu Root, who negotiated with Pierpont Morgan during the coal strike of 1902. LIBRARY OF CONGRESS

reflected in the jagged penmanship, the grammatical lapses, the blanks left to be filled in later. "The managers of the different coal properties making up the Anthracite coal field wish their true position in the present strike understood therefore make the following statement of facts," the text began. After condemning the "course of violence" surrounding the mines and the "reign of terror" that put "every man wishing to work in fear of death or bodily harm," the document maintained that "the undersigned are not and never have been unwilling to submit all questions between them & their workmen to any fair tribunal for discussion."

Although the owners were not willing to enter into arbitration directly with the union or to come to any agreement that would not guarantee all miners the right "to work in safety and without bodily harm to themselves or their families," each company, recognizing "the urgent public need of coal," was "willing now as it always has been willing to submit to decision all questions between such company & its workmen as a body" and to place the "controversy" before a board of "persons named by the President of the United States if he will perform that public service.

"This upon the understanding that upon the constitution of such board the miners return to work & cease all interference with & persecution of non union men who are working or shall be working." And with that, on the eighth page, the document ended, without the signature of either of its authors.

With the hasty agreement in hand, Root and Morgan returned in the launch to the foot of Forty-Second Street, apparently in an attempt to elude the press. They had ordered a carriage, but it was late in coming, and for twenty minutes they stood in the rain, pestered by reporters. Morgan was testy, while Root answered their questions evasively but with a smile. When the carriage finally arrived, they rode to the Union Club, at Twenty-First Street and Fifth Avenue. After a few moments Root reemerged and went to the Pennsylvania Ferry at West Twenty-Third Street, where he sent several telegrams. Then he crossed to Jersey City and caught the 4:25 train to the capital. Morgan stayed inside the Union Club for the rest of the day, placing a long phone call to George Baer and receiving several visitors, including coal owners E. B. Thomas and John Markle. Finally, at nine o'clock that night, he and George Perkins took a cab to the Thirty-Fifth Street pier and boarded the *Corsair*.

The next morning, as Root made his report to the president, one group of mine owners met in New York and another in Philadelphia. Afterward, E. B. Thomas went to the Corner and conferred with Morgan in his private office. Later that evening, more comings and goings were reported on the *Corsair*. Word spread that the strike had been settled.

The next day, Monday, October 13, George Baer was called from Philadelphia to New York. That afternoon, Morgan and Robert Bacon left for Washington, arriving at 10:00 p.m. Despite the hour, they met Elihu Root at the Arlington Hotel, and at 10:15 all three men made the short trip to the temporary White House. Emerging an hour and a half later, they went around the corner to the Metropolitan Club, refusing to make any comment to the press. But not long afterward, George Cortelyou released a statement from the mine presidents, based on the agreement that Morgan and Root had negotiated aboard the *Corsair*.

But the document that Morgan had come to Washington to present to the president differed in several important respects from the handwritten draft that he and Root had worked out on Morgan's yacht. Pointedly addressed to "the Public" and not to the miners' union, the revised agreement included a lengthy chronicle of the strike from the owners' perspective and restated the operators' belief that the miners' wages were "fair and full." Moreover, the statement went so far as to stipulate the makeup of the president's commission: an Army or Navy engineer; a coal mining engineer; a federal judge from the eastern district of Pennsylvania; "a man of prominence, eminent as a sociologist"; and a man in the business of mining and selling coal.

The president was incensed that the owners wanted to dictate the number and qualifications of the committee's members, although he did express to various callers his "highest respect and admiration" for the pivotal role Pierpont Morgan had played in finally bringing them to the bargaining table. But the financier was making no guarantees. As he and Bacon arrived back in New York, he told reporters, "I hope the miners will accept the proposition made to President Roosevelt last night. I think if they do it will be for their own good. . . . But of course I can't tell what they will do. All I have to say is, that I am very well satisfied. As a direct statement from me, you may say that I do not know when the strike will end."

John Mitchell was jubilant that the owners had finally accepted the principle of mediation. Boarding a 3:00 a.m. train to Washington, he met on the morning of the 15th with the president and the commissioner of labor, Carroll Wright, to review the operators' offer. Although he took exception to the owners' depiction of the union, at length he agreed to the proposal, but on the condition that the president appoint two additional members, a labor leader and a Catholic clergyman. The president found this amendment reasonable, and they agreed on E. E. Clark, head of the Order of Railway Conductors of America, and John Spaulding, bishop of the Diocese of Peoria, Illinois.

Bob Bacon and George Perkins journeyed to Washington, arriving at 10:30 that night at the temporary White House, where the president, Elihu Root, and Carroll Wright were waiting. The mine presidents absolutely refused to accept Mitchell's additions to the committee, Bacon and Perkins reported, and even Pierpont Morgan could not prevail on them to change their minds. "It appeared" to Roosevelt "that the men who were back of them, who were in the narrow, bourgeois, commercial world, were still in a condition of wooden-headed obstinacy and stupidity and utterly unable to see the black storm impending." As the men argued, the Morgan partners grew "nearly wild" and "more and more hysterical," begging the president to force Mitchell to give up his demand for a labor representative and maintaining that a failure in the negotiations now would result in "violence and possible social war."

Then, after nearly two hours, Roosevelt was stunned when Bacon offhandedly mentioned that the owners had no objection to whatever individuals the president wished to appoint under the categories they had designated. "At last," he wrote, "I grasped the fact that the mighty brains of these captains of industry had formulated the theory that they would rather have anarchy than tweedledum, but that if I would use the word tweedledee they would hail it as meaning peace. . . . I instantly told them that I had not the slightest objection whatever to doing an absurd thing when it was necessary to meet the objection of an absurd mind on some vital point, and I would cheerfully appoint my labor man as the 'eminent sociologist.' It was almost impossible for me to appreciate the instant and tremendous relief this gave them." Telephone calls were placed to Morgan in New York and Baer in Philadelphia, and both men gave their immediate approval to Clark and Spaulding, along with the addition of

Carroll Wright to serve as the committee's recorder. In the end, the crippling, five-month strike had hinged on a point of semantics. Yet by failing to recognize E. E. Clark for the union leader he was, the agreement did serve to undercut the legitimacy of organized labor.

A telegram was sent to Mitchell, and at 2:15 a.m. George Cortelyou issued a press release with the names of the proposed commissioners. Besides Clark and Spaulding, the appointees included retired brigadier general John M. Wilson of the Army Corps of Engineers; E. W. Parker, chief statistician of the coal division of the U.S. Geological Survey and author of the government's annual report on American coal production; George Gray, judge of the Third U.S. Circuit Court of Appeals; and Thomas H. Watkins, a longtime coal merchant with offices in Scranton and New York. Anticipating questions as to how the head of the railway conductors' union qualified as "an eminent sociologist," the statement explained that the president assumed "that for the purposes of such a commission the term sociologist means a man who has thought and studied on social questions and has practically applied his knowledge."

Stocks rose sharply on Wall Street during the next session, and the wholesale price of coal dropped by a third or more in a single day. A frisson of relief rippled across the North, and although some voters still grumbled about presidential overreach, most were grateful for Roosevelt's shrewd and determined action. Thousands of letters and telegrams of congratulation arrived at the White House, from common folk and powerbrokers alike. Telegraphed Henry Cabot Lodge, "I am delighted beyond words. Best piece of work you have ever done. The country rejoices and knows it is all due to your effort." Wrote Secretary of State John Hay (who had been a friend of Roosevelt's father), "My dear Theodore, You have done a great service to the country—which is all you were thinking about. But the rest of us see that you have vastly increased your own power and prestige, and as these can never be used except for the public good, it is, all round, a big job well done."

John Mitchell was also appreciative, and the acquaintance that he and Roosevelt formed during the coal strike would grow into a warm and enduring friendship. Mitchell also publicly thanked Pierpont Morgan for following through on his promise to "do what was right when the opportunity for action came." Wrote Mitchell, "If others had been as fair and reasonable as Mr. Morgan was, this strike would have been settled a long time ago. . . . I am informed that he keenly felt his responsibility to the public in connection with the fuel famine, and has done his best to bring about the end. . . . I am credibly informed that he is friendly to organized labor. As an organizer of capital he concedes the right of labor to organize also and when labor organizations are fair and conservative he believes in dealing directly with them for the advantage of both employers and employees."

Before the miners had even voted to return to work, the president wrote Pierpont Morgan to offer his own appreciation: "It really does begin to look as if there was light ahead. And now, my dear sir, let me thank you for the service you have rendered to the whole people. If it had not been for your going into the matter I do not see how the strike could have been settled at this time, and the consequences that might have followed upon its being unsettled when cold weather set in are in very fact dreadful to contemplate. I thank you and congratulate you with all my heart."

On October 21, a miners' convention in Wilkes-Barre approved the settlement in a unanimous voice vote, followed by ten minutes of cheering. Most workers would return to their jobs two days later, but pump men, firemen, engineers, electricians, and carpenters would report at four o'clock that same afternoon to ready the mines. That night, coal country was alight with parades and fireworks. Like Roosevelt, the union leader was flooded with congratulations, and on October 29, the mines were closed again—in celebration of "Mitchell Day."

Though they had avoided recognition of the union, the coal operators were less enthusiastic than the miners about the pending arbitration. Robert Olyphant captured the owners' fame of mind when he grumbled to a newsman, "We have to be satisfied, whether we like it or not." Pierpont Morgan, while wanting to see the walkout ended, had been reluctant to involve himself, and now he was said to be annoyed at the role he had been made to play. Partially out of pique at the government's interference, it was reported, he was refusing all donations to Republican candidates in that year's election campaign.

Even without Morgan's financial help, Congress remained safely Republican that fall, with the G.O.P. retaining 210 seats in the House, versus 176 for the Democrats, and fifty-seven seats in the Senate, out of the total ninety. The Anthracite Coal Commission went to work immediately and met for nearly three months, inspecting the mines and hearing testimony from 558 witnesses. Its 257-page report, issued the following March, awarded the miners a 10-percent retroactive raise, reduced their workday from ten hours to nine, and established a six-member arbitration board to negotiate future disputes between miners and operators. Although the UMW didn't win all it had wanted—there was no curtailing of child labor, no improvement in living conditions, no new system for weighing coal, and no recognition of the union (which wouldn't come for another thirteen years)—the strike was universally seen as a victory for the miners.

For Roosevelt, the settlement marked the first major success of his administration, burnishing his personal popularity and enhancing his image as a decisive leader. It was also a victory for his vision of an empowered, activist executive. Back in early October, as he had drafted the statement that he read at the opening of the summit at the temporary White House, he had written that his mediation was not intended to set a precedent. But by the time he delivered the remarks he had deleted that claim, because he realized it wasn't true. The anthracite strike established the essential principle that the public had a vested interest in labor disputes, and it showed that government could be a successful arbitrator between workers and employers. In his annual message to Congress that December, Roosevelt argued that, just as it was natural for corporations to combine, it was expected for workers to form unions to protect their own interests, and that "both kinds of federation, capitalistic and labor, can do much good, and as a necessary corollary they can both do evil." And so "organized capital and organized labor alike should remember that in the long run the interest of each must be brought into harmony with the interest of the general public."

In the future, the government would continue to represent the public's interest in labor disputes. In 1913, during the administration of Woodrow Wilson, Congress would take a further step, passing the Newlands Labor Act, which established a federal Board of Mediation and Conciliation to arbitrate conflicts between the railroads and their employees. More than a century later, that group's successor, the National Mediation Board, still attempts to resolve disputes in the railroad and airline industries, while another, the Federal Mediation and Conciliation Service, offers conflict resolution services to labor and industry. The seed for both organizations had been sown in the Coal Strike of 1902.

Looking back years later, union leader Samuel Gompers called the strike "the most important single incident in the labor movement in the United States. . . . They secured the shorter work-day with higher pay, and from then on the miners became not merely human machines to produce coal but men and citizens, taking their place among the fairly well-paid, intelligent men, husbands, fathers, abreast of all the people not only of their communities but of the republic. The strike was evidence of the effectiveness of trade unions even when contending against trusts."

The strike would also prove a watershed in Pierpont Morgan's relationship with Theodore Roosevelt. Over the course of his presidency, Roosevelt would file more than forty anti-trust suits against the corporations, including meatpackers Swift & Co., the American Tobacco Company, and John D. Rockefeller's Standard Oil. However, after the Northern Securities suit, he would never again prosecute a firm controlled by the House of Morgan. This preference for Morgan companies would expose the president to damaging charges of favoritism and collusion. But in the meantime, the financier had already begun to play a controversial role in one of the signal accomplishments of Roosevelt's presidency.

CHAPTER FOUR

"The Mist of Mendacity"

EVER SINCE THE DAY IN SEPTEMBER 1513 WHEN SPANISH EXPLORER Vasco Núñez de Balboa scaled a mountain in what we now call Panama and glimpsed the ocean that we now call the Pacific, men had dreamed of constructing a canal across the slender isthmus. Over the next three centuries, Johann Wolfgang von Goethe, Benjamin Franklin, and Simón Bolívar had all embraced the vision of an interoceanic waterway. So had the preeminent naturalist of his day, Alexander von Humboldt, who after conducting the first extensive scientific exploration of Latin America, from 1799 to 1804, had proposed present-day Nicaragua as the most auspicious place for a crossing. Forty years later, American diplomat-archaeologist John Lloyd Stephens concurred in that judgment. Unlike Humboldt, Stephens had at least been to Nicaragua.

In 1846, the United States signed a treaty with the independent Republic of New Granada for the exclusive right to traverse its state of Panama via "any modes of communication that now exist, or that may be, hereafter, constructed." In exchange, the Americans agreed to guarantee New Granada's sovereignty over the region. Then, just over a year later, gold was discovered in California, and hundreds of thousands of forty-niners from the United States began to make the arduous dash across Panama, by foot, mule, and dugout, rather than hazard the long, perilous voyage around the tip of South America. In 1850, a U.S. company established the Panama Railroad to connect Colón on the Atlantic with Panama City on the Pacific. Though the line would run only forty-seven miles, disobliging topography, climate, insects, and disease would combine to exact five years, $8 million, and as many as ten thousand lives in its construction.

In the second half of the century, with the advent of the steamship, interoceanic canals became a priority for both commerce and warfare. In 1854, Ferdinand de Lesseps, a onetime French diplomat with no engineering experience (but a longstanding friendship with Mohammed Said, the reigning viceroy of Egypt), was awarded the right to construct a canal through Suez, connecting the Mediterranean with the Red Sea. When the route was opened, fifteen years later, the 120-mile sea-level channel was hailed as a technological marvel, and the charming, indefatigable de Lesseps was acclaimed a genius and a French national treasure.

In the United States, in 1870, President Ulysses S. Grant launched the first of seven expeditions to survey possible routes through Central America. After half a dozen years of exploration and study, the Interoceanic Canal Commission released its final, unanimous recommendation—in favor of Nicaragua. Though the isthmus was wider there than at Panama, the commissioners reasoned, the terrain was less mountainous, and graced with natural waterways that would reduce the amount of digging required. Nicaragua also lay some five hundred miles closer to the United States.

By then de Lesseps had turned his own sights on Central America, and had determined that any canal should run through Panama, along the route already blazed by the railroad. And rather than rely on locks to raise and lower ships over the rugged terrain, it must, as at Suez, be built at sea level. When a French expedition pronounced the task impractical, de Lesseps ordered a second survey, which spent all of two and a half weeks in Panama to confirm his prejudices. By the time they left Bogotá, in May 1878, the French had secured a concession, signed by the president of Colombia (as New Granada was now known) and ratified by its senate. For the exclusive right to build a canal through Panama and to operate it for ninety-nine years, France would make a one-time payment of 750,000 francs (at the time equivalent to $150,000) plus a share of the tolls. Critically, though the concession could be transferred to another private company, it could not be conveyed to the agency of any government.

The following May, under the aegis of the esteemed Société de Géographie de Paris, de Lesseps convened the Congrès International d'Études du Canal Interocéanique. Attended by 136 expert delegates from France, the United States, and twenty other European and Latin American countries, the congress was charged with settling two fundamental issues: the most expedient route for the canal and the most appropriate method of construction. The Americans arrived with surveys and maps and argued persuasively for a lock canal through Nicaragua. But de Lesseps was less concerned with fostering scientific exchange than with winning international endorsement, and over the course of the two-week meeting, trading on his charisma and renown, the hero of Suez maneuvered the delegates toward his preordained conclusion. The final vote was 74 to 8 for a sea-level canal at Panama, and to no one's surprise, de Lesseps was named director of the project. It was initially estimated that the work would require twelve years and $240 million, but on further consideration, de Lesseps reduced the estimates to eight years and $132 million. "Our work will be easier at Panama than at Suez," he explained.

De Lesseps next set about raising capital. When shares of the Compagnie Universelle du Canal Interocéanique, totaling 300 million francs, or $60 million, went on sale in France in December 1880, they were quickly bought out by more than a hundred thousand investors, including farmers, small business owners, and pensioners, all eager to be part of the patriotic (and judging from the success of the Suez Canal, lucrative) scheme. The following year, Drexel, Morgan, one of three companies named to the Compagnie Universelle's American committee, facilitated the sale of the American-owned Panama Railroad to the French.

When French engineers arrived on the isthmus in January 1881, they quickly discovered that Panama was not Suez. The area de Lesseps had selected for his canal was wild and remote, surrounded by dense jungle and accessible only by sea. As they began work, the French and their mostly West Indian workforce confronted implacable mountains and vegetation, debilitating heat, devastating rains and mudslides, merciless insects, and deadly epidemics of malaria and yellow fever. After four years of grueling labor, it was clear that the land would not yield to a sea-level canal. On the Paris Bourse the Compagnie Universelle's shares had already begun a long decline. But clinging to his original vision, de

Lesseps persisted in issuing new bonds, and hundreds of thousands of French investors continued to trust him with their savings.

In 1887, a young French engineer named Philippe Bunau-Varilla at last persuaded de Lesseps to accept a compromise with geography. The idea was to build a lock canal and open it to traffic to generate desperately needed revenue, while continuing to dredge an eventual sea-level canal. It was an ingenious solution, but it had come too late. When it was revealed that the revised project would require 600 million additional francs, public confidence finally collapsed. The French government grew tepid in its support, and subsequent bond offerings met with failure (including one, in 1888, that foundered after an unknown adversary planted a rumor that de Lesseps had died). In New York, Pierpont Morgan resigned from the company's American Committee.

With eight hundred thousand French men and women having invested 1.4 billion francs, or nearly $300 million, the Compagnie Universelle was the most spectacular failure in financial history. After a liquidator was appointed in February 1888, there was a panic on the Paris stock exchange. The national government fell. And in the ensuing scandal, it was revealed that tens of millions of francs had gone not for steam shovels and dredges but for bribes to journalists and government officials in exchange for their support. More than a hundred public figures were implicated, including a leading politician, Georges Clemenceau; the scientist Cornelius Herz; the engineer Gustav Eiffel; and Ferdinand de Lesseps and his son Charles. Though Ferdinand, like many other senior officials, was never put on trial, Charles was sentenced to a year in prison and fined 900,000 francs. His father passed away, in seclusion and ignominy, on December 7, 1894, at the age of eighty-nine. Since work began, the canal had claimed at least twenty thousand lives, most of them West Indian workmen.

Theodore Roosevelt had grasped the importance of sea power at an early age. While still an undergraduate at Harvard, he had begun writing his classic study *The Naval War of 1812*, and later, as assistant secretary of the navy, he had been instrumental in preparing the country for war with

Spain. During the fighting, the battleship USS *Oregon* was forced to make a dangerous, sixty-seven-day, sixteen-thousand-mile voyage from San Francisco, around the tip of South America, to reach the battlefront in Cuba. With victory, the United States added new possessions in the Pacific and the Caribbean, and the strategic necessity of the canal became more urgent still. And with American exports booming, not only with the traditional agricultural products such as cotton, grains, and meat, but with manufactured goods such as iron and steel, the need for a canal was undeniable from a commercial standpoint as well.

In 1850, after the United States and Great Britain had nearly come to war over the right to construct a canal through Nicaragua, the two countries had agreed to joint control of any waterway built across the isthmus. Now, after the collapse of the Compagnie Universelle, a group of English investors solicited Pierpont Morgan and his father, Junius, to act as financial agents for a company proposing a canal through Nicaragua, but the project never came to fruition. Moreover, after the failure of the French effort, the United States was adamant that any Central American canal be under American control. Early in 1900, after a negotiation of more than a year, Britain agreed to cede its claim if the United States pledged to keep the passage neutral and free of fortifications. Theodore Roosevelt, then governor of New York, was a staunch proponent of the canal, but he argued that the no-fortification clause would leave the waterway vulnerable to foreign seizure and render it a threat to national security, by cutting transit time for enemy ships as well as American vessels. The Senate agreed and refused to ratify the treaty, leaving Secretary of State John Hay to renegotiate the terms.

Nearly two years later, when a new agreement was reached, Roosevelt was president. In his first message to Congress, on December 3, 1901, he wrote, "No single great material work which remains to be undertaken on this continent is of such consequence to the American people as the building of a canal across the Isthmus connecting North and South America." The Senate ratified a revised treaty, without the no-fortifications clause, less than two weeks later.

The pact had cleared a crucial diplomatic obstacle. And whereas the French project had been undertaken by a private corporation, it was now understood that, over the objections of bankers like Pierpont Morgan, the American canal would be paid for, constructed, and operated by the federal government. But the old question remained: Where to build it? American engineers had a longstanding preference for Nicaragua, and the French debacle at Panama had done nothing to alter their opinion. One pivotal proponent of Nicaragua was John Tyler Morgan (no relation to Pierpont), longtime senator from Alabama, chairman of the Committee on Interoceanic Canals, and outspoken advocate of American expansionism. Besides the topographical advantages of Nicaragua, Morgan argued, the country was politically stable and known for its relatively healthy climate, whereas Panama was notorious for harboring both revolution and disease.

To weigh the merits of both routes, President McKinley had appointed the Isthmian Canal Commission (known as the Walker Commission, after its chairman, retired admiral John Grimes Walker). In November 1901, the group issued its report, in favor of Nicaragua. But the deciding factor, the commissioners wrote, was not any overwhelming advantage of that route but the relative cost: Whereas the French had placed the absurd value of $109 million on their holdings in Panama, the commission judged them to be worth only $40 million. Still, one commissioner in particular, prominent engineer George S. Morison, was not persuaded, and citing technical considerations, he wrote the minority report advocating Panama.

In December, Iowa congressman William Peters Hepburn introduced a bill authorizing $180 million to build a canal through Nicaragua. In early January, as the House considered the measure, the Compagnie Nouvelle du Canal de Panama, the successor of the defunct Compagnie Universelle, made a timely reduction in its asking price, to $40 million. But the concession came too late. On January 9, the Hepburn bill passed the House by a vote of 308 to 2.

President Roosevelt had been silent during these deliberations, but he had come around to George Morison's opinion that Panama was the better option, especially since the French had already done 40 percent of the required digging. After the vote on the Hepburn bill, the president met with the Walker commissioners and pressed them to change their recommendation in light of the Compagnie Nouvelle's new offer. By January 20, he had the revised report on his desk, now unanimous in favor of Panama.

A week later, John Coit Spooner, Republican senator from Wisconsin, introduced an amendment appropriating $40 million to buy the Compagnie Nouvelle's rights and equipment in Panama and authorizing the president to finish the canal. But since the French contract was transferrable only to a private company, not to a foreign government, the sale would require the approval of Bogotá. In the event that consent was not granted in a "reasonable time," or that clear title could not be obtained from the Compagnie Nouvelle, the president was authorized to begin negotiations with Nicaragua.

Many lawmakers still favored a canal in Nicaragua, which was seen as a fresh start following the French disaster. Some even began to murmur of a "Panama Plot," suggesting that Pierpont Morgan and other railroad interests, wishing to limit competition, were advancing Panama only to sow confusion and to delay the building of any canal, or at least one that wasn't theirs. On December 27, 1899, Morgan and other prominent names in American finance, including August Belmont; the firm of Kuhn, Loeb; and J. & W. Seligman, had filed documents in New Jersey to incorporate the Panama Canal Company of America, intending, according to the filing papers, "to acquire and complete the canal across the Isthmus of Panama."

Handling the incorporation for Morgan et al. was a prominent Wall Street lawyer named William Nelson Cromwell. No stranger to Panama, Cromwell was the general counsel and a director of the Panama Railroad, the American company whose sale to the French Morgan had facilitated. The Compagnie Nouvelle had retained Cromwell to find an American buyer for the moribund project, and he hoped that the Panama Canal Company of America would prove a viable purchaser, putting an American face on the venture even as his French clients maintained real control. But the Compagnie's stockholders refused to approve the transaction, in preference for a French company that was also trying to launch a new syndicate, and so Morgan and Cromwell's Panama Canal Company of America never progressed beyond its corporate filing.

William Nelson Cromwell, attorney
for Pierpont Morgan and clandestine
architect of American policy in Panama.
LIBRARY OF CONGRESS

But in hiring William Nelson Cromwell to represent their American interests, the Compagnie had engaged a powerful advocate. Born in Brooklyn in 1854, Cromwell had graduated from Columbia Law School, then cofounded the New York firm of Sullivan & Cromwell. With his flowing white hair and mustache and his clear blue eyes, he cut a striking figure. More to the point, he had proved himself an energetic, cunning advocate both in Washington, where he had forged extensive political connections, and in New York, where Pierpont Morgan had retained him for the reorganization of the Northern Pacific Railroad and the incorporation of General Electric and U.S. Steel. Since his appointment by the Compagnie Nouvelle, Cromwell had lobbied tirelessly for his client, courting newspapermen, cajoling Colombian officials, buttonholing lawmakers, pursuing Cabinet secretaries including Elihu Root and Philander Knox, and wooing the Walker commissioners. Without Cromwell's personal appeal, it seemed unlikely that President McKinley would have appointed the Walker Commission at all.

In 1900, as the country had looked toward the presidential election, Cromwell had persuaded Mark Hanna, chairman of the Republican National Committee, to amend the party platform in favor of a canal not in Nicaragua, but in "Central America." Shortly afterward, a rival claimed, Cromwell had delivered to the Republican campaign fund a check for $60,000, to be paid by the Compagnie Nouvelle. Though the allegation was never proven, in the brewing "Battle of the Routes,"

the principal advocate for Panama would be Mark Hanna, who
despite failing health remained
one of the Senate's most influential members.

The charge over the campaign
contribution was made by Philippe
Bunau-Varilla, the French engineer who had worked with de
Lesseps. In his early forties now,
with thinning dark hair and an
emphatic waxed mustache, Bunau-
Varilla had intense dark eyes that
Theodore Roosevelt compared to
those of a duelist. Along with
Cromwell, Bunau-Varilla would
prove a potent actor in the drama
of Panama, but whereas the American claimed no motivation other
than the pecuniary, the Frenchman
declared his primary interest to be

Philippe Bunau-Varilla, who claimed
that his primary motivation was "the
vindication of the French genius."
LIBRARY OF CONGRESS

the restoration of his country's honor. By all accounts the two men loathed
each other, and even as they labored toward the same end, they advanced
their individual agendas, then squabbled over the credit for their success.

Though he claimed to be from a wealthy family, Bunau-Varilla was
born out of wedlock and raised in modest circumstances. After attending
the prestigious École Polytechnique on a scholarship, he had reported
for work in Panama in 1884. Less than a year later, at the age of twen-
ty-seven, he had found himself, for several punishing months, acting
supervisor of the entire project. Later he left the Compagnie Universelle
but remained in Panama, working as a private contractor on the canal
and, in a manner never entirely explained, amassing a personal fortune.
Eventually, he and his brother Maurice came to own more than $400,000
of stock in the Compagnie Nouvelle, which would be worthless if no one
were willing to purchase the French concession.

In the summer of 1899, when the Walker Commission arrived in Paris on a fact-finding mission, Bunau-Varilla met with George Morison and other members and argued for the advantages of Panama. After the commission opted for Nicaragua, he redoubled his efforts, distributing thirteen thousand copies of his pamphlet *Panama or Nicaragua?* and addressing large, influential audiences in Cincinnati, Cleveland, Boston, Chicago, and Philadelphia. In New York, Pierpont Morgan, who followed the canal debate with great interest, was among the members who invited him to address the state's Chamber of Commerce. In Washington, Bunau-Varilla was granted interviews with Mark Hanna and President McKinley, but when he visited the office of the Senate's champion of Nicaragua, John Tyler Morgan, the two nearly came to blows before Bunau-Varilla made a diplomatic retreat.

In March 1902, Morgan's Committee on Interoceanic Canals voted 7 to 4 in favor of the Hepburn bill, and the chances of a canal through Panama seemed next to nil. Then in early May, a catastrophic eruption of Mount Pelée, on the Caribbean island of Martinique, leveled the city of St. Pierre and killed thirty thousand people. During his barnstorming tour, Bunau-Varilla had warned of the threat posed by volcanoes in Nicaragua as well, and he now wrote Roosevelt, Hanna, Spooner, and Senator Morgan to remind them of the danger. In mid-May, as the Senate was preparing to debate the Hepburn bill, Nicaragua's Mount Momotombo also erupted, and though the damage was relatively minor, the proponents of Panama felt that Nature had underscored their argument. To accentuate the point, Bunau-Varilla sent each senator a Nicaraguan postage stamp, depicting an erupting Momotombo, mounted above the typed caption: "An official witness of the volcanic activity of Nicaragua."

Opening debate on the Spooner bill on June 4, John Tyler Morgan reminded his fellow senators that Panama also experienced its share of seismic instability. Then, for two and a half hours, he detailed that route's other drawbacks, including notoriously unhealthful conditions and unceasing political turmoil. Building a canal in Panama was bound to result in war with Colombia, he argued, since the region's chronic instability would sooner or later require the United States to secure the isthmus by force.

The next day, Mark Hanna took the floor. Eschewing polemical brimstone, the senator spoke plainly, relying on data supplied by Cromwell and displaying simple, effective charts created by Bunau-Varilla. One by one, he ticked off the practical advantages of the Panama route, which not only was less prone to volcanic eruption, but was shorter, straighter, and faster to traverse; required fewer locks; would be cheaper to operate; and boasted superior harbors on either end and a ready-built railroad. It was a masterful presentation, and the Senate eventually voted in favor of the Spooner bill, 67 to 6. A week later, the House, which earlier had supported the Hepburn bill, reversed itself and approved the Spooner measure by 260 to 8. Some representatives had apparently decided that a Panama Canal was preferable to no canal, while others were hoping that the French could not deliver a good title or that Colombia would not agree to the transfer, in which case Nicaragua would remain the only viable option.

With the passage of the Spooner Act, the drama shifted from Congress to the State Department, where John Hay was charged with securing Colombia's approval. At Mark Hanna's recommendation, Roosevelt and Hay embraced William Nelson Cromwell as their principal adviser, and in the coming months Cromwell would play an extraordinary ex-officio role as intermediary between Washington and Bogotá.

The United States and Colombia had begun negotiations even before the passage of the Spooner Act, and by April 1902 they had arrived at a memorandum intended to serve as the basis of a potential treaty. Under the memorandum, Colombia consented to transfer the Compagnie Nouvelle's assets to the United States and agreed to rent the Americans a ten-kilometer-wide canal zone on a hundred-year, renewable lease. In exchange, Washington agreed to pay a one-time fee of $7 million plus an annual amount to be negotiated; to recognize Colombia's sovereignty in the canal zone (although the method of administering the zone had yet to be determined); to keep the waterway neutral and open to ships of all nations; and to cede the defense of the canal to Colombia, except in times of crisis.

But the Spooner Act called for a perpetual, not a hundred-year, lease and reserved exclusive administration of the canal zone to the United States. When Washington sought to renegotiate the terms of the memorandum to include these changes, Bogotá resisted. Discussions continued throughout the summer and autumn, through a change of ambassadors in Washington and yet another revolt in Panama. In December, apparently at Cromwell's suggestion, the United States increased its offer to $10 million plus a $100,000 annual payment to begin after ten years. Still Bogotá held to its principles.

The Americans could have waited until October 1904, when under the terms of the Compagnie Nouvelle's contract with Colombia, the agreement could be canceled if the canal had not been completed. Exempt from paying $40 million to the French, Washington would presumably have had more financial leeway to tempt Bogotá. But there was no guarantee that even then the two countries could come to terms, or that an interloper wouldn't step forward to tie up the rights. A Colombian senator had already approached the German government to gauge their interest, in case negotiations with the United States broke down.

By January 1903, Roosevelt and Hay had lost patience. On the 21st, the secretary of state wrote the Colombian envoy, Tomás Herrán: "I am commanded by the President to inform you that the reasonable time provided in the [Spooner Act] for the conclusion of the negotiations with Colombia . . . has expired." The United States, he said, would increase the annuity to $250,000, but he was "not authorized to consider or discuss any other change." If Colombia did not give its immediate consent, the Americans would break off negotiations and begin discussions for a canal through Nicaragua. Satisfied that they had won all the concessions they were likely to extract, Bogotá acquiesced, and the following afternoon the two ministers signed the Hay-Herrán Treaty. In recognition of the crucial part Cromwell had played, Hay presented him with the signing pen.

The treaty was sent to the Senate, where John Tyler Morgan again led the opposition, pressing for some sixty amendments. As he had during the debate over the Spooner bill, Cromwell lobbied the senators doggedly, and when the roll was called on March 17, the treaty was ratified by a vote of 73 to 5.

The previous October, after journeying to Paris to inspect the documents, Attorney General Knox had reported that the Compagnie Nouvelle's title was sound. Now the single remaining obstacle to the transfer was for the Colombian senate to ratify the treaty that its ambassador had already signed. But Colombia had only recently ended a costly, three-year civil war, and the nation's leader, José Manuel Marroquín, enjoyed a tenuous grip on power. If he acceded to the treaty, he would face the wrath of his countrymen, who bitterly resented the erosion of national sovereignty that the document represented. But if he didn't agree, he would forego the Americans' money, which the country urgently needed, and he would face the real possibility of secession by the chronically restless state of Panama, which was desperate for the benefits the canal would bring. So, hoping to make the treaty more palatable at home, Marroquín tried to make it more lucrative. In addition to the $10 million indemnity from the United States, he now demanded a share of the $40 million to be paid to the Compagnie Nouvelle.

In truth, Colombia had been pressuring William Nelson Cromwell on this point for two years. But in the interest of protecting his French clients, Cromwell had persuaded Bogotá to defer their claim until the all-important Spooner bill had passed Congress—by which time, he hoped, it would be too late to increase the asking price. Now, as Colombia insisted on the additional payment, Cromwell decried their "blackmail."

Neither Roosevelt nor Hay held a high opinion of Latin American governments in general or the Colombian administration in particular, and they readily agreed with Cromwell's characterization. In April, Hay sent the American ambassador in Bogotá a strongly worded communiqué, apparently drafted by Cromwell, ordering him to tolerate no delay that would offer Colombia a chance to negotiate a separate settlement with the Compagnie Nouvelle. "Neither the canal nor the railroad company is or can be a party" to the treaty, Hay wrote; "nor can the United States permit its international compacts to be dependent in any degree upon the action of any private corporation. Such a course would be consistent neither with the dignity of either nation nor with their interests."

Stalling for time and glad to deflect responsibility, Marroquín called a special session of the Colombian congress to consider the treaty. In early June, as the lawmakers prepared to meet, Hay went further, warning in decidedly undiplomatic language, "If Colombia should now reject the treaty or unduly delay its ratification, the friendly understanding between the two countries would be so seriously compromised that action might be taken by the Congress next winter which every friend of Colombia would regret." In a letter to his secretary of state, Roosevelt was even blunter. "I fear we may have to give a lesson to those jack rabbits," he wrote. In case Bogotá did not acquiesce, he began drafting plans to seize the canal route by force.

On June 13, Cromwell spent much of the day in conference at the White House and afterward sent his press agent to the Washington bureau of the *New York World.* The following morning, on page one, the newspaper published an astonishing prediction. "President Roosevelt is determined to have the Panama canal route," the piece began. "He has no intention of beginning negotiations for the Nicaragua route. . . . The State of Panama will secede if the Colombian Congress fails to ratify the canal treaty. . . . The citizens of Panama propose, after seceding, to make a treaty with the United States, giving this Government the equivalent of absolute sovereignty over the Canal Zone. . . . There will be no increase in price or yearly rental. . . . President Roosevelt is said to strongly favor this plan, if the treaty is rejected. . . . It is intended to wait a reasonable time for action by the Colombian Congress, which convenes June 20, and then, if nothing is done, to make the above plan operative." What of the treaty of 1846, whereby the United States guaranteed the sovereignty of Colombia? That agreement "is now construed as applicable only to foreign interference," the article explained, "and not to the uprisings of her own people."

In the Colombian congress, sentiment was running strongly against the treaty. In July the American ambassador was informed that in exchange for ratification, Colombia would now require $10 million from the Compagnie Nouvelle and an additional $5 million from the United States. Hay dismissed both demands out of hand. Roosevelt wrote his secretary of state, "Those contemptible little creatures in Bogotá ought to understand how much they are jeopardizing things and imperilling their own future."

On August 12, the Colombian senate voted 24 to 0 to reject the treaty. Though this had been expected, Roosevelt reacted with fury and disdain. On August 19, he wrote Hay, "It seems that the great bulk of the best engineers are agreed that that route is the best; and I do not think that the Bogota lot of jack rabbits should be allowed permanently to bar one of the future highways of civilization. Of course under the terms of the [Spooner] Act we could now go ahead with Nicaragua, and perhaps would technically be required to do so. But what we do now will be of consequence, not merely decades, but centuries hence, and we must be sure that we are taking the right step before we act."

Even as the president mulled his options, matters in Panama were taking their own course. As early as May 1903, a group of influential citizens in Panama City had begun plotting the state's independence. Among those brought into their confidence was an American, James Beers, who was port captain and freight agent for the Panama Railroad. Beers apparently reported the group's activities to his superior at the company, William Nelson Cromwell, who called him to New York for a consultation. In Panama, meanwhile, the would-be junta expanded to include other prominent members, several of whom also had ties to the railroad, including its chief physician, Manuel Amador Guerrero, who seemed eager to serve as the new country's president. In July, the conspirators apprised several Americans of their plans, including Hezekiah Gudger, the U.S. consul; J. Gabriel Duque, owner of the *Star and Herald* newspaper; Herbert Prescott, assistant superintendent of the railroad; and William Murray Black, a major in the U.S. Army Corps of Engineers. On August 4, Beers returned to Panama and passed along Cromwell's guarantee of aid. The plotters pressed ahead, and reports from Panama confirmed the growing likelihood of revolution.

In late August, Amador sailed for New York, hoping to secure more specific promises of help, including guns and money from Cromwell and military support from Washington. J. Gabriel Duque arrived on the same steamer, and during an extraordinary private meeting, Cromwell offered the newspaperman a loan of $100,000, to be used for purchasing arms and bribing the small Colombian garrison in Panama. Despite Duque's American citizenship, the lawyer also reportedly offered him the presidency of the breakaway country. Then Cromwell telephoned the State Department and arranged a meeting between Duque and John Hay for the following morning. During the interview, Hay was careful not to commit his government, although he made it clear that the United States intended to build a canal in Panama regardless of any objections in Bogotá.

But Duque was not as sympathetic to the revolution as Cromwell, Hay, and the others supposed, and on leaving the State Department, he contacted the Colombian embassy and reported all that he had heard about the plot. Outraged, Ambassador Herrán wrote Cromwell, warning that Colombia would hold him and his clients responsible for any disturbance in Panama and implicitly threatening to cancel the Compagnie Nouvelle's concession and to revoke its property rights. Shaken, Cromwell refused to meet with Amador again.

Alerted to events in New York, whether by Cromwell or some other source, Philippe Bunau-Varilla arrived from Paris on September 22. Two days later he met with Amador, who was still bewildered by Cromwell's sudden coldness. Then on the morning of October 9, Bunau-Varilla was in Washington, paying his respects to an old acquaintance, Assistant Secretary of State Francis B. Loomis, who was in charge of the department while John Hay spent some time at his summer home in New Hampshire. When Loomis offered to introduce him to President Roosevelt, ostensibly to discuss the long-running French political scandal known as the Dreyfus Affair, Bunau-Varilla eagerly accepted. Loomis made a telephone call to the White House, and a meeting was arranged for noon that same day.

Venturing into the raw, rainy weather, Loomis and Bunau-Varilla left the hulking State, War, and Navy Building and crossed the street to the White House. The president received the visitors in his second-floor office, and while Loomis stood nearby, Bunau-Varilla and the president made themselves comfortable. As they discussed the Dreyfus Affair, Bunau-Varilla searched for a chance to broach the subject foremost in his mind. Finally he ventured, "Mr. President, Captain Dreyfus has not been the only victim of detestable political passions. Panama is another."

"Oh, yes," Roosevelt answered, showing sudden interest. "That is true, you have devoted much time and effort to Panama, Mr. Bunau-Varilla. Well, what do you think is going to be the outcome of the present situation?"

"Mr. President, a revolution."

"A revolution. . . ." Roosevelt glanced toward Loomis. "A revolution. . . . Would it be possible? But if it became a reality, what would become of the plan we had thought of?" Then turning back to Bunau-Varilla, he asked, "What makes you think so?"

The Frenchman chose his words with care. "General and special considerations, Mr. President. As you know, the revolutionary spirit is endemic on the Isthmus. There is almost a certainty of seeing an endemic disease spread violently when the circumstances favourable to its development have reached their maximum. Colombia has decreed the ruin of the people of the Isthmus. They will not let things go any further without protesting according to their fashion. Their fashion is—Revolution."

Bunau-Varilla dared say no more, and the president apparently wanted to hear no more. The meeting ended soon afterward, but for both parties it had been worthwhile: For Roosevelt, it affirmed what his own sources had been telling him for months. And for Bunau-Varilla it confirmed that if there were a revolution, the United States would be prepared to seize the opportunity. But what form was American action likely to take? Clearly, an uprising by a few poorly equipped Panamanian patriots could succeed only with military intervention by the United States.

Soon after Hay's return from New Hampshire, Bunau-Varilla

Secretary of State John Hay.
LIBRARY OF CONGRESS

was summoned to a meeting at the secretary's home on Lafayette Square, an imposing structure bristling with turrets and gables and chimneys. When he arrived at 3:00, he found Hay waiting. As they began their conversation, Bunau-Varilla confessed his frustration with Colombia's intransigence on the treaty. Then he added, "When all the counsels of Prudence and Friendship have been made in vain, there comes a moment when one has to stand still and await events."

"These events," Hay asked, "what do you think they will be?"

"The whole thing will end in a revolution," he answered. "You must take your measures, if you do not want to be taken yourself by surprise."

"Yes," Hay said, "that is unfortunately the most probable hypothesis. But we shall not be caught napping. Orders have been given to naval forces on the Pacific to sail towards the Isthmus."

They spoke generally of the propensity of such countries for revolution. Then Hay told him, "I have just finished reading a charming novel, *Captain Macklin*," by Richard Harding Davis. "It is the history of a West Point cadet, who leaves the military academy to become a soldier of fortune in Central America. He enlists under the orders of a General, a former officer of the French army, who commands a revolutionary army in Honduras. The young, ambitious American and the old French officer, who as head of the army displays in all his acts the generous disinterestedness of his race, are both charming types of searchers after the Ideal." The secretary handed him the book. "Read this volume, take it with you, it will interest you." Though Hay could not speak directly what was on his mind, Bunau-Varilla left convinced that, in passing along the novel of collaboration between the noble Frenchman and the energetic American in the wilds of Central America, the secretary had given him an unmistakable signal.

Returning to New York, Bunau-Varilla met with Amador at the Waldorf-Astoria and personally offered collateral for a $100,000 loan to fund the revolution. Citing the importance of swift action, he also insisted that the uprising be launched within a week of Amador's arrival in Panama. And he extracted a promise that after independence, Panama would engage him to negotiate the canal treaty with the United States. Reassured, Amador sailed for home.

The Panamanian Revolution began on precisely the day that William Nelson Cromwell's press agent had predicted to the *New York World* three months before. On November 2, at 5:30 in the afternoon, the USS *Nashville* anchored in the harbor at Colón, on Panama's Atlantic Coast. Although the ship's orders commanded it only to protect the railroad and maintain the peace, to the insurgents the gunboat's appearance was an undeniable signal of American support.

A little before midnight, the Colombian warship *Cartagena* also entered the harbor, with five hundred troops aboard. Their commander, General Juan Tobar, landed the soldiers early the next morning, and the situation suddenly seemed dire for the would-be revolutionaries. But James Shaler, the seventy-one-year-old American superintendent of the Panama Railroad, contrived to separate the Colombian officers from their men, telling Tobar that the governor had ordered the detachment to continue immediately across the isthmus to Panama City. Shepherding the officers aboard a special train of only one carriage, Shaler assured them that the troops would follow as soon as other rolling stock became available.

Fifty miles away, in Panama City, Manuel Amador secured the loyalty of the Colombian garrison, paying $65,000 to the commanding general, Esteban Huertas, and $50 to each enlisted man. After Tobar and his staff arrived, they were arrested. A Colombian warship, the *Bogotá*, was anchored in the harbor, and on hearing reports of revolution, the captain lobbed half a dozen shells into the city; then after taking fire from a shore battery, the ship withdrew. The state and municipal government declared their loyalty to the junta, and in the central square toasts were raised to President Roosevelt and the United States.

In Colón, the stranded Colombian soldiers spent the night camped in the street. Early the next morning, the *Nashville*'s senior officer, Commander John Hubbard, disembarked a detachment of forty sailors, beginning a tense standoff at the railroad's warehouse. Finally, on the afternoon of November 5, the Colombian officer in charge, Colonel Eliseo Torres, agreed to board his men on a mail ship, the *Orinoco*, which was moored in the harbor, in exchange for $8,000 and two cases of champagne. Another American gunboat, the *Dixie*, appeared that evening, the second of ten U.S. warships that would arrive off Panama's Pacific and Atlantic coasts over the next week. After the departure of the Colombian soldiers, the *Dixie* landed four hundred marines, effectively securing Colón for the revolutionaries. The official proclamation of independence was read the next morning outside Colón's government building. The revolution's single casualty had been a Chinese shopkeeper who had been asleep in bed when the *Bogotá* shelled Panama City.

The junta honored its promise to appoint Philippe Bunau-Varilla its envoy to Washington, and in a White House ceremony held on November 13, just ten days after the revolution, the United States became the first government to officially welcome the new country to the community of nations. At the event, Roosevelt asked Bunau-Varilla, "What do you think, Mr. Minister, of those people who print that we have made the Revolution of Panama together?"

"I think, Mr. President," the Frenchman responded, "that calumny never loses its opportunity even in the New World. It is necessary patiently to wait until the spring of the imagination of the wicked is dried up, and until truth dissipates the mist of mendacity."

As word of the United States's role became public, the uprising in Panama would prove the single most controversial episode of Roosevelt's presidency. Though most Americans supported his actions, there was also widespread criticism. In the Senate, John Tyler Morgan called the canal treaty a "usurpation" and ventured that Panama had "no more right to appoint a Minister to the United States than that country had to consecrate a saint. [Bunau-Varilla] came as a swift-winged messenger of falsehood, dispatched on his mission by the Panama Canal Company."

Many newspapers launched their own scathing critiques. Under the headline "Stolen Property," the *New York Times* editorialized: "Let us not deceive ourselves. We get our canal by spoliation, by robbing Colombia of her Isthmian territory, by breaking treaty faith, by wrong and dishonor. . . . [T]his territory through which we are to build the canal is stolen property, [and] our partners in the theft are a group of canal promoters and speculators and lobbyists who come into their money through the rebellion we encouraged, made safe, and effectuated." The *New York Evening Post* called the affair "the most ignominious thing we know of in the annals of American diplomacy. . . . This overriding of the rights of the weaker is the work of the advocate of 'a square deal'! The preacher to bishops has shown that, for him at least, private morality has no application to public affairs."

In response, both Roosevelt and Hay stressed the perfect propriety of what they had done. The secretary of state assured newsmen that the government's actions were "not only in the strictest accordance with the principles of justice" but were the only possible course "in compliance with our treaty rights and obligations." On January 4, 1904, in a special message to Congress, the president responded to his critics point by point. "No one connected with this Government had any part in preparing, inciting, or encouraging" the revolution, he claimed, and the United States had "received a mandate from civilization" to build the canal. The claims were clearly self-serving, but it appears that Roosevelt genuinely believed his version of events. Years afterward, in his autobiography, he betrayed no appreciation of the domestic constraints on Marroquín and was still attributing Colombia's actions to simple dishonesty and greed. If Elihu Root had not been on government business in Britain, maybe he would have been able to curb the president's impulses. But in the event, Roosevelt, characteristically, reduced the complex conflict to a morality play, in which the "blackmail" of the "corruptionists" was impeding the advance of "civilization."

In private, Roosevelt was heard to say, "I took Panama because Philippe Bunau-Varilla brought it to me on a silver platter." But the diminutive Frenchman's part in the affair was not at an end. Neither was Pierpont Morgan's. After the unsuccessful launching of the Panama Canal Company of America and the federal government's assumption of control in all matters relating to the canal, Morgan had been relegated to the role of observer in the drama of Panama. But now, as the new country's "Envoy Extraordinary and Minister Plenipotentiary near the Government of the United States of America," Bunau-Varilla arranged for the financier to extend Panama a loan of $100,000 until it received the $10 million indemnity from the United States. Bunau-Varilla also appointed Morgan as Panama's financial agent, charged with receiving and investing those funds.

Following Panama's recognition by the United States, Bunau-Varilla and John Hay began to draft the treaty that would transfer the canal zone to American control. And they needed to work with undiplomatic speed, because on November 10 a special commission, including Manuel Amador, had left Panama, en route to Washington. Although Bunau-Varilla remained "the authorized party to make treaties," Bogotá informed Hay, the commissioners would assist in the negotiations. But, fearing that their true purpose was to remove him from his post, or to claim credit for the treaty, or to otherwise undermine his work, Bunau-Varilla determined to have the crucial document signed before their arrival. (His apprehension was well founded, since the delegation carried a letter prohibiting Bunau-Varilla from acting without their consent.)

Resolved to give the U.S. Senate no excuse to delay ratification, Bunau-Varilla rewrote the Hay-Herrán Treaty in terms more favorable to the United States. Panama, it agreed, would accept $10 million for transferring the French concession to the United States, plus annual payments of $250,000, which would begin in 1913. Whereas Colombia had been prepared to cede a canal zone six miles wide, Panama would authorize ten miles. Instead of granting a hundred-year lease, the agreement would run "in perpetuity." And the United States would have a free hand in administering the canal zone, exercising all the rights of a sovereign power. On November 17, after working through the night, he delivered the document to the secretary of state. Understandably pleased, Hay set his stenographers to drawing up the signing copies, and the treaty was executed at Hay's house at seven o´clock on the evening of the 18th, barely two weeks after the revolution.

Amador and his party had arrived in New York the night before, but unaware of the hasty negotiations taking place in the capital, they had lingered in Manhattan and met with William Nelson Cromwell, whom they appointed Panama's fiscal agent and legal representative in the United States. As they stepped off the train in Washington, at nine o'clock on the night of the 18th, Bunau-Varilla was on hand to greet them. On hearing that the treaty was already signed, one of the emissaries slapped him across the face.

Bunau-Varilla cabled the text of the treaty to Panama's foreign minister, then followed up with a warning that any delay in ratification would cause the United States to withdraw its ships and to begin negotiations with Nicaragua. The Panamanian government accepted the bluff and within twenty-four hours telegraphed its guarantee that the pact would be ratified without delay. The U.S. Senate took considerably longer in its deliberations, but on February 23, 1904, following heated debate in which the cons were again led by John Tyler Morgan, the treaty passed by a vote of 66 to 14.

Having realized his long-delayed dream of redeeming French honor, Bunau-Varilla resigned his diplomatic post and returned to Paris. In addition to the $453,000 that he and his brother would recoup for their stock in the Compagnie Nouvelle, he was presented his country's highest award, the Legion of Honor, in recognition of his service.

Pierpont Morgan continued to play a central role in the finances of the canal. In light of his previous assistance to the American government and his ability to transfer enormous quantities of cash without ruffling world money markets, he was selected by the Roosevelt Administration and the Compagnie Nouvelle to handle the United States's $40-million payment to the French. In early April, he left on his annual trip to Europe, accompanied by his daughter Anne. While in Paris, he signed the contract governing the details of the canal transfer, and in late April American assistant attorneys general W. A. Day and Charles W. Russell executed the papers completing the purchase. The Compagnie Nouvelle had requested that payment be made in France rather than the United States and had consented to cover the associated expenses. To expedite the closing, a syndicate of Paris banks agreed to advance the $40 million, then take reimbursement from Morgan & Company over a period of weeks, as several installments of gold were shipped from New York to the Banque de France.

On May 4, at 7:30 a.m., in an understated ceremony inside Colón's Grand Hotel, Mark Brooke, a second lieutenant in the Army Corps of Engineers, took official possession of the Compagnie Nouvelle's property in Panama. Five days later, Treasury Secretary Leslie Shaw traveled to New York with a warrant for $40 million, the largest single check the government had ever issued (the second largest, for $7.2 million, had been paid to Russia for the purchase of Alaska, in 1868). Since the law required Morgan & Company to post security for the payment, $25 million in cash and federal, state, and municipal bonds was stacked in steamer trunks and suitcases, loaded onto a horse-drawn wagon, and conveyed to the U.S. Subtreasury Building, where it took more than three hours to count it all. Then the warrant was delivered to Morgan partners George Perkins and Charles Steele. For its work in facilitating the largest real estate transaction to date, Morgan & Company collected fees and commissions of less than $30,000.

As financial agent for the Republic of Panama, Morgan was also responsible for accepting the United States's payment for the canal. In early May, the bank received a treasury warrant for $1 million, to allow the young nation to meet immediate expenses (which, according to some reports, included generous payments to the country's founding fathers). Later that month, Morgan's bank accepted a warrant for the outstanding $9 million. After repaying the $100,000 loan, setting aside some working capital, and allotting $2 million for public works, the country was left with $6 million, which Morgan invested, very profitably, in New York City mortgages.

In making these arrangements, the banker dealt closely with Panama's legal representative in the United States, his longtime associate William Nelson Cromwell. Along with Bunau-Varilla and Roosevelt himself, Cromwell had played a determining role in events—the choice of Panama over Nicaragua, the timely allegations of Colombian "blackmail," the fomenting of revolution—doing all he could to ensure that his clients recouped every possible franc. In the end, stockholders in de Lesseps's bankrupt Compagnie Universelle got no part of the American payment, but the company's bondholders received 60 percent of the purchase price, or an average of $156 each, representing about 10 percent of their investment. The nearly seven thousand shareholders of the Compagnie Nouvelle did much better, recovering their principal plus interest of about 3 percent a year. For his years of effort, Cromwell billed his clients $832,499.38, including expenses, or some 2 percent of the purchase price. After the company contested this amount as excessive, a French arbitrator ultimately awarded the lawyer $228,282.71.

Partially owing to Cromwell's close ties to Pierpont Morgan, rumors had long circulated that the financier had played a hidden role in the sale of the canal. In 1899, Morgan had been one of the backers of the stillborn Panama Canal Company of America. And in March 1903, the *New York World* reported "reliable information" that a group of thirty American capitalists, supposedly including Morgan, had quietly bought up somewhere between a quarter and a half of the Compagnie Nouvelle shares. Since the old Compagnie Universelle's bonds were not registered but paid to the bearer, there was no record of who had received that portion of the payment.

John Tyler Morgan, the longtime opponent of the Panama route, spent years trying to prove that a secret Wall Street syndicate had invested in the canal and then resold their interest to the American government at a huge profit. In January 1906, as chairman of the Senate's Committee on Interoceanic Canals, he launched an investigation of the charges. William Nelson Cromwell was called to testify, but the lawyer so often refused to answer on the grounds of attorney-client privilege that Senator Morgan diagnosed him with a case of "lockjaw." The sparring continued for days, but in the end the lawyer divulged nothing. The lawmaker died in June of the following year, and the investigation was forgotten.

But on October 3, 1908, Joseph Pulitzer's *New York World* dedicated much of its front page to an extraordinary claim of corruption surrounding the canal. The article, the first of six appearing between October 3 and October 16, alleged that a New York syndicate had secretly paid $12 million for shares in the Compagnie Nouvelle, then had lobbied Congress to select the Panama route over Nicaragua and to pay the (in the editors' opinion) hugely inflated price of $40 million. And when negotiations with Colombia had stalled, they had abetted the revolution and promoted the treaty with the United States, producing a windfall for themselves. Among those implicated in the purported plot were Philippe Bunau-Varilla; William Nelson Cromwell; Pierpont Morgan; Douglas Robinson, Theodore Roosevelt's brother-in-law; and Charles Taft, the brother of William Howard Taft, the Republican candidate to succeed Roosevelt as president.

Cromwell denounced the article as a "lying fabrication" and claimed that, except for his legal fees, "neither me nor any one allied with me ever bought, sold, dealt in or ever made a penny of profit" on the canal. But it was Cromwell who had unwittingly brought the story to the *World*'s attention. In July and August, he claimed, he had been approached by blackmailers demanding $25,000 to suppress supposed evidence of corruption surrounding the canal. Instead of submitting, he had reported the threats to the district attorney. Then, on October 2, believing that the blackmailers were already in communication with the *World*, Cromwell sent an associate to the paper to deny their claims. But no one at the *World* seemed to know anything about the charges before Cromwell's man raised the issue. And so the paper's first story on the affair, published the following day, had served to publicize the very assertions that the lawyer wished to keep quiet.

William Howard Taft also telegraphed a denial to the *World*, and the newspaper later admitted that, other than Cromwell's statement to their editors, there was no evidence linking either his brother or the president's brother-in-law to any investment in the Compagnie Nouvelle. At first Roosevelt refused to answer the charges, but once his handpicked successor was safely elected, the outgoing president vehemently denied the existence of any syndicate and condemned as "slander" the "abominable falsehood that any American has profited from the sale of the Panama Canal."

On December 15, he sent a special message to Congress defending his actions in Panama and attacking the *World*. "The stories were scurrilous and libelous in character and false in every essential particular," he charged. "The wickedness of the slanders is only surpassed by their fatuity. ... They consist simply of a string of infamous libels." Not only did they libel individuals, they were "a libel upon the United States Government. Therefore, it was a high national duty to bring to justice this villifier of the American people. . . . The Attorney-General has under consideration the form in which the proceedings against Mr. Pulitzer shall be brought." The next day the newspaper responded: "If *The World* has libelled anybody we hope it will be punished, but we do not intend to be intimidated by Mr. Roosevelt's threats, or by Mr. Roosevelt's denunciations, or by Mr. Roosevelt's power. . . . So far as *The World* is concerned its proprietor may go to jail, if Mr. Roosevelt succeeds, as he threatens, but even in jail *The World* will not cease to be a fearless champion of free speech, a free press and a free people. It cannot be muzzled."

Roosevelt carried through on his threat, and on February 17, 1909, in the final days of his administration, a criminal indictment was returned against the Press Publishing Company (owner of the *World*); Joseph Pulitzer; two of the paper's editors, Caleb M. Van Hamm and Robert H. Lyman; and Delavan Smith and Charles R. Williams, proprietors of the *Indianapolis News*, one of many newspapers that had republished the *World*'s story. (Allegedly, the *News* was singled out because Roosevelt blamed their report for Taft's slim margin of victory in Indiana and for the Republicans' loss of the governorship and legislature there.) As the libeled parties, the indictment listed Theodore Roosevelt, William Howard Taft, Charles Taft, Douglas Robinson, Elihu Root, William Nelson Cromwell, and J. Pierpont Morgan.

The prosecution was extraordinary on several accounts. First, it was a generally accepted principle of law that the United States had no federal libel statute and that such matters were the province of the states. The venue for the case was also problematic; whereas criminal prosecutions are normally mounted in the jurisdiction where the offense occurred, the government had brought this indictment in the District of Columbia, on the grounds that both newspapers were distributed there.

The *World* answered with an editorial the following day, under the headline "A Political Persecution": "This persecution, if it succeeds, will place every newspaper in the country which circulates in Washington— and there are few of importance which do not circulate there—completely at the mercy of any autocratic, vainglorious President who is willing to prostitute his authority for the gratification of his personal malice. . . . The real offence of 'The World' is that for years it has consistently opposed on principle Mr. Roosevelt's jingoism, his militarism, his usurpations, his centralizing policies, his cowboy method of administration and his government by denunciation . . . Mr. Roosevelt is an episode. 'The World' is an institution. Long after Mr. Roosevelt is dead, long after Mr. Pulitzer is dead, long after all the present editors of this paper are dead, 'The World' will still go on as a great independent newspaper, unmuzzled, undaunted and unterrorized."

Rather than collaborate on the case, the U.S. attorney in Indianapolis, Joseph B. Kealing, chose to resign, writing Attorney General Charles Bonaparte, "I am not in accord with the Government in its attempt to put a strained construction on the law; to drag these defendants from their homes to the seat of the Government, to be tried and punished, while there is good and sufficient law in this jurisdiction in the State court. I believe the principle involved is dangerous, striking at the very foundation of our form of government."

In preparing its defense, the *World* hired a British corporate lawyer and member of Parliament, who traveled to Paris and obtained permission to open the Crédit Lyonnais vault where, in keeping with French law, the Compagnie Nouvelle's records had been sealed. But when the safe was unlocked, the documents were gone. Said the attorney, "I have never known in my lengthy experience of company matters any public corporation, much less one of such vast importance, having so completely disappeared and removed all traces of its existence."

One morning not long afterward, an editor at the *World* discovered on his desk a copy of a brief apparently written by William Nelson Cromwell to substantiate the $800,000 bill he had submitted to the Compagnie Nouvelle. Running to sixty-five thousand words, in French, the document detailed the lawyer's extraordinary and irregular efforts on behalf of his clients, but did not link him to any secret syndicate.

The *World* also sent reporters to Panama and Colombia in search of evidence that might substantiate their charges. Manuel Amador had since died, but other insurgents testified before a Panamanian court that they had not conspired with either Washington or the Panama Railroad Company in planning the revolution. Then Amador's son Raoul offered one of the reporters, Earl Harding, a letter his father had purportedly written him hinting at prior collusion with U.S. officials. Dated October 18, 1903, less than three weeks before the revolution, the document read, "The plan seems to me good. A portion of the Isthmus declares itself independent and that portion the United States will not allow any Colombian forces to attack." A treaty would be speedily concluded with Washington, it went on, and the new republic would remain "under the protection of the United States." As to financing the government, "already this has been arranged with a bank."

Harding also claimed that on March 5, 1909 (the day after Roosevelt left the White House), a freelance reporter named John Craig Hammond turned over to the *World* an original syndicate agreement in which a group of American investors agreed to purchase as many shares as possible of the Compagnie Nouvelle, for not more than 20 percent of par value, and to sell them for not less than 55 percent of par. Among the undersigned were J.P. Morgan & Company and other prominent bankers, including James Stillman and Isaac Seligman; Senator Chauncey Depew; Douglas Robinson; and Henry W. Taft (another brother of the incoming president). Hammond was also said to have produced a leather-bound ledger recording the contributions of the original sixteen members, plus investments by six additional contributors, who included "G. W. Perkins," "Nelson P. Cromwell," and "H. J. Satterlee." G. W. Perkins apparently referred to Morgan partner and Roosevelt friend George Walbridge Perkins. It was never determined who H. J. Satterlee might be, since Pierpont Morgan's son-in-law was Herbert L. Satterlee; Nelson P. Cromwell also remained a mystery, although some newspaper reports of the American Panama Canal Company back in 1899 had also listed that name as an investor.

The agreement's authenticity was never tested in court, because on October 15, 1909, federal judge Albert B. Anderson dismissed the government's case. In his sweeping verdict, the justice ruled that the suit violated both the First Amendment and the Sixth (which guarantees a trial in the state and district where the crime was allegedly committed). "To my mind that man has read the history of our institutions to little purpose who does not look with grave apprehension upon the possibility of the success of a proceeding such as this," he wrote. "If the history of liberty means anything—if constitutional guarantees are worth anything—this proceeding must fail."

The government had won a separate federal indictment against Pulitzer's company in New York, and after the dismissal in the District of Columbia, the administration shifted its case to that jurisdiction. After the *World*'s motion to quash the indictment was upheld in New York as well, the government appealed to the U.S. Supreme Court, which, on January 3, 1911, ruled in favor of the defendants. At his home in Oyster Bay, Theodore Roosevelt was approached by a reporter for the *World*, but the usually garrulous ex-president would only comment, "I have nothing to say."

When the United States took possession in May 1904, the canal was navigable for eleven miles inland from Colón, on the Atlantic Coast. The French had done some excavation along most of the route, although not all that work would prove useful to the Americans. Wherever they looked, the newcomers were impressed by the quality of their predecessors' engineering and construction in the face of overwhelming obstacles. But after years of disuse, the structures and machinery were seriously dilapidated. Before they could begin to dig, the Americans had to repair hundreds of buildings and construct dozens of new ones; modernize the railroad; and order new equipment, including ninety-five-ton Bucyrus steam shovels, three times the size of the rigs the French had had to work with.

There also remained the problem of disease. Putting to use recent discoveries in tropical medicine, American doctors launched a public health campaign unprecedented in scope. Teams of workers were dispatched to drain or cover standing water, fumigate buildings, and install window screens, all to eliminate the mosquitos spreading malaria and yellow fever. Thanks to their efforts, by the end of 1906 the dreaded "yellow jack" had been eradicated. Malaria was more stubborn, especially among the tens of thousands of black laborers from Barbados, whose work took them to more remote areas and whose barracks weren't equipped with niceties such as window screens. Most deadly of all for this group though was viral pneumonia, which was unknown on Barbados. In 1906, the death rate for white employees, who made up about 25 percent of the workforce, was seventeen per thousand, while for black workers it was fifty-nine. (But by 1914, the combined death rate would be just under eight per thousand—lower than for the general population of the United States. All told, during the decade of American construction, fifty-six hundred canal employees would succumb—fewer than five thousand of disease—versus the more than twenty thousand that had died from all causes during the French tenure.)

After making a fitful start, chief engineer John F. Wallace resigned in June 1905, in the midst of a yellow fever epidemic, to take a better-paying, less-taxing position in the private sector. As Roosevelt considered Wallace's replacement, he met at the White House with James J. Hill, Pierpont Morgan's partner in Northern Securities. Hill recommended for the job the man who had guided Hill's Great Northern Railroad to the Pacific, John Stevens. Now fifty-two, with thinning black hair and a push-broom mustache, Stevens was taciturn and tough, a natural leader who expected much from his men and inspired their undivided devotion. He was also, Hill said, the best construction engineer in America. On the verge of sailing for the Philippines to begin work on a railroad project there, Stevens was inclined to refuse the Panama appointment, but in New York he sought the advice of William Nelson Cromwell, who convinced him to sign on. And so even after the United States had begun work in Panama, Pierpont Morgan's attorney continued to throw an outsized shadow over the isthmus.

Stevens spent nearly a year planning and organizing before he resumed digging. By late 1906, almost twenty-four thousand workers were employed on the project, but they still didn't know whether they were building a sea-level or a lock canal. In January of that year a thirteen-man international board appointed by President Roosevelt had recommended the sea-level approach, which it was estimated would take twelve to thirteen years and cost $247 million, or about $100 million more than the alternative. But Stevens believed that a sea-level route would require at least eighteen years, versus eight for a lock canal. He was able to convince the president of his argument, and in June, the Senate

Roosevelt in Panama. LIBRARY OF CONGRESS

narrowly approved Stevens's plan. In November of that year Roosevelt, accompanied by his wife, Edith, made a two-week trip to Panama, the first time a sitting president had ever traveled outside the United States. Wearing a white suit and tramping through the rainy-season mud, he talked to everyone, asked everything, famously posed sitting in the cab of a steam shovel, and to all appearances had the time of his life.

In January 1907, physically and emotionally spent, Stevens resigned and was replaced by George Washington Goethals, a distinguished officer of the Army Corps of Engineers who had extensive experience building dams, bridges, and canals. Although Stevens had laid the foundation, most of the actual work remained—the lion's share of the excavation; the breaching of the continental divide at Culebra, three hundred feet above sea level; the building of the artificial Gatun Lake, then the world's largest, at 164 square miles; the design and construction of the mammoth locks. The dignified, demanding Goethals would spend the next seven years making the canal a reality. In 1908 alone, with their new Bucyrus shovels, workers removed thirty-seven million cubic yards of earth—nearly half of what the French had dug in almost seventeen years. By the end, Goethals would have nearly fifty thousand employees working under him.

Charged with overseeing the mammoth project was Roosevelt's close friend and new secretary of war, William Howard Taft. At the end of 1904, Taft made his first journey to the isthmus, to resolve some administrative issues and to patch up relations with Panama. (Accompanying him was William Nelson Cromwell, who remained Panama's representative in the United States.) Over the course of construction, Taft would make seven visits to Panama, including two as president. By the time Roosevelt left the White House, in March 1909, the canal was only half built, and it would not be finished until 1914, during the administration of Woodrow Wilson. In September 1913, as work was nearing completion, Panama was struck by a major earthquake; although buildings were damaged and landslides were loosed, the canal was unscathed.

In total, the U.S. government would spend $352 million on the canal, including the payments to Panama and the Compagnie Nouvelle. The project came in $23 million under the budget set in 1907 and six months ahead of plan. Including the expenditures by the Compagnie Universelle and the Compagnie Nouvelle, the canal had cost $639 million.

Finally, on January 7, 1914, the French crane boat *Alexandre La Valley* completed the first transit through the canal, without ceremony. On August 3 of that year, the *Cristobal*, a cargo ship belonging to the Panama Railroad Steamship Line, became the first oceangoing vessel to cross from the Atlantic to the Pacific. Among those onboard was Philippe Bunau-Varilla, who had journeyed from France to witness the restoration of French honor. But after all the intrigue and labor and sacrifice that had gone into making the canal a reality, the inauguration was relegated to the back of the world's newspapers; front pages were instead filled with reports of the war that had broken out that summer in Europe.

In 1921, the American government would reimburse Colombia $25 million for the loss of Panama. The proposal had been under discussion for years, and ex-president Roosevelt had been among those appalled by the idea. In 1914, he complained to Philippe Bunau-Varilla, "One of the rather contemptible features of a number of our worthy compatriots is that they are eager to take advantage of the deeds of the man of action when action is necessary and then eager to discredit him when the action is once over." Although American intervention in Panama would cloud relations between the United States and its southern neighbors for decades, Roosevelt justifiably called the canal "by far the most important action I took in foreign affairs during the time I was president." And to make the waterway a reality, the president, along with the Panamanian government and the Compagnie Nouvelle du Canal de Panama, had relied on the invaluable but controversial services of Pierpont Morgan and his indefatigable attorney William Nelson Cromwell.

CHAPTER FIVE

"Send Your Man to My Man"

ON MARCH 14, 1904, THE U.S. SUPREME COURT HANDED DOWN THE much-anticipated verdict in the case of *Northern Securities Co. v. United States*. By the thinnest of margins, the justices ruled that the railroad holding company created by Pierpont Morgan, James J. Hill, Edward H. Harriman, and John D. Rockefeller was an illegal combination under the Sherman Act. The verdict, which also affirmed the federal government's authority to regulate interstate commerce, would prove to be a watershed, the first of many rulings where the Act would be applied to dissolve unlawful monopolies.

President Roosevelt was lunching at the White House with John Hay and other guests when a telephone call brought the news. Though elated that his first major action to contain the trusts had been upheld, the president decided to make no immediate public comment. Instead, he deferred to Attorney General Philander Knox, who issued a statement reassuring business interests that the administration had no plans to "run amuck" with indiscriminate filings of other anti-trust suits. Wall Street, which had expected the government's case to be sustained, shrugged off the verdict. Asked for comment, Pierpont Morgan simply confirmed that of course he would respect the High Court's ruling.

The editors of the *New York Times* were less phlegmatic, decrying what they considered the Court's fetish over competition and condemning the Sherman Act as a "crude, ill-considered, harsh, destructive, and dangerous statute" under which "ancient rights hitherto held to be incontestable are abridged, industrial tendencies that promote the increase of

National wealth are suddenly checked, business is thrown into intolerable confusion . . . , and men who have supposed they were conducting lawful affairs in a lawful manner find themselves in peril of prosecution, fine, and imprisonment." But most newspapers and most Americans acclaimed the verdict and praised the president for pressing the case. The *New York Sun* suggested that "under this decision it becomes Mr. Roosevelt's duty to proceed impartially against every corporation or combination tending to restrain interstate commerce or to monopolize trade. . . . Against whom," it asked presciently, "will the Hon. Philander C. Knox be next directed to proceed? Will it be the Standard Oil Company?" The *New York World* noted, "Politically, the effect of the decision can hardly be exaggerated. It will greatly strengthen President Roosevelt as a candidate" for reelection in November. "People will love him for the enemies he has made."

Though it wasn't yet spring, Roosevelt was already looking toward fall. Of the four vice presidents who had come to the presidency on the death of their predecessor—John Tyler, Millard Fillmore, Andrew Johnson, and Chester Arthur—not one had ever been elected to another term. And so, ever since his hasty inauguration in the Wilcox library, Roosevelt had been desperate to shed the mocking title "His Accidency" and to win the office in his own right. As Henry Adams observed, "Theodore thinks of nothing, talks of nothing, and lives for nothing but his political interests. If you remark to him that God is Great, he asks naively how that will affect his election."

During his first term the president had posted some impressive achievements, beginning the arduous process of controlling the trusts, settling the coal strike, and securing the rights to the Panama Canal. But although his popularity was soaring, his road to election, or even nomination, was far from certain. Mark Hanna had warned McKinley against putting "that damned cowboy" on the ticket in 1900. Even so, during Roosevelt's first administration, he and Hanna had reached a productive détente, and the senator had supported many of the president's initiatives. But Hanna remained the Republicans' chief powerbroker, with cordial ties to Wall Street, and throughout his first term Roosevelt had brooded over the Ohioan's plans for 1904: Would Hanna support him or someone else for the nomination, or would he even make a run at the presidency himself?

With tradition prohibiting him from campaigning in 1904, in April of the previous year Roosevelt began a two-month, coast-to-coast tour intended to bolster his popularity with voters. Everywhere he went, from Chicago to Seattle to Salt Lake City, huge, cheering crowds turned out, giving him reason to hope that he could break the curse on accidental presidents.

While he was barnstorming, matters came to a head with Mark Hanna. When Senator Joseph Foraker, Hanna's intraparty rival in Ohio, suggested that the state's Republicans endorse Roosevelt at their convention in June 1903, instead of waiting until summer 1904, Hanna balked at making a commitment. Now Roosevelt forced the issue, telegraphing Hanna, "Of course those who favor my administration and nomination will endorse them, and those who do not will oppose them." Then he released the telegram to the press. Faced with the alternative of publicly opposing the sitting president and the party's likely nominee, Hanna assured Roosevelt that he would not contest his endorsement at the state convention. In a deft but merciless stroke, Roosevelt had defanged his only viable opponent for the nomination.

Pierpont Morgan, however, was not willing to cede the field so easily. That fall, over Thanksgiving dinner at his Madison Avenue home, the financier told Hanna that it was his "duty" to oppose Roosevelt, and he promised that Wall Street would support him if he "would only give the word." But Hanna's health had been declining for years, and he was in no condition for what was sure to be a brutal campaign, even if he were disposed to backtrack on his commitment to the president. In early February 1904 he was reported to be suffering from typhoid fever, and he died on the fifteenth of that month, just before his sixty-seventh birthday. "The country has lost one of the greatest men it ever had," lamented Morgan, who journeyed to Washington to attend the funeral, along with the president and myriad other officials of both parties. On June 23, at the Republican convention in Chicago, Roosevelt won his party's nomination, unanimously, on the first ballot.

The president would be campaigning at a difficult moment. The economy had gone into recession in 1902, and during the following year the Dow

Industrial Average had shed nearly 24 percent of its value. In an inter-view, Morgan attributed the decline to "undigested securities. . . . As for the general situation," he told a reporter, "you may state emphatically and unequivocally that it is most promising, with the country unqualifiedly prosperous. . . . In short, summing the situation up, not only is there pros-perity everywhere, but the promises are of a continuation of that prosper-ity for a long time to come."

Even so, the decline persisted. In a letter to his friend Henry Cabot Lodge, the president wrote, "The financial situation here looks ugly," and he ascribed the slump "chiefly, almost solely, to the speculative watering of stock on a giant scale, in which Pierpont Morgan and so many of his kind have indulged during the last few years. Of course," he grumbled, "if the panic spreads so as to affect the business world I shall have to pay for it."

But despite his private grousing, Roosevelt had worked to make him-self more palatable to Wall Street, toning down his attacks on the trusts and making a point of consulting with bankers. On October 8, 1903, he wrote Morgan, "Mr. Perkins tells me you may pass through Washington this fall. If so, I should much like to see you to talk over certain financial matters." But Morgan apparently felt no urgency in an invitation from the White House. Four days later, he responded: "I should like extremely to have an interview with you on the subject but, at the moment, it is absolutely impossible for me to leave owing to the absence of Mr. Perkins and the serious condition of affairs in this city. I will however commu-nicate with you in a few days. I am sure you will appreciate the reason for not immediately responding to your call." The president assured him, "There is no hurry whatever. I wished to speak to you about certain mat-ters of financial legislation, but it would probably be better to wait until Congress has assembled for the special session after November 9th."

It was to placate Wall Street that the Republicans nominated for vice president, over Roosevelt's objection, Charles Fairbanks, a conservative senator from Indiana who was closely allied with the railroads. Still, business interests failed to line up behind the incumbent, causing him to fret, "The big New York and Chicago capitalists—and both the criminal rich and the fool rich—will do all they can to beat me."

Of potential opponents, the president confided to Henry Cabot Lodge, the "most formidable Democrat" was Grover Cleveland, the former governor of New York who had worked with then assemblyman Roosevelt to pass civil service reform in the state and who had later won two nonconsecutive terms in the White House. The president was wary: "Pierpont Morgan and other Wall Street men have been announcing openly within the past fortnight that they should support Mr. Cleveland against me with all their power." It was true that Morgan, a lifelong Republican, did try to recruit Cleveland for a third term. But like Hanna, the sixty-seven-year-old ex-president begged off, citing poor health.

At the convention in Philadelphia that July, the Democrats nominated Alton B. Parker, the colorless chief judge of the New York Court of Appeals. The idea was to offer Wall Street a reassuring alternative to Roosevelt's anti-business bluster, and in the nation's financial capital, the *Times*, *Herald*, *World*, and *Evening Post* endorsed the Democrat, even though four years earlier they had all supported McKinley and Roosevelt. The reluctant exception was the *New York Sun*, whose backhanded endorsement read in full: "Theodore! with all thy faults—."

In the end, Morgan and Wall Street came around to the same opinion as the editors of the *Sun*—better to stand by the proven party of business, despite an unstable standard bearer, than to chance the party of Bryan, even with a proven ally at its head. Besides, considering Roosevelt's enormous popularity and Parker's spectacular blandness, it was clear which way the election was likely to go.

The Republicans turned to the politician's essential task, raising money. George Cortelyou, Roosevelt's former personal secretary, had been appointed head of the new Department of Commerce and Labor, but following the death of Mark Hanna he had left to become chairman of the Republican National Committee and manager of Roosevelt's reelection campaign. After TR's nomination, working with party treasurer Cornelius Bliss, Cortelyou began to solicit campaign contributions from America's largest banks and corporations. In October, Pierpont Morgan donated $100,000 in cash, then when approached again, gave another $50,000. Jay Gould's son George reportedly contributed

$500,000. Chauncey Depew's New York Central and George Perkins's New York Life made donations, as did Standard Oil, General Electric, and International Harvester. In all, the trusts and their wealthy investors donated just under $2.2 million to Roosevelt's campaign, or more than 70 percent of the Republicans' war chest.

In 1907, at Roosevelt's urging, Congress would pass the Tillman Act, outlawing corporate donations to candidates for federal office, but in 1904 there was nothing illegal in these contributions. Yet it didn't escape notice that, as former secretary of commerce and labor, George Cortelyou was soliciting donations from the very corporations he had been charged with regulating, on behalf of an incumbent who had the power to take the companies to court. In a two-page open letter signed by Joseph Pulitzer, the *New York World* charged, "You have not kept the faith, Mr. President, in your promise of publicity as to the affairs of the corporations. . . . When they give something to Mr. Cortelyou for your campaign . . . they regard your acceptance of their tribute as an implied promise of protection." Then the article demanded to know, corporation by corporation, how much money the Roosevelt campaign had accepted from the railroads, the steel trust, the oil trust, and the rest.

The president refrained from replying to Pulitzer's challenge at first, but when Alton Parker echoed the *World*'s demands, branding the corporate donations "blackmail," Roosevelt finally responded, calling the accusations "monstrous. If true they would brand both of us forever with infamy; and inasmuch as they are false, heavy must be the condemnation of the man making them. . . . The assertion that there has been made any pledge or promise or that there has been any understanding as to future immunities or benefits, in recognition of any contribution from any source is a wicked falsehood."

It may have been true that no quid pro quo was asked or given, but Roosevelt was almost certainly aware of Cortelyou and Bliss's activities. On October 26, he wrote Cortelyou ordering him to return a donation of $100,000 from Standard Oil. Then he followed up with a memo and a telegram repeating the instructions. Yet the money was never repaid (possibly because it had already been spent), as the president most likely understood even as he dictated the directives—which, like much of Roosevelt's correspondence, were intended at least as much for posterity as for the recipient.

On November 8, the president cast his own vote in Oyster Bay, then took a train back to Washington, arriving at 6:15 that evening. A telegraph line had been set up in the White House's Red Room, and by seven o'clock, as the returns trickled in, it was clear that the election was going his way. "How they are voting for me!" he exclaimed several times to the friends who had joined him and Edith. When the votes were counted, Roosevelt had won the greatest popular and electoral landslide to date, taking 33 of the 45 states, 336 of 476 electoral votes, and 7.6 million of the 12.7 million popular votes cast. "My dear," he told Edith, "I am no longer a political accident."

A little after nine o'clock a telegram of congratulation arrived from Judge Parker, and at quarter past ten the president left the living quarters and went down to the Executive Office Building, the suite of offices that had been constructed during the renovation of 1902 and that would later evolve into the West Wing. There he received the congratulations of the White House press corps. Then at 10:30 he called in his secretary, William Loeb, and as the reporters stood in a semicircle around his desk he leaned back in his chair and dictated a truly remarkable statement: "I am deeply sensible of the honor done me by the American people in thus expressing their confidence in what I have done and have tried to do," he said. "I appreciate to the full the solemn responsibility this confidence imposes upon me, and I shall do all that in my power lies not to forfeit it. On the fourth of March next I shall have served three and a half years, and this three and a half years constitutes my first term. The wise custom which limits the President to two terms regards the substance and not the form. Under no circumstances will I be a candidate for or accept another nomination."

It wasn't a decision taken in the enthusiasm of the moment but a step he had been considering for some time. Still, by declaring himself a lame duck, he had squandered precious political capital and weakened his position with the more conservative elements of his own party. And not least of all, he had committed himself to vacating the office that he loved perhaps more than any other man who had ever held it. He would later say that he would have cut off his hand for the chance to take back his promise.

In contrast to his first, somber swearing-in in Buffalo, Roosevelt's second inauguration, on March 4, 1905, was a boisterous affair, played out before tens of thousands of his cheering countrymen. Standing on the U.S. Capitol's east portico, bathed in brilliant sunshine and buffeted by a brisk north wind, the president repeated the oath of office, then spoke for a scant ten minutes on the responsibilities faced by Americans both at home and in the world. "Much has been given to us, and much will rightfully be expected from us," he reminded them. "Our relations with the other powers of the world are important, but still more important are our relations among ourselves. . . . Modern life is both complex and intense, and the tremendous changes wrought by the extraordinary industrial development of the half century are felt in every fibre of our

Roosevelt's second inauguration, March 4, 1905. LIBRARY OF CONGRESS

social and political being. . . . Upon the success of our experiment much depends, not only as regards our own welfare, but as regards the welfare of mankind."

The entire ceremony was over in fifteen minutes. The president and his guests repaired to the White House for a luncheon, then mounted a reviewing stand across from Lafayette Park to take in the parade in his honor. For three and a half hours, the spectators were regaled by thirty-five thousand marchers—a hundred bands playing everything from fife-and-drum ditties to ragtime riffs; scores of elected officials; platoons of newsboys and schoolboys; servicemen representing every branch of the armed forces; retired Rough Riders; a troop of cowboys from Deadwood, South Dakota; and a half dozen Indian chieftains, including the Apache warrior Geronimo. By the time the last marcher straggled by, darkness had fallen and the guest of honor could no longer even see the salutes offered in his direction.

The night before, in a quieter moment, Roosevelt had told a friend, "Tomorrow I shall come into my office in my own right. Then watch out for me." Buoyed by his huge victory at the polls, the president set an ambitious course for his new term. And there was no higher priority than reconciling the needs of the corporations with the rights of workers and the public. By intervening in the coal strike in 1902, he had established the federal government as the people's representative in disputes between workers and employers. Now he hoped to strike a dynamic balance between labor and industry. "Somehow or other," he wrote English historian George Trevelyan, "we shall have to work out methods of controlling the big corporations without paralyzing the energies of the business community and of preventing any tyranny on the part of the labor unions while cordially assisting in every proper effort made by the wage workers to better themselves by combinations."

He had chosen Northern Securities for his first assault against the trusts because he realized that any attempt to control the corporations must start with the industry that, more than any other, propelled the nation's economy. And few people, except for their investors, doubted that the railroads were in need of reform, with rates skewed by lack of competition and by preferential tariffs granted to large companies, to the detriment of farmers and other small customers. In his annual message to Congress in December 1905, the president urged, "The immediate and most pressing need, so far as legislation is concerned, is the enactment into law of some scheme to secure to the agents of the Government such supervision and regulation of the rates charged by the railroads of the country engaged in interstate traffic."

The president had already taken steps in this direction. In 1903, he had signed the Elkins Act, which prohibited railroads from offering rebates to favored customers. But the law, which had been promoted by the Pennsylvania and other large lines eager to phase out the expensive rebates, had done little to reduce shipping costs. In January 1906, William Hepburn, chairman of the House Committee on Interstate and Foreign Commerce, introduced a bill empowering the Interstate Commerce Commission to set limits on the rates that railroads could charge. The measure passed quickly and virtually unanimously in the House, but when Republican senators tried to derail the bill, Roosevelt marshaled such popular support for the law that the railroads and conservative members of his own party were forced to concede. Approved in May, with only three senators opposed, the law represented a major victory for the president and a milestone in federal regulation of the nation's business.

The following month, goaded by the president and the muckraking press, Congress passed two other groundbreaking laws, the Meat Inspection Act and the Pure Food and Drug Act, meant to protect consumers from adulterated and misbranded foods and medicines. Also in June the president signed an Act for the Preservation of American Antiquities, which gave him the authority to proclaim national monuments on federal land to preserve the nation's historical and scientific treasures. By the end of his second term, Roosevelt would also set aside sixteen million acres of new national forests and create five national parks and some fifty wildlife refuges. In international affairs, he would declare the United States's right to intervene in Latin American countries in cases of "chronic wrongdoing" or governmental impotence. And to extend American power abroad, he would order the construction of dozens of new warships and launch sixteen battleships and fourteen thousand sailors on an unprecedented, fourteen-month, around-the-world cruise. He would also negotiate an end to the Russo-Japanese War, for which he would be awarded the Nobel Peace Prize, the first Nobel presented to an American.

During his new term the president would also establish a wary but extraordinary collaboration with the nation's preeminent financier. Recognizing his own lack of economic expertise—"When it comes to finance or compound differentials, I'm all up in the air," he would later admit—Roosevelt would occasionally invite Morgan to the White House to confer on business matters. But more often, the two communicated through intermediaries. Principal among these go-betweens was Morgan's partner George Perkins, who had met Roosevelt when TR was governor of New York and who in the intervening years, as Morgan's "secretary of state," had become a trusted confidant of both men.

In December 1902, Roosevelt had appealed to Perkins to lobby Congress on behalf of the bill that would create the Department of Commerce and Labor. "I know your interest in the Department of Commerce bill and you know my plans in reference to filling the position," the president wrote him. "Will you not at once try to get whatever influence you can bear on Speaker [of the House David] Henderson on its behalf? I write this because you told me you were anxious to do all you could to secure the passage of the bill." And, he directed, "Do what you can with Marshall Field and others in Chicago to see that Representative [James] Mann (who is to prepare the report on the bill for the Interstate Commerce Committee of the House) makes a thoroughly sensible report."

The next day, Perkins wrote that he had "already been at work on the Illinois end of the matter" and had dispatched "two gentlemen" from Chicago to Washington to see Congressman Mann. "As to the other gentleman you mention [Speaker Henderson], I am at work on that also. I am personally very anxious to see the Department of Commerce bill become a law," he assured Roosevelt, since "our interstate relations, as well as our relations with foreign countries, require the establishment of such a department. In my judgment, the time is ripe for it, and the man you have selected is ripe for the work. Please command me in any way that I can be of service in the matter."

With the legislation floundering in Congress, the president welcomed Perkins's help. Opposition centered not so much on the department itself but on its Bureau of Corporations, an investigative arm that would have the power to subpoena corporate records. But while the bill was under consideration, Roosevelt leaked to the press telegrams from John D. Rockefeller's attorney, John D. Archbold, expressing Rockefeller's hostility to the law. When it was revealed that the founder of the hated Standard Oil was opposed, public enthusiasm surged, and Congress responded by rushing the measure through both houses, including the controversial Bureau of Corporations.

Roosevelt signed the new department into existence on Valentine's Day 1903, and in appreciation for Perkins's lobbying, sent him one of the pens used. (The other went to the department's first secretary, George Cortelyou.) In his letter of thanks, Roosevelt wrote Perkins, "Your interest in the legislation was strongly indicated at different times during the year or more of active discussion of the bill in Congress, and upon a number of occasions you represented to me the wishes of commercial organizations and business interests in behalf of the establishment of such a department."

Although it's not surprising that the administration would be eager to create a Department of Commerce and Labor, as a way of reining in the corporations, it may not be obvious why a partner of Pierpont Morgan would be so enthusiastic about the new agency. But to capitalists like Perkins and Morgan, federal regulation promised important benefits. For one thing, by halting aggressive practices such as railroad rebates, government control would dampen the fierce competitive pressures that Morgan had always condemned as inefficient and destabilizing. Naturally, from his point of view it would have been better for business to police itself. But failing that, federal regulation was preferable to chaos, or to the plethora of state laws that were the likely alternative.

Morgan and Roosevelt also shared an aversion to radicalism in all its forms. Although the president's intent was undeniably progressive, to limit the power of the trusts, there was also an essentially conservative element to his program, since he hoped that incremental reform would inoculate America against the threats of socialism and anarchism that were infecting Europe. Morgan also sought to avoid social and political upheaval at all costs, and like Roosevelt, he believed (as he had shown during the coal strike) that government intervention could protect industry from its own worst impulses.

As the president said, "The dull purblind folly of the very rich men, their greed and arrogance . . . and the corruption of business and politics, have tended to produce a very unhealthy condition and excitement in the popular mind." Although Roosevelt wanted to curtail what he considered the abuses of the trusts, he recognized the necessity of the corporations, praised them for their contribution to the nation's well-being, and was eager not to restrict them so severely that economic growth was made to suffer. And so Perkins could write him, "You know that I have the highest hopes for the new Department [of Commerce and Labor], and sincerely believe that it will be of very great practical use to our Government and our vast business interests."

Another Morgan partner, Elbert Gary, cofounder and chairman of U.S. Steel, also fostered the growing collaboration between the administration and the House of Morgan. Perkins had recommended Gary to Roosevelt as someone who shared the president's philosophy on corporate regulation, and in December 1902, Roosevelt had invited the steel executive to the White House. The men had taken an immediate and mutual liking, and the meeting would be the first of many. Their friendship grew so warm, in fact, that some board members of U.S. Steel, including Pierpont Morgan, took exception, and after the Supreme Court issued the Northern Securities verdict, the directors debated a motion to ban the chairman from any future visits. Gary managed to deflect the resolution, and his meetings with Roosevelt continued. A few years later, Morgan would discover just how crucial it could be to have a partner in such good stead with the president.

One of the first fruits of the unlikely partnership between Morgan and Roosevelt came early in the new administration. In May 1904, International Harvester, which George Perkins had organized two years earlier, was found to be accepting illegal rebates from an Illinois railroad. Company president Cyrus McCormick Jr. approached Attorney General William H. Moody and James R. Garfield, commissioner of the Bureau of Corporations, and suggested that the administration and the company come to an understanding: In the future, if government examiners discovered any area where Harvester was breaking the law, before mounting a prosecution the Bureau would give it a chance to correct the violation. Moody and Garfield agreed, though the arrangement wasn't formalized immediately.

Elbert Gary was eager to come to a similar understanding concerning U.S. Steel. In November 1905, as he and Roosevelt were discussing the need to control the trusts, he saw his opening. "I don't know, Mr. President, whether you are trying to hit me over the shoulders of the companies of which you speak, but I make you this promise. If at any time you feel that the Steel Corporation should be investigated, you shall have an opportunity to examine the books and records of all our companies, and if you find anything in them that you think is wrong, we will convince you that we are right or we will correct the wrong."

"Well," Roosevelt told him, "that seems to me to be about the fair thing."

Nothing concrete came from this discussion until January, when Congress called on the Bureau of Corporations to investigate the nation's largest trust, U.S. Steel. That same month James Garfield paid a quiet call to Gary's New York office in the Empire Building, on Lower Broadway.

"The President tells me," Garfield said, "that some months ago you said that, if at any time the administration felt that it should investigate the Steel Corporation, your books were open to us."

"Yes," answered Gary. "I did. And they are."

But many details remained to be agreed, including how the administration planned to use the information it gathered, and it was September before U.S. Steel began to turn records over to the Bureau. In November, hoping to put their arrangement on a more formal footing, Gary and U.S. Steel director Henry C. Frick went to the White House to meet with the president, Commissioner Garfield, and Victor Metcalf, who had replaced George Cortelyou as secretary of commerce and labor.

U.S. Steel, Gary assured his hosts, did not question the constitutional authority of the Bureau of Corporations to investigate the trusts. On the contrary, his company desired "to cooperate with the Government in every possible way that is consistent with the proper protection of . . . [stockholders'] rights and property." The corporation would gladly release data to federal investigators, and in return asked only that it be kept confidential and be used "by the president alone for his guidance in making such suggestions to Congress concerning legislation as might be proper, expedient, and for the actual benefit of the general public." If there were any difference of opinion between Gary and Garfield about whether the material should be published, the issue would be referred to the secretary of commerce and labor, and if necessary, to the president. It was agreed that the company and the administration would go forward under these terms.

But in December 1906 Congress threatened to intrude again on the alliance between Morgan interests and the White House, when it called for the Bureau of Corporations to investigate International Harvester. In January Elbert Gary, George Perkins, and other executives sat down with officials from the Bureau in Gary's apartment in the Waldorf-Astoria to discuss the impending action. The understanding between regulators and International Harvester had not called for the company to proactively share information with the government, as U.S. Steel was doing. Now reassuring his visitors that his own company was pleased with its treatment by the Bureau, Gary expressed hope that the same terms could be extended to Harvester. Over two days of meetings, the men came to an understanding, and in May Harvester became the second Morgan company to deliver data to the Bureau of Corporations.

Then that summer, Roosevelt's new, more aggressive attorney general, Charles Bonaparte, began to prepare a suit against Harvester for alleged violations of the Sherman Act. In August, George Perkins saw the president at Sagamore Hill and argued that no action should be taken until the Bureau of Corporations completed its own examination. Back in Washington, Perkins conferred with Bonaparte and with Herbert Knox Smith, the Bureau's head. In September Smith assured the president, "I have no knowledge of any moral grounds for attacks on [International Harvester]. The attitude of the Morgan interests generally, which control this company, has been one of active cooperation. . . . It is a very practical question whether it is well to throw away now the great influence of the so-called Morgan interests [by bringing the lawsuit], which up to this time have supported the advanced policy of the administration, both in the general principles and in the application thereof to their specific interests, and to place them generally in opposition." The president agreed, and he instructed Bonaparte not to proceed against the company.

Both Roosevelt and Morgan appreciated the advantages of behind-the-scenes negotiations as opposed to drawn-out, public legal battles, and as time went on, they had reason to be pleased with the bargain they had struck. James Garfield reported that the Bureau of Corporations never found any significant violation in the activities of U.S. Steel and that not one of its competitors ever complained of unfair practices by the company. And Perkins wrote Morgan that, thanks to Steel's cooperation with the government "we have anticipated a great many questions and situations that might have been unpleasant." As a result, he boasted, the company was "looked upon in Washington with more favor than perhaps any other."

Through such unofficial understandings, Roosevelt and Morgan were nudging government and business toward a new relationship. For most of the nation's history, federal intervention in the economy had focused on general measures to encourage industry and commerce—granting patents and copyrights, building roads and canals, levying tariffs to protect American manufacturers—until Roosevelt had embarked on his agenda of reform and regulation. Now not only was the president inserting the executive branch into private enterprise to an unprecedented degree, he was inviting business's collaboration in the process. Recognizing the benefits of accommodation, the House of Morgan was particularly forthcoming and was singled out for considerations accorded no one else.

Even though this cooperation was mutually beneficial, it would not have been possible without an element of trust. As he did in most matters, Roosevelt cast his dealings with the business community in starkly personal terms. And so it was important that, although he and Morgan didn't enjoy what could be called a friendship, they did share experiences and attitudes—social class, a Victorian sense of morality, a craving for stability, a preference for pragmatism over dogma, a genuine concern for the welfare of the country—that together formed the basis of a common, if wary, understanding. At least as crucial was the fact that the president and Morgan shared a network of trusted friends who could mediate between them.

Roosevelt relied to an extraordinary degree on his own moral judgment, rather than impersonal legal dicta, to guide him in his dealings with the trusts. In consultation with advisers, both in government and in business, he would review the activities of the corporations and determine which were, in his words, "good" and "evil." Evil trusts, those that he found unaccommodating or "selfish"—such as Standard Oil and the American Tobacco Company—would find themselves the target of federal prosecution. But "good" trusts, those that were judged cooperative and that advanced the national interest, no matter how large or monopolistic they became—such as U.S. Steel, the largest trust of all—would be permitted to pursue their business, albeit under government supervision.

In the coming years, Roosevelt would prosecute some forty corporations for anti-trust violations, but no Morgan company would ever again be among them. So the quintessential trust builder and the original trust buster had finally arrived at the personal accommodation that Roosevelt had angrily rejected in 1902, when Morgan had gone to the White House during the initial shock over National Securities and offered to have his "man" speak to the president's "man" and "fix it up." And George Perkins and Elbert Gary had become the principal fixers.

⁓

Both Roosevelt and Morgan were committed to enhancing American prestige abroad, the president to bolster the country's influence in the world, the financier to keep foreign capital flowing into the economy. And so sometimes their collaboration extended overseas, as it had with the purchase of the Panama Canal. During Roosevelt's second term, its influence was felt as far as Asia.

In 1895, Morgan and forty other investors had incorporated the American-China Development Company, which controlled certain railroad and mining concessions in that country. Planning to build a railroad running the six hundred miles between Canton and the river port of Hankow, the company encountered strong anti-foreign sentiment in China, and by 1905 fewer than thirty miles of track had been laid. Raising tensions further, Chinese merchants began a boycott of American goods that year, in retaliation for the Chinese Exclusion Acts, which, introduced in 1882 and extended in 1892 and again in 1902, had put a virtual end to immigration from that country. The American-China Development Company negotiated from the Chinese a generous fee of $6.75 million for canceling the concession, and rather than risk proceeding in the face of such strong local opposition, Morgan was inclined to accept the offer.

Representing the company in the negotiations was Elihu Root. After Roosevelt's election, Root had stepped down as secretary of war and resumed his law practice, working with Pierpont Morgan on the court-ordered dissolution of Northern Securities and the reorganization of the Equitable Life Assurance Society. But in July 1905, Roosevelt appointed Root secretary of state, replacing the late John Hay. Hired as assistant secretary was longtime Roosevelt friend Robert Bacon, who had left Morgan & Company in 1903, following a nervous breakdown brought on by stress and overwork. (Apparently Bacon found government work less taxing. He would serve as assistant secretary until early 1909, then, on Root's resignation, become secretary of state for the last month of Roosevelt's term; during the Taft Administration he would be appointed ambassador to France, and during World War I would be an aide to General John Pershing.)

After discussing the American-China Development Company with Morgan, Henry Cabot Lodge reported to the president that the financier didn't consider the investment "serious enough to make him at his age enter on a struggle with the Chinese," especially since Morgan wasn't sure that the administration, if pressed, would defend the company's interests. As word spread that Morgan was considering a withdrawal from China, some in the administration objected. Before his death, Hay had spoken out against the divestiture, calling it a setback for American interests and an impediment to future concessions from the Chinese. Lodge agreed, warning the president that the loss of the railroad would be "a blow to our prestige and to our commerce in China which we want to foster in every way."

On July 18, Roosevelt wrote: "Now, my dear Mr. Morgan, it is not my business to advise you what to do. From the standpoint of our national interests, I take entirely Lodge's view. I cannot expect you or any of our big business men to go into what they think will be to their disadvantage. But if you are giving up this concession, if you are letting the railroad slip out of American hands, because you think that the Government will not back you up, I wish to assure you that in every honorable way the Government will stand by you and will do all that in its power lies to see that you suffer no wrong whatever from the Chinese or any other Power in this matter. . . . My interest of course is simply the interest of seeing American commercial interests prosper in the Orient."

On August 7, over a private luncheon at Sagamore Hill, the president again assured Morgan that the U.S. government would "insist that China shall carry out its side of the agreement regarding the concession." He asked, "Can your company delay action for a few weeks longer? If so, I'll call a halt in emphatic terms to the Chinese Government." The following day, the Chinese minister, Chentung Liang Cheng, arrived for dinner at the Roosevelt estate.

But Roosevelt's intervention had come too late. On August 28, Morgan sailed the *Corsair* to Oyster Bay for another luncheon, and he and the president agreed that, in the face of opposition from the Chinese, the only feasible course was to sell the railroad. The next day, the company's board of directors voted to accept the offer, and the president issued a statement praising the financier for his cooperation: "Mr. Morgan has consulted with the Administration and shown every desire to do what American interests in the Orient demanded, and only consented to the arrangement proposed by the Chinese Government in view of the fact that the attitude of the Chinese Government rendered it obvious that there was no other course which he could take with due regard to the interest of the stockholders he represented."

Despite the occasional foray into foreign policy, the alliance between Morgan and Roosevelt was felt mostly at home. In 1907, the president assured Charles Sanger Mellen, president of the New York, New Haven & Hartford Railroad Company, that the federal government would not intervene even as he bought up street railways, steamship lines, and the important Boston & Maine Railroad. Mellen's purpose was to assemble a vast transportation monopoly, and his actions prompted widespread outrage. But Roosevelt and other notable progressives viewed the Morgan-controlled corporation as one of the "good" trusts, promising a much needed economic boost to Massachusetts and all New England.

That fall, the Roosevelt Administration continued to look the other way when Elbert Gary, chairman of U.S. Steel, began to convene a series of meetings with managers from rival producers. At these so-called Gary dinners, the executives, whose companies accounted for 90 percent of American iron and steel production, freely shared the prices they intended to charge in the near term. Since no agreement was made to maintain prices at a fixed level, Gary and the others believed that they were abiding by the letter of the Sherman law and acting only "to maintain so far as practicable the stability of business and to prevent . . . the wide and sudden fluctuation of prices which would be injurious to everyone interested in the business." The administration apparently agreed that such information sharing had a salutary effect on the industry, and made no attempt to curtail the dinners.

But the extraordinary collaboration between the forces of Roosevelt and Morgan would bear no more important results than during the financial crisis known as the Panic of 1907, when the world economy teetered on the verge of collapse.

Washington was dry but unseasonably cold on the morning of November 4, 1907, as Elbert Gary and Henry Frick stepped down from their Pullman and strode past the locomotive that had carried them through the night. Looking like a pair of ordinary businessmen come from New York, they attracted no notice as they left the depot, boarded a common hansom, and ordered the driver to the White House. It was nearly eight o'clock. Two hours before the market opened. Two hours to persuade the president and fend off disaster.

It wasn't the first time that the House of Morgan had pleaded with Mr. Roosevelt to intervene in the crisis. In March, Pierpont Morgan had made front-page news when he had traveled to Washington and, during a two-hour meeting at the White House, had warned the president that the administration's aggressive stance toward the trusts was contributing to the mounting sense of economic unease. Asked to issue a statement that he had no intention of advocating further federal regulation of the railroads, Roosevelt begged off, saying, "I do not like to seem to talk just for the effect upon the stock market." Morgan also asked the president to convene a committee of prominent railroad executives, as a way to "allay the public anxiety now threatening to obstruct railroad investments and construction." Roosevelt agreed, but though he continued to meet with individual railroad men from time to time, no such summit was ever held. Meanwhile, as spring turned to summer and then to autumn, the stock market continued its steady slide.

Business had been suffering all year under a worldwide shortage of cash, brought on by everything from high railroad debt to a lag in gold production to the previous year's catastrophic earthquake in San Francisco. Then in October, a syndicate of F. Augustus Heinze and other speculators failed spectacularly in its attempted corner of United Copper, spelling disaster for the banks and brokerage houses holding their millions of dollars of debt. On October 22, when the Knickerbocker, one of the nation's largest trust companies, failed, stocks plunged to their lowest level in nearly seven years.

Many Americans both on Wall Street and on Main Street blamed the crisis on Roosevelt's aggressive attitude toward big business, but even as disaster loomed the president seemed not to grasp the seriousness of the situation, first joining a bear hunt in Louisiana and then bragging that he had Wall Street "on the run." By then, Pierpont Morgan had hurried back to New York from Richmond, where he'd been attending an Episcopal Church conference, and had taken matters in hand. With a dozen New York banks on the verge of failure, he had acted as the country's central banker of last resort and raised nearly $90 million to prop up faltering financial institutions and even the City of New York. Belatedly, Secretary of the Treasury George Cortelyou joined the effort, releasing more than $35 million in gold from federal reserves and authorizing Morgan to lend the money where he believed it would do the most good.

But by the evening of Sunday, November 3, it appeared that all the desperate work of the past two weeks had been for naught, when it was revealed that the important brokerage house of Moore & Schley was on the point of bankruptcy. The brokerage had borrowed $30 million, posting as collateral the stock of the large southern steel producer Tennessee Coal, Iron & Railroad. The shares were originally valued at $130 but now were worth much less, perhaps as little as $60. On Monday morning, Moore & Schley's loans would be called in and the brokerage would fail, dragging its many creditors down with it. Before the dominos stopped tumbling, the U.S. financial system would collapse and the world would be mired in a depression.

The only way to avoid catastrophe was for Moore & Schley to divest its shares of TC&I. And the only company large enough to consider such an acquisition was Morgan's United States Steel. The U.S. Steel board was reluctant to take on the troubled TC&I, but in a series of heated meetings, Morgan persuaded his fellow directors that the company's mineral deposits alone were worth the investment. Over the weekend, the two corporations agreed on a price of $100 per share. But then, before Morgan would consummate the sale, he insisted, during a frantic all-night conference of a hundred of the city's most important bankers, that the solvent New York trust companies loan the endangered trust companies an additional $25 million to see them through the crisis. Though the other bankers balked, Morgan eventually prevailed, and as the men straggled out of his marble library at sunrise, it appeared that the crisis had finally been stemmed.

But Gary had raised another prerequisite for his company's acquisition of TC&I. "Before we go ahead with this," he told Morgan, "we must consult President Roosevelt."

"But what has the president to do with it?" demanded Morgan, who for two weeks had been shouldering the brunt of the crisis.

At this point the Morgan company was already producing more than half the country's steel. If they proceeded without the president's blessing, Gary explained, the government might file suit to stop the sale or bring an anti-trust case against them. Morgan saw the wisdom in the plan, and he realized that Gary, as a trusted friend of Roosevelt, was the ideal man to make the approach. It was agreed that U.S. Steel director Henry Frick would accompany him. A telephone call was placed to the White House, and the president's personal secretary, William Loeb Jr., scheduled a meeting for first thing the following morning.

Early on November 4, Gary and Frick's hansom stopped before the simple neoclassical entrance that Charles McKim had designed for the Executive Office Building, which was connected to the White House proper by a long, low colonnade. Passing through a lobby crowded with wooden desks and chairs, the men reached the spacious office occupied by Loeb and other aides. The president was still at breakfast, Loeb explained, and would see no one before ten o'clock.

But, Gary told him, it was crucial that their business be decided by the time the market opened. "This is a serious matter, and I think that if you will tell him just what Mr. Frick and I are here for, he will see us." Adamant, the secretary merely directed them to seats in a small anteroom.

Just then they caught sight of the tall, slender figure of James R. Garfield, the former commissioner of corporations, who in March had assumed the position of secretary of the interior. Together Garfield and Gary had negotiated the groundbreaking détente between U.S. Steel and the administration. Now Gary and Frick frantically explained their mission, and Garfield hurried down the corridor toward the residence, promising to intercede on their behalf. The emissaries retook their seats, as the minutes ticked toward the market's opening.

Before long the president appeared and ushered them into his office. The "president's room," as it was called to distinguish it from the office that he still maintained upstairs in the White House, was modest and businesslike, smaller than the secretary's office next door. As in Loeb's room, the walls were covered in forest green and the woodwork painted a stark white. The president's desk was ample but plain, facing a fireplace with a white wooden mantle, beside which a large globe had been placed. He showed his visitors to some green upholstered chairs.

Since Attorney General Bonaparte was out of the capital, the president sent word to Elihu Root to join them. Gary and Frick then began the explanation for their hurried visit. There was a financial firm in New York, they said, whose identity they would rather not divulge. It was a large firm, and it was certain to fail this week, perhaps even today, if it did not receive assistance. Among its assets were a majority of the shares in Tennessee Coal & Iron, whose directors had urgently applied to United

States Steel to purchase its stock. Their corporation would prefer not to buy the company and in fact had recently refused an opportunity to do so, but now they found it the only way to stem the current panic on Wall Street and avoid a general industrial smash-up.

The president answered that of course he could not counsel them whether to purchase the company or not. But, he assured them, he certainly felt no duty to object to the sale. He called in a stenographer, and as his visitors listened, he dictated a letter relaying the particulars of their conversation for Attorney General Bonaparte (and for posterity).

During the conference a White House telephone line had been kept open to the New York office of George Perkins, who was hugely relieved to hear of the president's position. When the news reached Wall Street, just after the opening bell, the market surged. After weeks of uncertainty and desperate behind-the-scenes maneuvering, the Panic of 1907 was at last contained. And crucial to the rescue of the nation's financial system had been the warm regard and mutual trust established between Roosevelt and Gary. Such was the president's confidence in the Morgan partner that he took him at his word, asking very few specifics before committing his administration's support. And such was Gary's trust in Roosevelt that he would risk tens of millions of dollars based on the president's verbal assurance.

Still, after the crisis had passed, Gary was eager to have a written record of their meeting. On November 7, he wrote Elihu Root reiterating the circumstances that had led U.S. Steel to want to purchase TC&I, then added, "I understood the President to say that while he would not and could not legally make any binding promise or agreement, he did not hesitate to say from all the circumstances as presented he certainly would not advise against the proposed purchase. If consistent, will you kindly write me if the above statement is in accordance with your understanding and recollection."

Four days later, Root responded. "I have your letter. . . . It fully agrees with my recollection of the interview to which you refer. . . . I have sent a copy of your letter with this answer to the President with a recommendation that it be transmitted to the Department of Justice for filing there."

On November 19, the president confirmed to Root: "Mr. Gary states the facts as I remember them." Later, Gary would be happy to have documentation of their conversation.

The aftereffects of the panic were still being felt across the country. Short of cash, many banks not only stopped making loans but limited depositors' withdrawals and began to pay customers and other banks with IOUs in lieu of cash. Factories were forced to close or to cut their workers' hours. But the country had, narrowly, avoided economic collapse. Some detractors, including Wisconsin senator Robert La Follette, accused Pierpont Morgan of engineering the panic for personal gain. But most Americans were grateful for Morgan's intervention, and the banker found himself (briefly and uncharacteristically) lionized by the public and the press. Wrote the *New York Tribune*'s financial columnist, H. Allaway, "What Mr. J. P. Morgan represents in our national crisis seems finally burned into the comprehension of the whole country. Bitterest cynics abandon their cynicism; sane, healthful, comprehending men acclaim this man's service, his wisdom, his courage, his disinterested patriotism. Without J. P. Morgan business interests to-day would be captainless; if prosperity is saved it is Morgan who has wrought its salvation."

But it wouldn't be long before the extraordinary collaboration between the Morgan interests and the Roosevelt Administration would come under fire as too accommodating to the very corporations the president had once vowed to rein in. Wrote the *New York Sun*, "The past has shown that in raising campaign funds [the president] is unembarrassed by ordinary considerations of official propriety or common decency. . . . A Tammany grafter taking his toll of suffering and shame could not have been more direct. . . . Who but Theodore Roosevelt could so steal 'the livery of the court of heaven' by clothing that which closely bordered on executive blackmail in a cloudy veil of smug hypocrisy?"

The *New York Evening World* argued that the president "had great and admitted wrongs to contend with. He merely blustered and threatened. He had powerful criminals to punish. He ignored most of them, and by his violent methods made the administration of justice in the case of others almost a nullity. He inveighed mightily against malefactors and undesirable citizens. He nevertheless entertained some of them in the

White House. He demanded law and more law for the punishment of wealthy offenders. He then suspended law in the interest of the Steel Trust. . . . It is a remarkable showing of undisciplined fury in one man and of meek submission in millions of men equally free."

As with his election-night rejection of a third term, Roosevelt would pay a price for his ready acceptance of the TC&I merger in particular and his easy, personal relationship with J.P. Morgan & Company in general. Within a few years, his preference for the House of Morgan would help to immerse him in the bitterest chapter of his career and to divide the party he had championed for decades.

CHAPTER SIX

The Bull Moose and the
Lion of Wall Street

Tuesday, March 23, 1909

NEW YORK HAD NEVER SEEN A DEPARTURE QUITE LIKE IT. A FEW MIN-
utes past eleven o'clock, the SS *Hamburg* slipped from its berth in Hoboken. As the black-hulled, twin-masted liner churned into the Hudson
and glided past the Manhattan skyline, Theodore Roosevelt perched
on the bridge beside the captain, wearing a rumpled khaki uniform
and waving a broad-brimmed hat. Onshore, factory whistles blared and
skyscraper windows and roofs grew black with cheering crowds. As the
Hamburg passed forts Hamilton and Wadsworth, which guarded the
Narrows between Brooklyn and Staten Island, their batteries gave a
twenty-one-gun salute. Buzzing around the ship was a fleet of smaller
craft. Crowded aboard one of the vessels, the steam tug *John J. Timmins*,
were sixty dignitaries and friends of the Colonel (as Roosevelt preferred
to be called since leaving the White House, just three weeks earlier).
Among the congressmen and judges, military men and business executives were Elbert Gary and William Loeb, who was now serving as
collector of customs for the Port of New York.

Earlier, at the terminal in Hoboken, old friends and colleagues such
as Elihu Root, Henry Cabot Lodge, and James Garfield had come to
offer their goodbyes. But five hundred well-wishers and souvenir hunters
had also mobbed the Colonel, snatching the leather briefcase from his

hand, lifting the gray slouch hat from his head, and cutting several buttons from his new uniform jacket. Safely aboard the *Hamburg*, he'd been shown to the Emperor William Suite, which the Kaiser had occupied on two transatlantic voyages. In Roosevelt's honor, jute tapestries and armor had been hung on the walls. There were also new carpets and silk curtains done in harmonious shades of blue and green. Besides a parlor and dressing room, the suite boasted a pair of bedrooms, one for Roosevelt and one for his nineteen-year-old son, Kermit. Rooting in his father's luggage, Kermit had found a hat to replace the one that had been filched, and the Colonel had climbed up to the bridge to join the captain and salute the crowds.

Kermit had taken a leave of absence from Harvard to make this journey, which had been christened the Smithsonian-Roosevelt African Expedition. Expected to last nearly a year, the safari would collect natural history specimens for the Smithsonian's United States National Museum in Washington. Andrew Carnegie had donated to the venture, and Roosevelt had accepted $50,000 from *Scribner's Magazine* for twelve articles, later collected in the bestselling book *African Game Trails*. The Colonel was particularly keen to bring home large trophies such as elephants, rhinos, and lions. But Pierpont Morgan seemed to be rooting for the other side. "Wall Street," he quipped, "expects every lion to do its duty."

Roosevelt had always been drawn to the wilderness, and Africa had fascinated him since boyhood. Having left the White House just three weeks before, at age fifty, he needed a grand undertaking to engage his restless energy. But the safari promised more than the hunt of a lifetime. That morning, on the train from Oyster Bay to Hoboken, newsmen had asked several times if he would ever make another bid for the presidency. Each time he had simply smiled his inimitable smile and called back, "Good-bye! Good-bye! Good luck!" It was largely to avoid such questions that he was making this journey. As he wrote a friend, "My main reason for wishing to go to Africa for a year is so that I can get where no one can accuse me of running [for a third term] nor do Taft the injustice of accusing him of permitting me to run the job."

Three years earlier, another longtime friend, the educator Nicholas Murray Butler, had warned him, "Your most difficult task will come when you finally leave the White House. . . . It will be a lot harder for you, Theodore, to be an ex-President than President." At the end of his second term, he was as beloved by the public as ever. Even his bitter opponent Senator "Pitchfork Ben" Tillman of South Carolina called him "the most popular President the country has ever had," and Mark Twain judged him "the most popular human being that has ever existed in the United States." If he had run again he would certainly have been reelected. But, ignoring the "still, small voice" within him, he had honored the pledge he had made on Election Day 1904 and had not sought another term.

But who could take his place? Perhaps because of his ambivalence at leaving office, he put off endorsing a successor, sowing disorder in his party and provoking speculation that he intended to run for a third term after all. In December 1907, less than a year before the election, William Loeb persuaded him that he must name a candidate. Possibilities included Charles Evans Hughes, the progressive governor of New York; Philander Knox, Roosevelt's former attorney general and now a senator from Pennsylvania; and Elihu Root, TR's longtime friend and now his secretary of state. Roosevelt confided to another friend, "I would walk on my hands and knees from the White House to the Capitol to see Root made president." But the sixty-two-year-old was in fading health, and his recent legal work for J.P. Morgan & Company had done nothing to endear him to the electorate.

The president turned to another loyal friend, William Howard Taft, who had served him first as governor of the Philippines and since 1904 as secretary of war, trusted adviser, and chief troubleshooter. But most of Taft's government experience had come in the judicial system, including stints as a state judge in his native Ohio, solicitor general of the United States, and a justice on the Sixth U.S. Circuit Court of Appeals. His lifelong ambition had been to serve on the U.S. Supreme Court, but when Roosevelt had offered him a seat, twice, he had declined on both occasions, pleading unfinished business in his current post.

It's possible that Taft's only interest was to place duty above ambition, but his wife, Nellie, and his half-brother Charley were urging him to hold out for the presidency. One night during Roosevelt's second term, after dinner at the White House, Roosevelt, Will Taft, and Nellie retired to the library, where the president took a seat, closed his eyes, and facetiously intoned, "I am the seventh son of a seventh daughter. I have clairvoyant powers. I see a man before me weighing three hundred and fifty pounds. There is something hanging over his head. I cannot make out what it is; it is hanging by a slender thread. At one time it looks like the presidency—then again it looks like the chief justiceship."

"Make it the chief justiceship," said Taft.

"Make it the presidency!" pleaded Nellie.

Now it appeared that Mrs. Taft's wish was on the way to being granted. To Roosevelt, Taft seemed a natural choice, not only because of their friendship, but because he could be counted on to continue the president's progressive agenda. As Roosevelt wrote George Trevelyan, "I have the profound satisfaction of knowing that he will do all in his power to further every one of the great causes for which I have fought and that he will persevere in every one of the great governmental policies in which I most firmly believe." And since the genial, cautious Taft had made few enemies over his long government career, perhaps he could even heal the rift between the conservative and the progressive wings of his own party. Expecting Taft to prove more reliably pro-business than his predecessor, Wall Street was enthusiastic about the choice. The House of Morgan was sufficiently keen that it donated $150,000 to the Taft campaign.

At the Republican convention in Chicago, delegates seemed to be in danger of stampeding for Roosevelt, giving him a forty-nine-minute ovation and roaring, "Four, four, four years more!" The convention chair, Henry Cabot Lodge, finally managed to end the demonstration only by reminding the crowd that the Colonel's decision was "final and irrevocable" and that any delegate seeking to place Roosevelt's name in nomination "impugn[ed] both his sincerity and his good faith, two of the President's greatest and most conspicuous qualities." Taft was duly nominated on the first ballot, although to Nellie Taft's chagrin, his ovation lasted only half as long as Roosevelt's.

Unlike his friend, Taft was not a natural politician or an energetic campaigner. Even so, in November he easily defeated the Democrats' perennial populist William Jennings Bryan, although the margin of victory in the popular vote was a little more than half of what Roosevelt's had been in 1904. On Inauguration Day there was a blizzard in Washington, causing the ceremony to be moved indoors to the Senate chamber. Said Taft to Roosevelt, "I always said it would be a cold day when I got to be President of the United States."

———~———

"Always excepting Washington and Lincoln," Roosevelt had written George Trevelyan, "I believe that Taft as President will rank with any other man who has ever been in the White House." Yet rumors of a rift between the longtime friends had begun even before the inauguration. During the campaign, Taft had assured Roosevelt that he would retain several Cabinet members who had expressed interest in staying on, including James Garfield, secretary of the interior, but then the new president had reversed himself and decided to replace them with his own men after all. Worse, several of Taft's appointees were corporate lawyers, "conservative men who know what they are talking about," as the new president put it, men who could initiate reforms "without injury to the business interests of the country." George Perkins bragged that he had selected several of the new Cabinet secretaries himself, including banker Frank MacVeagh as treasury secretary and corporate lawyer George Wickersham as attorney general. And even the positions he hadn't chosen, he assured Pierpont Morgan, were "filled to our entire satisfaction." But Roosevelt and the voters were less impressed with the roster. They had supported Taft on the expectation that he would continue TR's progressive programs, but already the new president seemed to be taking a turn toward the right.

Part of the problem was that Taft was not a gifted leader. Whereas Roosevelt relished a good fight, whether in the political arena or the boxing ring, Taft shied away from controversy. While Roosevelt was decisive—impetuous, his critics would say—Taft seemed passive and irresolute. Coming under the sway of powerful conservative Republicans such as Senator Nelson Aldrich of Rhode Island and Speaker of the House Joseph Cannon, he signed a controversial tariff bill that, rather than providing badly needed relief, raised levies on some essential goods (even as it, at the request of Aldrich's card partner Pierpont Morgan,

Roosevelt and his hand-picked
successor, William Howard Taft.
LIBRARY OF CONGRESS

eliminated the tariff on works of art at least twenty years old.) Then Taft compounded his misstep by stubbornly praising the measure as "the best tariff bill the Republican party ever passed."

Over the course of his presidency, Roosevelt had espoused a nimble, dynamic policy toward the corporations, calling for new legislation to enhance the government's authority and preferring regulation over litigation (as in the détente he had negotiated with the House of Morgan). But Taft, a jurist by experience and by temperament, took a more legalistic view. Believing that the government already had the tools it needed to control the trusts, he chose not to push for additional laws but to concentrate on enforcing the statutes already in place, especially the blunt instrument of the Sherman Act. Whereas Roosevelt depended on his own moral sense to ferret out the "evil" trusts in need of control, Taft preferred the impartial application of law and the breakup of all monopolies, the "good" and the "wicked" alike. In his single administration Taft would bring half again as many anti-trust suits as Roosevelt had during his two terms. Yet, even as the welter of prosecutions alienated the business community, the public was left with the impression that Taft was retreating from the progressive spirit of the times.

Taft also seemed to take a rightward stance on conservation, a crucial element of the Roosevelt legacy. To replace ardent conservationist James Garfield as secretary of the interior, he chose Richard A. Ballinger, a westerner who advocated more aggressive development of the country's natural resources. Just months into the new administration, Ballinger had a public falling-out with Roosevelt's friend and close adviser Gifford

Pinchot, who as chief of the Forest Service had played a central role in formulating TR's wilderness policy. The dispute would drive another wedge between Taft and Roosevelt—and at its center were a handful of investments made in Alaska by Pierpont Morgan.

While Roosevelt was still president, Morgan and the Guggenheim family had formed the Alaska Syndicate, to mine copper and coal near the Kennicott Glacier in the southeastern part of the state. After Roosevelt left office, an Interior Department investigator named Louis Glavis discovered mineral claims by thirty-two individuals, encompassing 5,280 acres, that were about to be transferred to the Alaska Syndicate, for whom Ballinger had once worked as legal representative. Glavis suspected that the transfer violated the Alaska Coal Act, which Roosevelt had signed in 1908, prohibiting the filing of dummy claims, that is, ones made with the intention of selling them to secondary investors at a profit. Convinced that Ballinger would validate the claims, Glavis conferred with Pinchot, who urged him to bring the matter to Taft's attention. But after Glavis personally delivered his fifty-page report to the president, Taft ordered Ballinger to dismiss the investigator "for filing a disingenuous statement unjustly impeaching the integrity of his superior officers." When Pinchot wrote a letter to Senator Jonathan Dolliver critical of Taft's handling of the matter, Pinchot was fired as well.

Even on safari, Roosevelt had been following developments in Washington, and on hearing of Pinchot's dismissal he was livid. It was "a very ungracious thing for an ex-President to criticize his successor," he wrote Pinchot; "and yet I cannot as an honest man cease to battle for the principles [for] which you and I and Jim [Garfield] . . . and the rest of our close associates stood." He confessed, "I very keenly share your disappointment in Taft, and in a way perhaps feel it even more deeply than you do, because it was I who made him President."

In spring 1910, Roosevelt packed for home, taking more than five-hundred big-game trophies destined for the Smithsonian and his personal collection. En route, he made a triumphal, six-week tour of Europe, giving speeches, meeting with monarchs, and being received, as one reporter put it, as "something more than a king." In May, at the request of President Taft, he represented the United States at the funeral of England's Edward

VII, riding in the official procession along with European heads of state. Then on June 18, the Colonel marked the end of his African adventure with a colossal parade up Broadway and Fifth Avenue, replete with ticker-tape, military bands, and hundreds of thousands of cheering New Yorkers, said to be the largest crowd ever assembled in the city. As in Europe, many of the revelers assumed that, despite his earlier disavowal, Roosevelt would eventually announce his campaign for a third term.

In the coming months, the rift between Roosevelt and Taft only widened. The Colonel publicly criticized his successor's tariff policy and his negotiation of arbitration treaties with Britain and France, under which all disputes between the nations would be submitted to a tribunal in The Hague. In August 1910, Roosevelt launched a three-week speaking tour of sixteen western states, addressing large, enthusiastic crowds wherever he went. The announced purpose was to shore up struggling Republican candidates in the midterm elections, but many suspected the real motive was to test the waters for a presidential run in 1912.

In a speech in Denver on August 29, Roosevelt shocked members of both parties by arguing that the Supreme Court, in failing to rein in the corporations, was serving as an impediment to social justice. Then, two days later, in a ninety-minute address at Osawatomie, Kansas (where in 1856 John Brown had led abolitionists in battle against pro-slavery forces), Roosevelt laid out the most sweeping argument he had ever made for an expanded federal government. Calling his program the "New Nationalism" (a phrase borrowed from Herbert Croly's 1909 book *The Promise of American Life*), he argued for equality of opportunity for all Americans, for the need to put "the national need before sectional or personal advantage," and for the necessity of freeing federal and state governments from "the sinister influence or control of special interests. . . . This New Nationalism," he went on, "regards the executive power as the steward of the public welfare. It demands of the judiciary that it shall be interested primarily in human welfare rather than in property, just as it demands that the representative body [the legislative branch] shall represent all the people rather than any one class or section of the people."

To advance his philosophy, Roosevelt laid out a comprehensive program of reform, including primary elections, public accounting of campaign contributions, recall of elected officials, stronger conservation laws, and inheritance and graduated income taxes. But much of the speech was devoted to the corporations. Quoting Abraham Lincoln, Roosevelt declared, "Labor is the superior of capital and deserves much the higher consideration," and he demanded that "the citizens of the United States must effectively control the mighty commercial forces which they have called into being." Toward this end, he advocated an impartial commission to propose meaningful tariff reform, as well as new workmen's compensation regulations and protections for working women and children.

His friend Taft was among the many Americans disturbed by Roosevelt's radical notions. When the president was informed of the speech, while golfing, his response was to hurl a club. Later he wrote his brother Charley that Roosevelt was "going quite beyond anything that he advocated when he was in the White House, and has proposed a program which it is absolutely impossible to carry out except by a revision of the Federal Constitution." The speech's resemblance to an election platform was also inescapable, and understandably threatening to the incumbent. Then, on Election Day, Taft's prospects were further clouded when the Republicans, hopelessly split between eastern conservatives and western progressives, lost their majority in the House for the first time in sixteen years and saw their majority in the Senate reduced from twenty-nine to ten.

In December, Taft confided to his military aide, Archie Butt (also a close friend of the Colonel), "It is very hard to take all the slaps Roosevelt is handing me at this time, Archie. I don't understand Roosevelt. I don't know what he is driving at except to make my way more difficult. It is hard, very hard, to see a devoted friendship going to pieces like a rope of sand." In time, those grains of sand would be swept away, undermining the reputations of both men. And the single most divisive aspect of their feud would center on the special consideration that the Roosevelt Administration had accorded the House of Morgan.

In the 1908 election, Morgan had been an enthusiastic supporter of Taft's candidacy and a generous donor to his campaign. According to Henry

Cabot Lodge, there was no one in the country "more anxious for Taft's success than Morgan." But by November 1909, Lodge reported to Roosevelt, the financier was already "very much disappointed in Taft." Like the Colonel's irritation, Morgan's disaffection would only grow, as Taft proved less friendly to corporate interests than Wall Street had hoped. Even so, he had not anticipated that Taft would make an assault on his own U.S. Steel.

Nearly three years before, as Roosevelt was preparing to leave office, the Senate had begun to investigate U.S. Steel's purchase of Tennessee Coal & Iron, including the president's reported endorsement of the sale. But, citing his earlier promise to Elbert Gary, Roosevelt would release only nonconfidential information to the Senate committee, writing Kermit that Congress would get nothing more from him "unless they were prepared to go to the length of trying to have [him] impeached." The obstruction had the desired effect, and in the absence of more detailed data, the Senate was unable to come to any conclusion regarding the propriety of the merger.

But congressional interest in the affair was not sated. In August 1911, the Colonel was called to testify about his involvement with TC&I, this time before a House committee chaired by Augustus Stanley, a Democrat from Kentucky. In his testimony, Roosevelt vigorously defended his actions of November 1907, reminding the congressmen that the country had been on the verge of financial collapse. "I would have been derelict in my duties," he said, "I would have shown myself a timid and unworthy public officer if in that extraordinary crisis I had not acted as I did act."

That fall, the Taft Administration seized the initiative, in a way that could not have been less flattering to Roosevelt, or more infuriating. On October 26, 1911, the day before the Colonel's fifty-third birthday, Attorney General Wickersham (one of the Cabinet officers that Perkins had boasted of personally selecting) filed suit in federal court, charging that U.S. Steel had achieved "great and dangerous power . . . over the trade and commerce of the country" and demanding the company's dissolution under the Sherman Act. Pierpont Morgan, Elbert Gary, Henry C. Frick, and George Perkins were among the defendants named individually. As evidence of monopolistic constraint of trade, the government pointed to the Gary dinners as a transparent attempt at price-fixing. More explosively, it cited the TC&I merger that Roosevelt had personally approved in 1907.

Not that the former president had colluded to break the law, the attorney general allowed; rather, he "was not made fully acquainted with the state of affairs" concerning the merger, and Gary and Frick had not been forthcoming about the motive for the transaction or the substantial benefits that would accrue to U.S. Steel. In acquiring TC&I, the corporation had swallowed an important competitor that controlled the largest ore and coal deposits of any company except U.S. Steel itself. And if the president "had been fully advised, he would have known that a desire to stop the panic was not the sole moving cause" for the purchase. In other words, Morgan's men had duped him.

It wasn't Taft's practice to review the documents before such suits were filed, and in their discussions the attorney general had neglected to mention that one of his central arguments would implicate Roosevelt. The Colonel was predictably furious. In an editorial in the November 19th issue of *The Outlook*, he responded, "Any statement that I was misled or that the representatives of the Steel Corporation did not thus tell me the truth as to the facts of the case is itself not in accordance with the truth." The addition of TC&I had a negligible impact on U.S. Steel's production, he pointed out, before going on to condemn Taft's fundamental approach to controlling the trusts: "Nor should we persevere in the hopeless experiment of trying to regulate these industries by means only of lawsuits, each lasting several years, and of uncertain result." In place of litigation, the country "should enter upon a course of supervision, control, and regulation of these great corporations," through the Bureau of Corporations or some other federal agency. "We demand that big business give the people a square deal; in return we must insist that when any one engaged in big business honestly endeavors to do right he shall himself be given a square deal; and the first, and most elementary, kind of square deal is to give him in advance full information as to just what he can, and what he cannot, legally and properly do. It is absurd, and much worse than absurd, to treat the deliberate lawbreaker as on an exact par with the man eager to obey the law, whose only desire is to find out from some competent Governmental authority what the law is, and then live up to it."

The night that Taft read the piece he told Archie Butt, "I really feel so blue and depressed that I shall spend the evening alone." Before the U.S. Steel suit, his friendship with Roosevelt had been riven by grievances both political and private, including some, like the contretemps over the Alaska Syndicate, that had involved Pierpont Morgan. But after the lawsuit, rapprochement became unthinkable. In the coming months the animosity between the two men would only fester, until it imperiled their own futures and that of their party. In December 1911, the Colonel decided to challenge Taft for the Republican nomination. And in the battle to follow, the House of Morgan would continue to be a major source of contention.

⚊ ⚊

Roosevelt's reasons for seeking a third term were complex, ranging from a desire to defend his legacy and further the progressive cause, to remorse for having put Taft forward as his successor, to dissatisfaction with retirement and resentment over perceived slights by his onetime protégé. But the Colonel insisted that vanity and personal ambition did not play—and must not appear to play—a role in his decision. "As far as I know my own soul," he wrote Herbert Hadley, Republican governor of Missouri, "I am telling you the exact truth when I say that I do not wish and will not take this nomination unless it comes to me as a public duty. I would not touch it if it were to come in such fashion as to look like the gratification of a desire on my part again to hold the Presidency. If I am to be nominated, it must be made clear that it is because the people think that at this time I am the man to do the job which in their interests they want done."

Progressive Republicans had already been trying to prod him into the race. Roosevelt for President clubs had appeared across the nation, and his personal appearances had been met with renewed cries of "Four years more!" In November 1911, a group of Republicans from Taft's home state of Ohio, including former secretary of the interior James Garfield, gave Roosevelt their endorsement. When a group of progressive Republican governors urged him to run, he suggested that they write an open letter asking his intentions. "The letter to me might simply briefly state the writer's belief that the people of his State, or their States, desire to have me run for the Presidency, and to know whether in such a case I would refuse the nomination," he helpfully suggested. "If it is the sincere judgment of men having the right to know and express the wishes of the plain people that the people as a whole desire me, not for my sake, but for their sake, to undertake the job, I would feel in honor bound to do so."

The governors complied, and their letter was published on February 10. Roosevelt planned to announce his candidacy on the 24th of that month, but three days beforehand, after a particularly incendiary speech in Columbus, Ohio, he confided to an inquisitive friend, "My hat is in the ring!" The comment immediately found its way into the newspapers (popularizing an enduring political metaphor), and the next day Roosevelt extended the pugilistic allusion: "Well, the fight is on; I am stripped to the buff." The formal announcement came on the evening of February 25, when he released a simple reply to the Republican governors: "I will accept the nomination for President if it is tendered to me, and I will adhere to this decision until the Convention has expressed its preference. . . . Therefore I hope that so far as possible the people may be given the chance, through direct primaries, to express their preference as to who shall be the nominee of the Republican Presidential convention." The third candidate for that honor would be progressive Wisconsin senator Robert La Follette, who had announced his candidacy in June.

Aware of the difficulties in bucking the Republican machine, Roosevelt decided that his only possible route to the nomination was to leverage his tremendous personal popularity and to dominate the primaries in the dozen states that would hold them (for the first time) that year. Even so, he seemed to go out of his way to alienate all but the most extreme elements of his party. In his address in Osawatomie, he had put forth a more radical program for the country than he had ever espoused as president, and in the earlier speech in Denver, he had attacked the Supreme Court.

In his remarks in Columbus, he had shocked progressives and conservatives alike with a revolutionary proposal concerning the judicial system. "Justice between man and man," he'd begun, "between the state and its citizens, is a living thing whereas legalistic justice is a dead thing. Moreover, never forget that the judge is just as much the servant of the people as any other official." It followed, therefore, that when "any considerable number of the people feel that the decision [of a court] is in defiance of justice" or of the Constitution, they should have the right to force a popular vote to determine whether the verdict be reversed, "subject only to action by the Supreme Court of the United States."

The prospect of putting court decisions to a popular vote was more than even some of Roosevelt's closest friends could bear. Elihu Root complained to Robert Bacon, the ex-Morgan partner who had briefly succeeded Root as Roosevelt's secretary of state, "Theodore has gone off on a perfectly wild program. . . . I wish to fall upon your neck and weep. I wish to walk up and down in your congenial and unrestraining presence and curse and swear and say things which I would not have repeated for the world." Henry Cabot Lodge was equally appalled, writing Roosevelt, "I have had my mishaps in politics, but I never thought that any situation could arise which would have made me so miserably unhappy as I have been during the past week." To reporters he would say only, "The Colonel and I have long since agreed to disagree on a number of points."

What about Roosevelt's pledge not to seek a third term? He'd been speaking about three consecutive terms, he now explained. "Frequently when asked to take another cup of coffee at breakfast, I say 'No thank you, I won't take another cup.' This does not mean that I intend never to take another cup of coffee during my life; it means that I am not accepting the offer as applying to that breakfast, and that my remark is limited to that breakfast." Many Americans were not persuaded by the homey but strained analogy.

Finally, Taft struck back. On April 24th, Attorney General Wickersham filed an anti-trust suit against International Harvester, the other Morgan corporation that Roosevelt had singled out for particularly favorable treatment. The Justice Department had been mulling a suit since the previous summer, and in a meeting with the attorney general, George Perkins had suggested that Harvester and the government come to a mutual accommodation rather than resort to litigation. Wickersham

Henry Cabot Lodge. LIBRARY OF CONGRESS

had met several times with Harvester attorneys but, frustrated by lack of progress in the negotiations, he filed the complaint.

On the same day, in an obvious political maneuver, Wickersham released to the Senate a sheaf of documents revealing Roosevelt's extraordinary collaboration with the Morgan companies. Consisting of correspondence from Roosevelt, Attorney General Bonaparte, and other members of the administration, the archive made front-page news across the country. "Roosevelt Halted Harvester Suit," broadcast the headline in the *New York Tribune*. "That President Roosevelt looked on the International Harvester Company, George W. Perkins, president; the United States Steel Corporation and other 'Morgan interests' as 'good trusts,' against which the stringent provisions of the Sherman anti-trust law should not be enforced, is the deduction drawn," the article continued. It was lost on no one that George Perkins, organizer of International Harvester and an architect of the Roosevelt-Morgan détente, was now a major contributor to the Colonel's campaign. Roosevelt responded that Harvester had received no special treatment from his administration. And, he claimed, when the issue was discussed at a Cabinet meeting, then Secretary of War Taft had "heartily concurred" with the chosen course of action. In dealing with Harvester and "in all other cases of the kind," he said, "I considered nothing but what was demanded by right and justice."

The Harvester prosecution was announced less than a week before the Massachusetts primary. On the 25th, stumping in that state, Taft launched his own bitter attack against Roosevelt, whom he called a "dictator who, once he received a third term, would cling like a leech to the White House and never leave it until death removed him." The next day, in a speech at Worcester, Roosevelt resumed the offensive. "I do not think that Mr. Taft means ill," he ventured; "I think he means well. But he means well feebly, and during his administration he has been under the influence of men who are neither well meaning nor feeble. It is this quality of feebleness in a normally amiable man which pre-eminently fits such a man for use in high office by the powers of evil." As the campaign wore on, the mutual recriminations became even nastier, with Taft labeling Roosevelt a "demagogue" and a "dangerous egotist" and Roosevelt calling him a "fathead" and a "puzzlewit" with "brains less than a guinea pig." As Elihu Root observed, Roosevelt was "essentially a fighter and when he gets into a fight he is completely dominated by the desire to destroy his adversary." But the brawl took a toll on the naturally less pugnacious Taft, who sat in his railroad car and wept to a reporter, "Roosevelt was my closest friend."

When the primary results were in, Roosevelt had won more popular votes than both of his Republican opponents combined and had taken nine of the twelve contests, including a decisive win in Taft's home state of Ohio. Entering the convention, held in June in Chicago, Roosevelt claimed 469½ delegates to Taft's 454½. But 254 of these seats were contested, with Roosevelt supporters claiming they had been unfairly displaced by machine hacks, especially in the South. As the Credentials Committee sorted through the claims and counterclaims, the auditorium was rocked by parades, demonstrations, and fistfights on the convention floor. The wrenching duty of chairing the meeting fell to Elihu Root, who, following his conscience, consistently ruled in favor of the incumbent, even as he confided to a friend, "I care more for one button on Theodore Roosevelt's waistcoat than for Taft's whole body." Ultimately, the party granted 235 of the contested delegates to Taft and 19 to the Colonel. In protest, Roosevelt instructed his delegates to abstain, and Taft was nominated on the first ballot, 561 to 107, with 41 votes for La Follette and 344 abstentions.

Furious, claiming that the nomination had been stolen, Roosevelt bolted from the party he had represented for more than thirty years. Meeting in a Chicago hotel suite, he and his supporters, among them governors, senators, and prominent journalists, founded a new party, the Progressive, or Bull Moose (from Roosevelt's claim that he felt "as strong as a Bull Moose"). But where would the money come from to finance a national campaign? As Roosevelt paced the room and his followers looked on, two millionaires with close ties to Pierpont Morgan huddled in a corner. One was George Perkins. Although he had left Morgan & Company in late 1910, after Morgan had tired of his stubborn independence, Perkins still sat on the boards of more than a dozen Morgan corporations. Hunched with Perkins was self-made newspaper mogul Frank Munsey, who had extensive holdings in Morgan companies such as U.S. Steel and International Harvester. At length, the two men approached Roosevelt and laid their hands on his shoulders. "Colonel," they told him, "we will see you through."

The Progressives then turned to other wealthy donors who had close ties to the House of Morgan, including Willard Straight, who had represented J.P. Morgan & Company in China. But Perkins and Munsey would prove the largest contributors, donating more than $100,000 each. In a frenetic whirl of activity, the new party elected a national committee, opened headquarters in Chicago, New York, and Washington, and assembled a slate of candidates to contest state and local elections. In August, Roosevelt was duly nominated at the party convention, held in the same Chicago auditorium where the Republicans had earlier named Taft. For his running mate, the Colonel chose Hiram Johnson, governor of California.

At the Democratic convention in Baltimore, public opinion was running so high against Wall Street that William Jennings Bryan was able to cajole the party into pledging not to nominate any candidate "who is the representative of or who is under any obligation to J. Pierpont Morgan . . . or any other members of the privilege-hunting or favor-seeking class." As the convention opened, Woodrow Wilson seemed a long shot for the nomination. As governor of New Jersey, he had introduced a series of popular reforms that had received national press attention. But Wilson's progressive agenda had not endeared him to the right wing of his party, and when the presidential campaign season opened in 1912, his feuds with Democratic bosses and his limited experience in government seemed to favor more tested and more conservative candidates such as Speaker of the House James Beauchamp "Champ" Clark of Missouri. During the Democratic primaries that spring, Wilson won only five of thirteen contests, and so arrived at the convention with 248 delegates versus Clark's nearly five hundred.

But when Roosevelt had thrown his hat into the ring he had also created an opening for Wilson. Democratic strategists realized that by splitting the Republican Party, the Bull Moose had presented their best chance of retaking the White House in sixteen years, ever since the second administration of Grover Cleveland. And they recognized that it was the magnetic Roosevelt, not the somnolent Taft, who blocked their path. If the Democrats chose a traditionalist, he and Taft would split the conservative and moderate vote and throw the election to Roosevelt, the only progressive in the race. But if they put forward another progressive, Roosevelt and Taft would split the Republican vote, likely handing the presidency to the Democrats. At the convention, this strategy prevailed, and after an agonizing forty-six ballots Wilson was nominated, in one of the great upsets in American politics.

The fourth contender for the presidency was charismatic, fifty-six-year-old labor organizer Eugene V. Debs, candidate of the Socialist Party, who was making his third attempt at the office. With Roosevelt, Taft, Wilson, and Debs in the race, the election would prove a passionate, four-way battle of ideas, which historians have called the most fascinating election in American history. Featuring the introduction of state primaries, weakened influence by party bosses, a longer and more expensive campaign season, and expanded roles for the press and for women (1.3 million of whom were eligible to vote that year, in six states), the election of 1912 has also been called the first truly modern campaign.

The central issue was not whether to rein in the corporations but how, and each candidate strove to position himself as the true bulwark against the trusts. The Progressive platform (which also advocated expanded primaries; the direct election of U.S. senators; women's suffrage; initiative, referendum, and recall; the creation of a nonpartisan government commission to study tariff revision; inheritance and income taxes; the end of child labor; and other measures to protect workers and consumers) called for "a strong National regulation of inter-State corporations," including "a strong Federal administrative commission of high standing, which shall maintain permanent active supervision over industrial corporations. . . . Thus," it reasoned, "the businessman will have certain knowledge of the law, and will be able to conduct his business easily in conformity therewith . . . freed from confusion, uncertainty and fruitless litigation."

The Republican platform declared its opposition "to special privilege and to monopoly," while omitting most of the specific reforms put forward by the Progressives. But on many issues related to business, the parties' programs were remarkably similar. Like the Progressives, the Republicans called for the appointment of an expert commission to study the tariff. And like the Progressives, they recognized the need for banking reform but were noncommittal as to what shape that might take. To control the trusts, the G.O.P. proposed legislation to define specific acts "that uniformly mark attempts to restrain and to monopolize trade," and they supported the creation of a Federal Trade Commission, "thus placing in the hands of an administrative board many of the functions now necessarily exercised by the courts." Both Republicans and Progressives, then, would formalize and extend to all corporations the same type of extrajudicial regulation that the Roosevelt Administration had offered the Morgan companies.

In August, Roosevelt set out on a ferocious, ten-thousand-mile barnstorming tour, from New York to San Francisco and back again, routinely filling auditoriums with such huge, fervent crowds that newspapermen began comparing him to John the Baptist. Taft, meanwhile, honoring the tradition that a sitting president not actively campaign for reelection, spent the summer at his seaside home in Beverly, Massachusetts, while surrogates traveled the country on his behalf.

But he didn't refrain from attacking the Progressive candidate. In his acceptance speech at the Republican convention, Taft had pointed with pride to his aggressive prosecution of the trusts and had warned against demagogues such as Roosevelt, who were advocating "dangerous changes in our present constitutional form of representative government and our independent judiciary." Now he condemned the Progressives' close ties to the House of Morgan and criticized Roosevelt's tabling of the Harvester investigation. As for the Bull Moose, he said, "letting the people rule when reduced to its lowest terms, it seems, is letting the Steel Trust rule."

It was a theme the Progressives would hear throughout the campaign. George Perkins had been named party chairman against the wishes of many of the Colonel's advisers, who understood that to the press and public Perkins remained as closely associated with Pierpont Morgan as if he were still a partner in the firm. Over the course of the campaign the dapper businessman proved a lightning rod for critics—

Democrats, Republicans, and Progressives alike—who accused Roosevelt of conniving with the very corporations he claimed to want to subdue. The impression of collusion between Morgan and Roosevelt was only magnified when Morgan's son-in-law Herbert Satterlee (who had been appointed assistant secretary of the navy in the final days of the Roosevelt Administration) declared his support for the Bull Moose and Morgan's daughter Anne started attending Progressive Party meetings. In June, a Senate subcommittee chaired by Moses Clapp of Minnesota began investigating contributions to Roosevelt's 1904 campaign from wealthy donors, including Pierpont Morgan, E. H. Harriman, George Gould, William K. Vanderbilt, and John Archbold of Standard Oil.

Wilson was also eager to distance himself from Wall Street, and he was chagrined to learn that he had been endorsed by *Harper's* magazine, whose principal creditor was none other than Pierpont Morgan. Among its progressive planks, the Democrats' platform called for the reinstatement of the income tax, the popular election of U.S. senators, the extension of presidential primaries, and a prohibition on corporate political contributions. While acknowledging the need for banking reform, the Democrats opposed the creation of a central bank, which they feared would be subject to "dominion by what is known as the money trust."

Like his opponents, Wilson made control of the trusts the centerpiece of his campaign. But whereas Roosevelt wanted to enhance the power of the federal government as a means of countering the corporations, Wilson argued that monopolies must not be regulated but eliminated. Toward this end he advocated, in the words of the party platform, "the prevention of holding companies, of interlocking directors, of stock watering, of discrimination in price, and the control by any one corporation of so large a proportion of any industry as to make it a menace to competitive conditions." Only then, he maintained, would smaller businesses be free to thrive and restore competition to the marketplace. In keeping with his vision of a smaller federal government, he suggested that issues such as women's suffrage and child labor be decided by the states, and he opposed laws establishing a minimum wage. "No government has ever been beneficent when the attitude of the government was that it could take care of the people," he warned. "Let me tell you that the only freedom exists where the people take care of the government." To emphasize the flowering of personal and economic liberty that would ensue, he called his program "the New Freedom."

To Roosevelt, both the Republicans and the Democrats were fossilized reactionaries. "The trouble with Mr. Wilson," he charged, was that he was "thinking of government as embodied in an absolute king or an oligarchy or aristocracy. He is not thinking of our government which is a government by the people themselves. The only way in which our people can increase their power over the big corporation that does wrong, the only way in which it can protect the working man in his conditions of work and life, the only way in which people can protect children working in industry or secure women an eight-hour day in industry or secure compensation for men killed or crippled in industry, is by extending instead of limiting the powers of government. . . . We propose to use the whole power of the Government to protect all those who, under Mr. Wilson's laissez-faire system, are trodden down in the ferocious, scrambling rush of an unregulated and purely individualistic industrialism."

In early October, in the midst of the heated contest, Roosevelt and Morgan were called to testify before the Clapp Committee, which was investigating campaign contributions dating back to 1904. In his testimony, John Archbold claimed that Cornelius Bliss, Republican Party treasurer at the time, had coerced him into contributing $125,000 to the campaign. The committee was eager to expose such pressure, along with any quid pro quo that may have been promised Archbold or any other donor.

Testifying on October 3, Morgan amiably admitted to giving the Republicans $150,000 in 1904. But, he said, "I want it distinctly understood that J.P. Morgan & Company never made a single subscription to any election with any promise or expectation of anything or return in any way, shape, or manner, and we never made it without we deemed it advantageous for the Government and the people." When asked whether the recipients expressed their appreciation for his donations, Morgan grumbled, "No. Gratitude has been rather scarce in my experience." The following day, Governor Thomas R. Marshall of Indiana, Woodrow Wilson's running mate, suggested, "If that is all he gave, he is a tightwad," since the TC&I merger "netted Morgan $69,000,000. I repeat that if he only gave back $100,000 of it he is a tightwad." When he took the stand, Roosevelt devoted the morning to defending his honor, barely pausing to let the committeemen interject a question. When Atlee Pomerene of Ohio suggested that the Colonel must have known that the trusts hoped for some consideration in exchange for their contributions, Roosevelt admitted receiving corporate donations but adamantly denied promising anything in return. As for Archbold, he told the senators, "His complaint is that he did not get anything for the contributions he made." After the midday recess, Pomerene asked hypothetically whether some campaign contributors might expect to receive favors from his administration. "It is, of course, impossible for me to say," Roosevelt answered, "that any man who gives a dollar may not have an idea that he ought to get something for that dollar. I do not know. But if I tell him he will not get anything for it, then it is his own fault if he goes ahead and gives it."

"As a practical man," Pomerene pressed, "would you naturally think that some of these people might be expecting favors?"

"As a practical man of high ideals," Roosevelt countered, "who has always endeavored to put his high ideals into practice, I think any man who would believe that he would get any consideration from making any contribution to me was either a crook or a fool." Finally, after two and a half more fruitless hours of cross-examination, the witness was excused, having made no concession of any kind. Observed the *New York Times*, "The Clapp Committee behaved very well when it appeared before Col. Roosevelt on Friday."

Later that month, George Perkins offered what may have been the most contentious testimony before the committee, heatedly denying that he was funding the Progressive campaign in gratitude for Roosevelt's earlier quashing of the anti-trust suit against International Harvester. When confronted with the rumor that the Progressives were bankrolled by $3 million from the trusts, including Harvester, Perkins exploded. "In the long list of unmitigated lies put out in this campaign," he fairly shouted, "that one probably deserves to be placed at the head because it is the largest. There is not a scintilla of truth in it from A to Z." Asked whether he considered Harvester a legal corporation, he answered, "Not only legal but moral as well, and in the interest of the producer and the consumer." Did he feel the same way about U.S. Steel? "Amen," he told the senators.

In the end, the Clapp Committee found no evidence of illegality. Even so, the senators had achieved their principal purpose, of painting Roosevelt as a hypocrite and a tool of big business and sapping momentum from his campaign. Taft came out no better, since it was revealed that in 1908 he had also accepted a contribution of $150,000 from the House of Morgan. And so Woodrow Wilson emerged as the prime beneficiary of the committee's labors.

After offering his testimony, the Colonel resumed the campaign. But as he traveled the country, addressing huge audiences, he had no inkling that a would-be assassin was stalking him. A German immigrant named John Schrank believed he had been visited by the spirit of William McKinley, who had named Theodore Roosevelt as his true assassin and commanded Schrank to avenge his death. Leaving his home in New York City, Schrank pursued the candidate for a month, through eight southern and midwestern states. Three times, in Atlanta, Chattanooga, and Chicago, he came close to Roosevelt but missed his opportunity. Then, on the evening of October 14, outside a Milwaukee hotel, he finally struck.

Though shot in the chest at close range, and bleeding profusely, Roosevelt insisted on being driven to the auditorium, where ten thousand supporters were waiting. When it was announced from the stage that he had been shot, someone in the crowd shouted, "Fake!" Upon which Roosevelt opened his coat to display his bloody shirt and waistcoat. But not to worry, he assured the audience, "It takes more than that to kill a bull moose." Then he proceeded to speak for eighty minutes before finally consenting to being taken to the hospital. In his breast pocket were discovered his metal spectacles case and the folded, fifty-page manuscript of his speech, both pierced with a neat round bullet hole. Apparently the Colonel's myopia and long-windedness had saved his life. In the words of Senator Joseph Dixon, manager of the Progressive campaign, "That must have been a great speech if it could stop a bullet that way."

Although the Bull Moose sustained no permanent injury from the bullet (which he carried in his ribcage for the rest of his life), the shooting curtailed his campaigning that year. But on October 30, two weeks after the assassination attempt, he did return to the hustings for a final appearance, in New York's Madison Square Garden. In intense pain, he stood onstage for forty-five minutes beseeching the overflow crowd to quiet their cheers and let him speak. When he was finally able to begin, his audience was surprised to see his habitual combativeness replaced by the unaccustomed gravity of a valedictory, as though he believed this to be his last public address. And in place of a call to arms, he offered a simple statement of Progressive principles. "We propose to lift the burdens from the lowly and the weary," he told the throng, "from the poor and the oppressed. . . . We intend to strike down privilege, to equalize opportunity, to wrest justice from the hands that do injustice. . . . We recognize no differences of class, creed, or birthplace. . . . We are striving to meet the needs of all these men, and to meet them in such fashion that all alike shall feel bound together in the bond of a common brotherhood where each works hard for himself and for those dearest to him, and yet feel that he must also think of his brother's rights because he is in very truth that brother's keeper. . . . I believe we shall win, but win or lose I am glad beyond measure that I am one of the many who in this fight have stood ready to spend and be spent, pledged to fight while life lasts the great fight of righteousness and for brotherhood and for the welfare of mankind."

On November 5, the election played out as the Democratic strategists had hoped. With Roosevelt and Taft splitting the Republican vote, Woodrow Wilson was elected the nation's twenty-eighth president, taking 6.3 million ballots, versus 4.1 million for Roosevelt and 3.5 million for Taft. Eugene Debs, the Socialist candidate, won 900,000 votes, the highest proportion (6 percent) that his party had ever earned, or ever would again. Though Wilson received only 41 percent of the popular vote, in the Electoral College he won forty states and 435 votes. Roosevelt took six states and 88 electoral votes, while Taft trailed with two states and eight electors, making 1912 the only time before or since that a third party has outpolled either the Republican or Democratic candidate.

The *New York Times* was exultant. "The victory of Wilson, the victory of the Democrats, was predestined in our politics," it editorialized. "The

Republican Party had betrayed its trust. It had come to be recognized not as a party of the people, but as an instrument of business interests, of interests seeking special favors." The contest had been a referendum on how to balance the needs of the people with those of the great corporations, as personified by Pierpont Morgan, the man who more than any other had propelled their rise and defended their interests as America had transformed itself into the leading industrial power of the world. In 1912 a vote for Roosevelt or Taft, to many, was a vote for Morgan, whose largesse had funded their previous elections, just as Morgan's ex-partner George Perkins was underwriting that year's Progressive campaign. Roosevelt's collaboration with the House of Morgan, especially their accommodation over U.S. Steel and International Harvester, had alienated voters, and it had been a principal factor in his falling-out with Taft, which in turn had split the Republican Party and resulted in the election of Woodrow Wilson. From before the first primary until Election Day, although his name had appeared on no ballot, the specter of Pierpont Morgan had hung over the campaign of 1912 and, in no small measure, had influenced its outcome.

On election night, Roosevelt met with reporters in his library at Sagamore Hill. "Like all other good citizens," he told them, "I accept the result with entire good humor and contentment." To James Garfield he wrote, "We have fought the good fight, we have kept the faith, and we have nothing to regret." Taft received the news at his home in Cincinnati. To a friend he confided, "I'll be very glad to ride down Pennsylvania Avenue with Governor Wilson. It wouldn't have been so easy if things had been different," that is, if Roosevelt had won, "but I would have taken the ride just the same."

—✦—

Whereas Roosevelt's valedictory had come in October, before ten thousand cheering followers in Madison Square Garden, Pierpont Morgan's public farewell came in December of that year, in Washington, before several hundred congressmen, aides, newsmen, and spectators. They were all crammed into a hearing room in the House Office Building, where the Banking and Currency Subcommittee, chaired by Louisiana congressman Arsène Pujo, was conducting an investigation of the so-called money trust, the handful of New York bankers said to exercise disproportionate control over the country's economy. "The trust of trusts," the *New York Times* called them, "without whose favor all other trusts must languish to a lingering death."

As the nation's preeminent financier, Morgan was considered the nexus of the money trust, and his testimony before the Pujo Committee was much anticipated. On the afternoon of Wednesday, December 18, he appeared briefly before the panel and testified to rudimentary facts such as his address, place of employment, and the names of his partners. Then the committee adjourned until the following morning, when, it was understood, the real examination would begin.

On the 19th, Morgan arrived at the House Office Building just before 10:30, accompanied by his son, Jack, his daughter Louisa, and a dozen partners and attorneys. As he entered the committee room, he

Morgan, accompanied by his son, Jack, and his daughter Louisa, arrives for his testimony before the Pujo Committee. LIBRARY OF CONGRESS

swung his black walking stick and fussed with his silk top hat. Then, flanked by Louisa and one of his lawyers, he seated himself in the front row, in the section reserved for witnesses. During his testimony, the other attorneys would sit close behind, murmuring information and advice.

The committee's counsel, prominent corporate lawyer Samuel Unter-myer, began the questioning. "Mr. Morgan, can you give the committee a statement of the total amount of deposits of your banking firm in New York as of the 1st of November, 1912, including all deposits?"

"I have not got it here, sir," Morgan answered.

"Can you approximate it?"

"I should think one hundred millions."

Having established the financial heft of the House of Morgan, Untermyer launched into his interrogation of the seventy-five-year-old witness, probing his investments in banks, railroads, insurance companies, and some of America's largest corporations. Always deploring the spot-light, the financier fidgeted with his horn-rimmed glasses, which he put on and took off as the need arose. His answers were generally terse, not hostile but guarded. Yet he appeared in good humor and fine mental fet-tle. Maintaining a Jovian aloofness, he spoke in generalities and pleaded ignorance of the details, since he no longer directed his firm on a daily basis. More than anything, he underplayed his own influence.

Trying to induce him to admit to monopolistic tendencies, Unter-myer asked, "You are opposed to competition, are you not?"

"No," Morgan answered, "I do not mind competition."

"You would rather have combination, would you not? . . . Combina-tion as against competition?"

"I do not object to competition, either. I like a little competition."

"Is that the reason you want to control everything?"

"I want to control nothing."

Then what about the "vast power" he wielded?

"I do not know it, sir."

"You admit you have, do you not?"

"I do not think I have."

"You do not feel it at all?"

"No, I do not feel it at all."

The witness even denied his influence at 23 Wall Street. "Your firm is run by you, is it not?" Untermyer asked.

"No, sir."

"You are the final authority, are you not?"

"No, sir."

"You never have been?"

"Never have."

Concerning Morgan's sway over the nation's financial affairs, the counsel asked, "You do not think you have any power in any department of industry in this country, do you?"

"I do not."

"Not the slightest?"

"Not the slightest."

"And you are not looking for any?"

"I am not seeking it, either."

"This consolidation and amalgamation of systems and industries and banks does not look to any concentration, does it?"

"No, sir."

"It is for the purpose of concentrating the interests that you do amalgamate, is it not?"

"If it is desirable, yes. . . . If it is good business for the interests of the country to do it, I do it."

As for the control of credit, the presumed means by which the money trust exerted its power, Untermyer asked, "Is not the credit based upon the money?"

"No, sir."

"It has no relation?"

"No, sir; . . . none whatever. . . . I know lots of men, business men, too, who can borrow any amount, whose credit is unquestioned."

"Is that not because it is believed that they have the money back of them?"

"No, sir; it is because people believe in the man. . . . I have known a man to come into my office, and I have given him a check for a million dollars when I knew he had not a cent in the world."

"Is not commercial credit based primarily upon money and property?"

"No, sir; the first thing is character."

"Before money or property?"

"Before money or anything else. Money can not buy it. . . . A man I do not trust could not get money from me on all the bonds in Christendom."

The very idea of a money trust, Morgan claimed, was a figment of the imagination. "There is nothing in the world that you can make a trust on money. . . . [Someone] may have all the money in Christendom, but he can not do it."

For nearly four hours, the two men sparred, as Roosevelt had done before the Clapp Committee. When it was over, Untermyer declared himself satisfied, but the consensus was that Morgan had given a masterful performance, "dominating," as one reporter put it, "and yet not domineering."

Immediately afterward, Morgan sailed for Egypt, accompanied by Louisa and a party of friends. But as their steamship neared the European coast, he appeared nervous and depressed. He seemed in better health after an excursion in Spain and Monaco. Then in early February, while cruising up the Nile, he experienced a sudden mental breakdown, including agitation, nightmares, and paranoid delusions. One of his doctors was summoned from New York, and by March 10, Morgan felt well enough to travel to Rome. But ensconced in the royal suite of the city's Grand Hotel, he became incoherent once more. On March 30, he lapsed into unconsciousness. The following day, at five minutes past noon, with Louisa holding his hand, Morgan died.

The Italian death certificate credited his demise to "psychic dyspepsia," possibly brought on by a series of strokes. His family began the long journey across the Continent, accompanying his remains. In Rome, a military escort conducted his casket through the streets, and in Paris private citizens decked it with flowers. At Le Havre, on April 5, the mourners boarded the SS *France* and sailed for home. Nine days later, Morgan was interred in the family plot in his hometown of Hartford, Connecticut. In New York, the stock exchange was closed in his honor.

Morgan's will, comprising thirty-four pages, included dozens of bequests to friends, employees, and charities. Although it made generous provision for his wife, Fanny, and daughters, Louisa, Juliet, and Anne, the bulk of the estate was left to his son and partner, Jack. Considering the enormous shadow he had cast over American finance, many observers were surprised that Pierpont had left only $80 million, much of that in works of art. "And to think," sniffed John D. Rockefeller, "he wasn't even a rich man." And although Morgan was by any measure well compensated for his work, there was no doubt that if his primary goal had been to amass a personal fortune, he would have died even wealthier. But (like Theodore Roosevelt) he had been driven by a sense of personal responsibility and a desire for control more than the promise of monetary gain.

It was widely remarked, even among his contemporaries, that Morgan's passing signaled the end of an era. Wrote the *New York Times*, "We may look upon Mr. Morgan's like again—there were great men before and after Agamemnon—but we shall not look upon another career like his. The time for that has gone by. Conditions have changed, and Mr. Morgan, the mighty and dominant figure of finance, did more than any other man to change them." In the complex commercial world he had helped to create, no individual would ever again be able to wield such power: Morgan had made his own kind obsolete.

As for Theodore Roosevelt, after his defeat in 1912 the Bull Moose didn't spend much time in second-guessing, any more than he had after leaving the White House in 1909. In late 1913, again with his son Kermit, he joined a Brazilian expedition charged with mapping a tributary of the Amazon called the Rio da Dúvida, or River of Doubt. Only four years had passed since his African safari, but Roosevelt was unprepared for the rigors of the Amazon Basin, including dangerous rapids, violent inhabitants, and near starvation. Although the group did manage to trace the 400-mile waterway (now known as the Rio Roosevelt), the Colonel suffered from high fevers and a near-fatal leg infection, and he limped home fifty pounds lighter and in permanently reduced health.

After war broke out in Europe, Roosevelt castigated his nemesis Woodrow Wilson for America's lack of military preparedness; then, after the United States finally entered the fighting in April 1917, he took the Democrat to task for his prosecution of the war. To many the criticism seemed born of frustration that Wilson, and not he, had been called to lead the country in time of war. Like most Progressives, Roosevelt reconciled with Republican leaders, including Taft, and by 1918 he was considered the frontrunner for the party's nomination two years hence. But he continued to suffer from rheumatism, heart disease, and other ailments. His legendary strength seeped away, and at four o'clock on the morning of January 6, 1919, he died peacefully in his sleep at Sagamore Hill, of a pulmonary embolism. He was sixty years old. His son Archie telegraphed his brothers, who were serving with the army in Europe, "The old lion is dead."

After William Howard Taft's historic drubbing in the election of 1912, it may have seemed that his long and distinguished government career had come to an end, but Taft's later years would be among the most satisfying and productive of his life. After leaving the White House, he taught constitutional law at Yale University for eight years. Then, in 1921, President Warren Harding appointed him to the position he had coveted for decades, Chief Justice of the U.S. Supreme Court, making Taft the only individual in American history to lead two branches of the federal government. As chief justice, he proved not only an astute judge but an exceptional administrator, injecting a new efficiency into the federal judiciary. After nine years he retired due to poor health, and he died on March 8, 1930 at the age of seventy-two.

Pierpont Morgan's relationship with Theodore Roosevelt had not been simple or easy, and the two would never be mistaken for friends. With their profoundly different ideas on the proper roles of government and business, the trust builder and the trustbuster represented divergent currents of American history. Both were colossal figures and titanic personalities, and they could easily have become sworn enemies. But under his father's tutelage, Morgan had learned to think in the long term, and to recognize that his businesses could not prosper if the country did not prosper. Drawing on their shared values—a strict moral code, a strong sense of duty, a genuine concern for the public good—Morgan and Roosevelt were able to overlook their personal and philosophical differences and come together to resolve national crises such as the Anthracite Coal Strike and the Panic of 1907.

Yet the importance of their collaboration surpasses any specific achievement. Both men had begun their careers in the age of laissez-faire, when government exerted practically no restraint over private enterprise. Then, as industry and banking assumed unprecedented levels of complexity and power, the need for greater oversight grew more urgent. Early in his administration Roosevelt had attempted to use the big stick of the Northern Securities lawsuit to intimidate Morgan and other would-be monopolists. But like many of his colleagues, Morgan accepted the necessity of federal regulation, and even welcomed it over the alternative of either ruinous, unfettered competition or more-intrusive regulation by the states. Though Roosevelt rebuffed Morgan's first attempt at accommodation, offered immediately after the Northern Securities filing, in time he came to see the wisdom of a negotiated truce versus protracted judicial warfare. By the end of his presidency, Roosevelt had not only accepted détente with the Morgan companies but had bestowed on them a preference not accorded any other corporations. In his final, quixotic campaign of 1912, his intimate ties with the House of Morgan had sealed his falling out with Taft and had unsettled voters, setting the stage for his defeat.

Yet the collaboration between Roosevelt and Morgan had established a new paradigm for how business and government would work together. The Taft years, with their more measured pace of reform and their return to the litigious pattern that Roosevelt had abandoned, stand as an exception to this new pattern. But Woodrow Wilson, despite his campaign posturing, would adopt many of Roosevelt's policies, including stronger federal control of the economy. Like Roosevelt, he would prefer regulation over litigation. And he would institutionalize Roosevelt and Morgan's détente within the bureaucracy of the federal government.

The Pujo Committee, in its investigation of the money trust, had helped to set the nation on this new regulatory course. The committee's majority report found no illegal conduct, and it acknowledged the "important and valuable part that the gentlemen who dominate this inner group [Morgan, Stillman, and Baker] and their allies have played in the development of our prosperity." But for all his adroit parrying, Morgan had not convinced the committeemen of his insignificance. On examining the evidence, the lawmakers not only confirmed the existence of a money trust but found it even more destructive of competition than the industrial monopolies that had been prosecuted under the Sherman Act.

"There is an established and well-defined identity and community of interest between a few leaders of finance," the report concluded, "created and held together through stock ownership, interlocking directorates, partnership and joint account transactions, and other forms of domination over banks, trust companies, railroads, and public-service and industrial corporations, which has resulted in great and rapidly growing concentration of the control of money and credit in the hands of these few men." Quantifying this hegemony, the committee identified five institutions holding 341 interlocking directorships in 112 corporations, which together were valued at more than $22 billion. Among the banks singled out for their undue influence, J.P. Morgan & Company led the list, followed by firms such as First National Bank of New York; National City Bank; and Kuhn, Loeb.

"If the arteries of credit now clogged well-nigh to choking by the obstructions created through the control of these groups are opened so that they may be permitted freely to play their important part in the financial system," the report continued, "competition in large enterprises will become possible and business can be conducted on its merits instead of being subject to the tribute and the good will of this handful of self-constituted trustees of the national prosperity." Toward this end, the committee recommended more than two dozen corrective measures, including new regulations governing stock exchanges and the banking industry.

But the impetus for bank reform had deeper roots, reaching back to the Panic of 1907. By the early years of the century the United States had built the world's largest economy, but it remained the only industrialized nation without a central bank. The bank's opponents—in Wilson's day as in Andrew Jackson's—were suspicious of bankers and federal officials, both of whom they believed favored the interests of eastern, urban elites.

Yet after the near calamity of 1907, it was clear that America's archaic, decentralized banks could no longer sustain a modern industrial economy. Nor could the government rely on private citizens to rescue the financial system in times of crisis. And not least, the country could not entrust its economic security to persons who might not prove as scrupulous and public-spirited as Pierpont Morgan.

Among those aroused out of complacency after 1907 was Nelson Aldrich, one of the Senate's most powerful members and chairman of its Finance Committee (and card partner of Pierpont Morgan). Throughout his long tenure, the conservative Republican from Rhode Island had been a staunch ally of business and a formidable opponent of most types of regulation. But now, nearing the end of his career, Aldrich determined to make banking reform the capstone of his life's work. As chairman of the National Monetary Commission, which Congress had created in May 1908, he studied widely and deeply on the subject, and he traveled to Europe, where central banks had long been the norm. He was also swayed by the ideas of colleagues such as Assistant Secretary of the Treasury A. Piatt Andrew, National City Bank's Frank Vanderlip, J.P. Morgan & Company's Harry Davison, and especially Kuhn, Loeb's Paul Warburg, who had embraced the creation of a central bank as a personal crusade. In November 1910, during a clandestine, weeklong conference at the isolated resort of Jekyl Island, Georgia, Aldrich and his coconspirators hammered out a proposal for what they called the National Reserve Association of the United States (to avoid the politically loaded term "central bank"). And it was true that the organization they envisioned was not a central bank, at least not in the sense of a European-style, government-run institution; instead, the Reserve Association would seek to balance regional and national control, and it would be run by bankers for bankers.

When the Aldrich Plan was made public, the banking industry reacted with predictable enthusiasm. But progressives, who were in the political ascendancy, condemned the lack of public accountability and feared that the new institution would only fortify the so-called money trust. In 1912, under pressure to respond to the Aldrich Plan, House Democrats convened the Pujo Committee, at whose hearings Pierpont

Morgan dueled with Samuel Untermyer. But during that year's presidential campaign, bank reform took a back seat to the issue of government control over the corporations.

Following the election, Woodrow Wilson and the new Democratic Congress introduced a welter of progressive measures, including a graduated income tax and a significant reduction in the tariff. Wilson also favored banking reform, but the crucial issue of control remained unsettled—would the Reserve Association fall under centralized or regional authority, and would it be managed by the government or by bankers?

In December 1913, Congress answered both questions with the Federal Reserve Act, a political masterstroke that proved acceptable to (though not uniformly popular with) Democrats and Republicans, national and state banks, Wall Street, populists, progressives, and conservatives. Mirroring the federal structure of the country itself, the Federal Reserve would consist of twelve private, regional banks under central, government control. Among its responsibilities, the new institution would set short-term interest rates, supervise the banking industry, determine monetary policy, and act as lender of last resort, assuming the role that Pierpont Morgan had been obliged to play during the Panic of 1907.

The greatest accomplishment of Wilson's famously productive first term—and one of the signal financial reforms of the century—the Federal Reserve System would create a more flexible currency, modernize the banking system, and prepare the United States for leadership on the world financial stage. It would also guarantee that no private individual would ever again be called on to rescue the economy from collapse. Ben Strong, the young banker who had helped to stem the panic in 1907, was appointed first governor of the Reserve Bank of New York, the system's largest and most important.

In 1914, Wilson signed another significant piece of financial legislation with far-reaching consequences. A clarification and strengthening of the Sherman law, the Clayton Act prohibited specific practices such as price discrimination and predatory pricing, limited interlocking directorships, confirmed workers' rights to form unions and to conduct peaceful strikes, and banned corporate mergers that would produce monopolies. That same year, Wilson signed into existence the Federal Trade Commission, the successor of the Bureau of Corporations. With broad powers to enforce laws against unfair competition and deceptive practices, the FTC, working with the Department of Justice, would investigate companies, identify unfair or deceptive practices, and take appropriate measures to prevent or curtail them. Although the Commission could file suit in federal court, it also was empowered to issue cease-and-desist orders, to seek voluntary compliance through consent decrees, and to review proposed mergers to determine whether they would create an illegal monopoly, and if so, to disallow them.

Under Woodrow Wilson, federal control of the corporations shifted away from the reactive, judicial remedies of William Howard Taft and back toward the proactive, regulatory methods favored by Theodore Roosevelt. By codifying the informal understanding struck by Roosevelt and Morgan, and by extending it to all corporations rather than a favored few, the Clayton Act, the Federal Reserve, and the Federal Trade Commission marked the beginning of a new regulatory era. Under this paradigm, government would have more tools to protect workers and consumers from corporate abuses, and corporations, faced with the more-dire alternatives, would accept and even welcome a measure of federal control. And so the Progressive years would replace the old model of laissez-faire with a new balance between government and business, an unprecedented relationship offering benefits for corporations, the government, and the public alike.

For the rest of the century and beyond, Theodore Roosevelt's progressive legacy would be carried forward not by his own party, which after Taft would swing permanently to the right, but by Democrats such as Wilson, Franklin Roosevelt, and Lyndon Johnson. Through succeeding administrations of both parties, liberals would argue that Washington still favored big business over ordinary citizens, while conservatives would claim that excessive regulation was strangling innovation and American competitiveness. In the future, the equilibrium between these competing interests would shift depending on the party in control of Congress and the White House and the composition of the Supreme Court.

Today, the trend is once again away from government regulation. Throughout the twentieth century and the beginning of the twenty-first, a series of federal laws imposed limits on corporate campaign contributions. But recent Supreme Court decisions have chipped away at these reforms and given new impetus to what Theodore Roosevelt once called "the combination of business with politics and with the judiciary which has done so much to enthrone privilege in the economic world." With corporate contributions flooding political campaigns and with an executive branch under the direction of multimillionaires and billionaires, the current trend is toward stripping away measures protecting workers, consumers, investors, and the environment.

In fact, as we compare the current political landscape with that of the early 1900s, perhaps what is most striking is not how much has changed over the past century but how little. As during Roosevelt and Morgan's time, our urgent domestic issues include the extent of corporations' influence over the political process, the proper size of government, the appropriate degree of federal control over private enterprise, and the growing divide between rich and poor. And so the pendulum set in motion by Theodore Roosevelt, with added impetus from Pierpont Morgan, appears to have reached its momentary apogee and to have begun its contrary swing, still seeking, as it has for the past hundred years, the ideal accommodation of government, business, labor, and the public interest.

ACKNOWLEDGMENTS

MY THANKS TO THE DEDICATED STAFF AT THE FOLLOWING INSTITU-
tions: the Morgan Library and Museum, the Rare Book and Manuscript
Library of Columbia University, the New York Public Library, the
Library of Congress, the Wilson Library at Millsaps College, and the
Hinds County (Mississippi) Library System. Without your expert and
timely assistance, this book would have been impossible.

My special thanks to Clay Jenkinson, Sharon Kilzer, Pamela Pierce,
Pamela Kukla, and the other staff members of the Theodore Roosevelt
Center at Dickinson State University. Among the many forms of assistance that the center offers to Roosevelt scholars and aficionados is an
extensive online digital library featuring tens of thousands of letters and
other documents that were previously available only through a personal
visit to the Library of Congress or to the Houghton and Widener
Libraries at Harvard University. You can sample the center's amazing
resources at www.theodorerooseveltcenter.org.

I am indebted to the readers who generously shared their time and
expertise to help me make this a better book, including J. Lee Annis, Paul
Aron, Sean Carr, John M. Hilpert, Clay Jenkinson, Edward P. Kohn, and
M. Kelly Tillery.

Thank you to my editors at Lyons Press, Keith Wallman and Gene
Brissie, for your interest in this project and your help in shepherding it
from idea to reality. To Ellen Urban, assistant managing editor, thanks for
your timeliness and fine eye for detail.

Thanks to my agent, Deirdre Mullane of Mullane Literary Associates, for your enthusiasm, editorial savvy, and expert advice, and not least
of all, your friendship.

And as always, I am most deeply grateful to my wife of forty years,
the writer Teresa Nicholas, my first reader, my partner, my love, *mi vida*.

NOTES

Listed below are the sources where I discovered the information cited, but please note that in many cases the same material can be
found elsewhere. Under each citation I have tried to list the most ger-
mane sources first. See the Bibliography for full citations.

PROLOGUE: "THIS, THEN, IS THE PLACE TO STOP THIS TROUBLE"
Page
xiii. Sunday, November 3, 1907: Some authors have erroneously written that these
events began on the evening of Saturday, November 2. I believe the mistake was
prompted by Benjamin Strong, who, working from memory (as quoted in Lamont), placed them on that day. In writing his later biography of J. P. Morgan
(hereafter referred to as JPM in Notes), Herbert Satterlee, who cites Strong's
account, apparently accepted his date without question. However, newspaper
reports from the time confirm that the all-night meeting in JPM's library actually began on the following evening, Sunday, November 3. Also, I have made a
few assumptions in my description of Strong's arrival on that evening—that he
would be carrying a briefcase and wearing a (dark) overcoat, that he would have
taken a cab uptown, and that reporters would have paid him no mind; I also
assume that he had brought "pages of figures" with him for his meeting with
JPM et al.
xiii. Events at JPM's library: Lamont, 78; *New York Evening World*, November 4, 1907;
New York Tribune, November 4, 1907; *New York Sun*, November 4, 1907; *New York
Times*, November 4, 1907; Strouse, 586–87; Chernow, 127.
xv. JPM promised to cut his cigar consumption to twenty per day: Chernow, 126.
xvi. "I can't say anything": *New York Tribune*, November 4, 1907.
xvi. "I wish to God": *Washington Times*, November 4, 1907.
xvi. Exchange between Strong and Stillman: Lamont, 80.
xvii. Financial situation before the panic: Bruner and Carr, 19ff; Strouse, 573.
xvii. Financial effects of San Francisco earthquake: Bruner and Carr, 13–15.
xvii. Bank of England nearly doubled interest rate: Bruner and Carr, 15.
xvii. Stocks were down 24 percent for the year: Bruner and Carr, 32.
xviii. "Malefactors of great wealth": Harbaugh, 311.

xviii. United Copper fiasco: Bruner and Carr, 37ff.

xviii. Charles Barney: Disgraced, Charles Barney shot himself to death on the morning of November 14, 1907, in the bedroom of his house at Park Avenue and Thirty-Eighth Street.

xviii. Patchwork of twenty-one thousand state and national banks: Strouse, 574.

xviii. By 1907 half the bank loans in New York City were using securities as collateral: Chernow, 122.

xviii. Background of trust companies: Strouse, 574; Chernow, 122; Bruner and Carr, 58, 67.

xix. "They are in trouble in New York": Chernow, 122.

xix. "We got three bears": Strouse, 576.

xx. "Dishonesty" and "his memory": *New York Tribune*, October 23, 1907.

xx. "Do I look as though those Wall Street fellows": Morris 2001, 498.

xx. JPM's efforts to stem the crisis: Bruner and Carr, 74–76, 84ff; Strouse, 575ff; Chernow, 122ff.

xx. "The consternation of the faces of the people": Chernow, 123.

xxi. "We are doing everything we can": Bruner and Carr, 86.

xxi. JPM's activities on Tuesday night: Bruner and Carr, 86–87.

xxi. Scene in JPM's office on Wednesday afternoon: Lamont, 76; Bruner and Carr, 90–91; Strouse, 578; Satterlee, 468ff.

xxi. "Have you anyone with you?" and rest of exchange between JPM and Strong: Lamont, 76.

xxiii. Twenty directors of TCA and Lincoln Trust weren't depositors at their own institutions: *New York Evening World*, November 4, 1907.

xxiii. JPM's activities Wednesday night: Strouse, 579; Bruner and Carr, 93–94; Satterlee, 471–72.

xxiii. "Gentlemen, the Bankers Trust Company": Strouse, 579.

xxiv. Events in JPM's office on Thursday afternoon: Bruner and Carr, 99–100; Satterlee, 474–75.

xxiv. "Mr. Morgan, we will have to close" and rest of dialogue between JPM and Thomas: Satterlee, 474.

xxiv. $19 million of the fund was committed: Strouse, 580.

xxiv. Ovation for JPM: Chernow, 125.

xxiv. Theodore Roosevelt's (Roosevelt hereafter referred to as TR in Notes) activities on Saturday, October 26: *New York Tribune*, October 27, 1907.

xxiv. "Those conservative and substantial business men": Bruner and Carr, 109–10.

xxv. TR's activities on Sunday, October 27: *Washington Herald*, October 28, 1907.

xxv. "There is some debate": *Washington Herald*, November 5, 1907.

xxv. JPM's meeting with George McClellan: Bruner and Carr, 111–12.

xxv. "We all realized the gravity of the situation" and "with scarcely a hesitation": Bruner and Carr, 112.

xxv. JPM called a delegation of clergymen: Chernow, 126.

xxv. Moore & Schley crisis: Bruner and Carr, 115ff; Strouse, 582–86.

xxvi. "It is very serious": Bruner and Carr, 116.

xxvi.   U.S. Steel's negotiation to buy TC&I: Strouse, 583–86; Bruner and Carr, 119, 129–31.

xxvi.   U.S. Steel earnings and cash position: Strouse, 573, 582.

xxvii.   "I have never been more concerned": Bruner and Carr, 128–29.

xxvii.   "I think the attitude of the present administration": Tarbell, 193.

xxviii.   "I wonder if you realize": Tarbell, 194.

xxviii.   U.S. Steel produced more than half the country's steel: Bruner and Carr, 117.

xxviii.   Events in JPM's library on Sunday, November 3: New York Evening World, November 4, 1907; Lamont, 78.

xxviii.   "I can't go on being everybody's goat": Chernow, 123.

xxviii.   "Before we go ahead with this" and rest of exchange between Gary and JPM: Tarbell, 200.

xxviii.   Gary and Frick's departure for Washington: Chernow, 127; Bruner and Carr, 131.

xxix.   Strong's report to JPM: Lamont, 80.

xxix.   Perkins's report to JPM: Bruner and Carr, 124.

xxix.   Strong discovered that the door was locked: Lamont, 80.

xxix.   JPM's meeting with trust bankers, including dialogue: Lamont, 81–82.

xxx.   "You look tired": Satterlee, 486.

xxx.   Scene as bankers left JPM's library: New York Evening World, November 4, 1907.

xxx.   "Nothing to say": Washington Times, November 4, 1907.

xxx.   "On good authority": Washington Evening Star, November 5, 1907.

xxx.   Gary and Frick's arrival at White House: New York Sun, November 5, 1907.

xxx.   Gary and Frick at White House, including dialogue: Tarbell, 200–201.

CHAPTER ONE: "I INTEND TO BE ONE OF THE GOVERNING CLASS"

1.   TR's inauguration: Wallace; Morris 2001, 11–15; N. Miller, 349–52; S. Miller; Buffalo Illustrated Express; New York Sun, September 15 and 16, 1901; New York Tribune, September 15, 1901; New York Times, September 15, 1901; Wilcox; Keating; weather data from Buffalo Morning Express, September 14, 1901, and National Climatic Data Center website (ncdc.noaa.gov).

4.   "Mr. Vice-President, I—" and other quotations during ceremony except as noted below: Buffalo Courier, September 15, 1901, as cited in Wallace.

4–5. "Where is the Bible?" and "You must swear him with uplifted hand": Keating.

5.   "Now—" and "I should like to see the members of the Cabinet": New York Sun, September 15, 1901.

5.   "It takes less in the way": Wilcox.

5.   "I have witnessed": New York Sun, September 16, 1901.

6.   TR's family background and biography until assuming the presidency: Morris 1979; N. Miller; Donald; Roosevelt 1913; Grondahl. Specific sources and quotations are referenced below.

6.   TR Sr. pledged $1,000, and JPM was a charter member of the Met: New York Times, March 15, 1871.

6. TR Sr. and JPM were trustees of the American Museum of Natural History: *New York Times*, November 10, 1875.
6. TR Sr. and JPM endorsed Hayes: *New York Times*, November 5, 1876.
6. JPM's firm contributed $5,000: Strouse, 165.
6. Gala dinner in honor of JPM's father: Strouse, 175.
7. "Sickly ... nervous and timid": Roosevelt 1913, 17, 32.
8. Roosevelt/Bulloch Civil War activities: N. Miller, 32–36.
8. JPM hired a substitute: Strouse, 109.
8. "The best man I ever knew" and following quotes: Roosevelt 1913, 8–9, 12.
8. "As I saw the last of the train": McCullough 1981, 162.
8. "Take care of your morals" and "I do not think there is a fellow in college": McCullough 1981, 165.
9. "The blackest day of my life": McCullough 1981, 187.
9. "He was everything": Kohn, 25.
9. "The one I loved dearest": Kohn, 19.
9. "The 'Machine politicians'": McCullough 1981, 180.
9. "I loved her as soon": N. Miller, 87.
9. "Purely a science of the laboratory": Roosevelt 1913, 29.
10. "Help the cause of better government": N. Miller, 98.
10. "Legalism": Roosevelt 1913, 61.
10. $125,000 inheritance and $8,000 annual income: N. Miller, 82 and 98, respectively.
10. Average American family earned less than $400: Long, 42.
10. "I could afford to make earning money": Roosevelt 1913, 62.
10. "The men in the clubs of social pretension" and following quotations: Roosevelt 1913, 63.
11. TR's nomination vote: N. Miller, 119.
11. *New York Times* endorsement: *New York Times*, October 30, 1881.
11. "Gentleman every way worthy of his parentage": *New York Tribune*, November 6, 1881.
11. "Owned by no man" and "untrammeled and unpledged": *New York Times*, November 1, 1881.
11. "Obey no boss": N. Miller, 120.
11. TR's margin of victory over Strew: *New York Tribune*, November 10, 1881.
11. "The wealthy criminal class": N. Miller, 147.
11. "Member of a prominent law firm": Roosevelt 1913, 85.
12. "The undersigned, members of both parties": *New York Sun*, November 5, 1882.
12. TR and JPM at the home of D. Willis James: *New York Times*, October 12, 1882.
12. TR's 1882 election results: N. Miller, 138.
14. For more on the cigar makers legislation, see Grondahl, 112–15.
14. "I worked on a very simple philosophy": Roosevelt 1913, 99.
14. "The light has gone out of my life": Morris 1979, 230.
15. "Made me perfectly heartsick": July 12, 1884. Theodore Roosevelt Digital Library, Dickinson State University (theodorerooseveltcenter.org); the original is in the Theodore Roosevelt Collection, Harvard College Library.

15. "Of all the men presented": June 8, 1884. Theodore Roosevelt Digital Library, Dickinson State University (theodorerooseveltcenter.org); the original is in the Theodore Roosevelt Collection, Harvard College Library.
15. JPM voted for Cleveland in 1884: Strouse, 241.
15. "(1) He is an honest man": Strouse, 242.
15. "The free choice of the great majority": June 8, 1884. Theodore Roosevelt Digital Library, Dickinson State University (theodorerooseveltcenter.org); the original is in the Theodore Roosevelt Collection, Harvard College Library.
15. "It has always been my luck": *New York Times*, August 1, 1884.
15. "I am by inheritance and by education": N. Miller, 160.
16. "I shall probably never be in politics": Morris 1979, 391.
16. JPM's background and biography until TR's inauguration: Strouse; Allen; Chernow; Sinclair. Specific sources and quotations are referenced below.
16. Joseph Morgan amassed an estate of more than $1 million: Chernow, 19.
18. "A good situation in a store or office": Strouse, 39.
18. Panic of 1857: Strouse, 71–74.
18. "You are commencing your business career": Strouse, 72.
19. "Never under any circumstances do an act": Strouse, 77.
19. "Do not let the desire of success": Strouse, 78.
19. "You are altogether too rapid": Strouse, 82.
19. "Suavity and gentle bearing": Strouse, 84.
19. "When I have responsibility laid upon me": Strouse, 107.
20. Courtship and wedding of JPM and Memie: Strouse, 78–97.
20. Illness and death of Memie: Strouse, 97–101.
20. "Poor Pierpont knelt by her": Strouse, 101.
20. JPM's career from the 1860s onward: Strouse; also see specific references below.
20. "Remember, my son": *New York Tribune*, December 11, 1908.
21. "Disappointed & pained to learn": Strouse, 111.
21. JPM's courtship and marriage to Fanny: Strouse, 114–16.
21. "Brusqueness of manners have made him personally unpopular": Strouse, 137.
22. Panic of 1873: Strouse, 150–55.
24. Drexel, Morgan showed a profit of more than $1 million: Chernow, 37.
24. JPM received $3 million in commissions: Chernow, 44.
25. Junius bestowed the ultimate praise: Chernow, 55.
25. "A success of which you may well be proud": Strouse, 253.
26. "Just and reasonable": Strouse, 257.
26. Ruled in favor of the railroads in fifteen of sixteen cases: Allen, 58–59.
26. Earning nearly a million dollars a year: Strouse, 194.
26. JPM's and Junius's combined fortune: Strouse, 216.
26. First private home in the city fully equipped with electric light: Strouse, 230.
27. Junius's estate valued at some $23 million: Strouse, 281.
28. "The brink of the abyss": Chernow, 74.
28. "I have come down to see the president" and "what suggestions have you to make": Chernow, 75.

28. Bonds sold out in two hours in London, twenty-two minutes in New York: Chernow, 76.
29. JPM's remuneration for the rescue was $300,000: Strouse, 350.
29. "We all have large interests dependent upon maintenance": Strouse, 349.
30. "I then believed, and now believe": Roosevelt 1913, 62.
30. TR's cowboy adventure cost him $40,000: Grondahl, 167.
31. "Wanted to put an end to all the evil": N. Miller, 205.
31. New York City's police bribes totaled nearly $10 million a year: Morris 1979, 500.
32. "You shall not press down upon the brow of labor": Bryan's "Cross of Gold" speech was made at the Democratic convention in Chicago on July 9, 1896.
32. 1896 election results, "glorious victory," and "we congratulate you": Strouse, 359.
32. McKinley campaign received millions from businesses and the wealthy: Strouse, 358.
33. "I rather hope that the fight will come soon": This has been widely cited.
33. JPM's hurried purchase of Cuban cigars and the commandeering of the *Corsair*: Strouse, 370.
34. "Great day of my life": This has been widely cited.
34. JPM contributed $10,000 toward TR's election: Strouse, 436.
34. "The combination of business with politics": Roosevelt 1913, 306–7.
35. "The exemption was of course put in": Carosso, 454.
35. "I want to get rid of the bastard": N. Miller, 335.
35. TR made a whirlwind tour through twenty-three states: For the definitive book on this episode, see Hilpert.
35. Louisa Morgan's wedding: Strouse reports that the Roosevelts were in attendance, and the *New York Times* ("Miss Morgan's Wedding," November 16, 1900) lists Mrs. Roosevelt, but not the vice president–elect, as having been there. But according to a November 16, 1900, article in the *New York Tribune*, both Roosevelts held a reception in Albany on November 15 for the State Federation of Women's Clubs.
35. "You see, it represents an effort": Strouse, 436.

CHAPTER TWO: "I AM AFRAID OF MR. ROOSEVELT"

37. JPM's schedule on September 14: *New York Evening World*, September 14, 1901.
37. Hanging of crepe on 23 Wall Street: "The City Draped in Black," *New York Tribune*, September 15, 1901.
37. Rumor that a spy had alerted JPM of McKinley's death: *New York Sun*, September 14, 1901. Satterlee writes that JPM heard of McKinley's death from a newspaper reporter at his office on Saturday, but he must be mistaken, since newspaper report makes it clear that the Drexel building was already swathed in crepe by then.
37. "President McKinley was a much-beloved man": *New York Evening World*, September 14, 1901.
37. Market results for Friday, September 13: *New York Tribune*, September 14, 1901.
37. Trading suspended on Saturday, September 14: "The City Draped in Black," *New York Tribune*, September 15, 1901.

38. The tariff raised prices from 5 to 75 percent: O'Toole, 207.
38. The government relied on the tariff for more than 40 percent of its revenue: *Historical Statistics of the United States 1789–1945*, 296.
38. "I am afraid of Mr. Roosevelt" and "Mr. Morgan is afraid of me": Carosso, 454.
39. "By no means as thoroughly awake": Roosevelt 1913, 100.
39. "An even greater fight must be waged": Roosevelt 1913, 174.
39. "Freedom for the strong to wrong the weak": Roosevelt 1913, 462.
39. 1895 and 1899 merger data: Kolko, 18.
40. "The principle of consolidation": Kolko, 14.
40. "Limited only by the specific restrictions": Roosevelt 1913, 388.
40. "Those who would seek to restore the days": Roosevelt 1913, 616.
40. "Behaving well": Roosevelt 1913, 625.
40. "Sinned": Roosevelt 1913, 610.
41. Roosevelt's boxing with Bacon: Scott, 29.
41. Perkins biography, meeting with JPM, and subsequent negotiations: Garraty.
42. Perkins supported TR for vice president at Republican convention: Kolko, 91.
43. "All right" and other dialogue between JPM and Perkins: Garraty, 85.
43–44. "Go slow," "searchlight," "of the highest character," "accept the publication," "so strong and dominant a character as Pierpont Morgan": Strouse, 439.
44. "Tremendous and highly complex industrial development" and other quotations from TR's message to Congress and stock market performance on that day: *New York Tribune*, December 4, 1901.
45. Formation of U.S. Steel: Strouse, 396–409; see specific references below.
46. Carnegie had accepted an option for the sale of U.S. Steel: Kolko, 20.
46. "I accept this price": Strouse, 403.
46. Carnegie added $240 million to his personal fortune: Strouse, 403.
47. Capitalization of U.S. Steel: Strouse, 405.
47. Federal budget was about $600 million: *Historical Statistics of the United States 1789–1945*, 296.
47. "A billion dollars of capital": *New York Tribune*, March 25, 1902.
47. "The high tide of industrial capital": Strouse, 406.
47. "Pierpont Morgan is apparently trying to swallow the sun": Strouse, 405.
47. U.S. Steel would produce more than half the nation's steel: Strouse, 404.
47. "It is probable there will be": Tarbell, 117.
47. Number of U.S. Steel shares traded in first two days and next week: Sinclair, 129.
47. U.S. Steel's earnings for 1902 and 1903, syndicates' and JPM's commissions: Strouse, 408.
48. Northern Pacific takeover fight: Strouse, 418–27; also see specific references below.
49. Northern Pacific stock shot from 127½ to 1,000: Strouse, 423–24.
49. "Perhaps the most controversial takeover fight in American history": Chernow, 88. It was in relation to the Northern Pacific affair that JPM made his famous remark, "I owe the public nothing." But as Strouse relates (p. xi), the comment was made after a reporter asked him whether he owed the public an explanation

of his actions during the takeover battle; Morgan was not making a blanket statement about his obligations to the American people.

49. Formation of Northern Securities: Strouse, 431–32.
49. "Did not believe in a night or week": Strouse, 432.
49. Operating ten thousand miles of track: Schwantes, 46.
49. "A startling menace to the commercial welfare": *New York Tribune*, November 28, 1901.
50. "Commercial slavery": *Minneapolis Journal*.
50. "Some time ago": Morris 2001, 89.
50. Description of JPM's dining room: Strouse, 227.
50. JPM's reaction to Northern Securities news: Sullivan, 412–14.
51. "It really seems hard that we should be compelled": Sinclair, 141.
51. "It has been a long time, indeed": *Washington Times*, February 21, 1902.
51. "Wall Street has been reminded": Mills.
51. "We do not propose to be made scapegoats": *New York Evening World*, February 21, 1902.
51. "We think President Roosevelt acted most unjustly": *New York Evening World*, February 20, 1902.
52. Worst storm of the season: *Washington Evening Star*, February 22, 1902.
52. Dinner at Chauncey Depew's house: *Washington Times*, February 23, 1902. Some authors have written that this dinner took place on the following night, but it is clear from two articles published in the *Washington Times* on February 23 (pages 2 and 7) that it occurred on the 22nd and that JPM's meeting with TR and Knox at the White House occurred on Sunday, February 23.
52. "Black" and "like a child": Morris 2001, 90.
52. The president telephoned: Some accounts have Depew initiating the call, but this seems unlikely to me considering the mood of the gathering.
52. "No, not a word of it" and "there is a strong belief": *New York Tribune*, February 24, 1902.
53. "Don't you realize that there's only one life": N. Miller, 341.
53. "Your *duty* to the Country": N. Miller, 342.
53. Hanna's decision not to run for president: Morris 2001, 299–300.
54. "Playmate": Morris 2001, 61.
54. "That is just what we did not want to do" and other dialogue from this meeting, except as noted below: Bishop, Vol. 1, 184–85.
54. "Prevent violent fluctuations": N. Miller, 368.
55. "I am neither a bull nor a bear": "Mr. Morgan Omitted," *Washington Evening Star*, October 2, 1902.
55. JPM's angry letter to TR: Sinclair, 142.
55. JPM was present when the Supreme Court read its opinion: *Washington Times*, February 25, 1902.
56. Dinner for Prince Henry at the White House: *Washington Evening Star*, February 25, 1902.
56. JPM's luncheon for Prince Henry: *New York Tribune*, February 27, 1902.

56. Formation of the International Mercantile Marine: Strouse, 458–76.
56. IMM capitalized at $170 million: Strouse, 465.
56. IMM controlled 136 ships, venturing as far as Australia; Germany added 329 ships to the combination: Strouse, 476.
57. 10 percent of overseas trade shipped on American vessels: Strouse, 458.
57–58. Shipping lines' profits were much lower in 1901 than they had been in 1900, and JPM had already invested almost $4 million in the merger: Strouse, 462.
58. "The proposed company": *New York Tribune*, April 20, 1902.
58. Perkins's June discussion with TR: Kolko, 69.
58. "John Bull does not like these foreign raids": *New York Tribune*, April 27, 1902.
58. "The [London] *Daily News* says": *New York Sun*, April 21, 1902.
59. License to Stay on the Earth: Satterlee, 381.
59. "Satisfied that it will be a very good thing": *New York Tribune*, October 19, 1902.
59. Poor financial performance of IMM: Strouse, 477–79.
60. The House of Morgan lost $2–3 million on IMM: Kolko, 24; Strouse, 478.
60. "The ocean was too big": Strouse, 480.
60. Business leaders on the *Titanic*: Daughtery.

CHAPTER THREE: "NO POWER OR DUTY"

61. "I feel better than I look": *Washington Evening Star*, September 25, 1902.
61. TR's arrival in Washington: *Washington Times*, September 25, 1902; *Washington Evening Star*, September 25, 1902.
61. Mrs. Roosevelt's journey and arrival: *Washington Times*, September 24 and 25, 1902.
62. TR's campaign itinerary: Morris 2001, 137–41.
62. TR's carriage accident: *New York Times*, September 4, 1902; *New York Sun*, September 4, 1902; *Berkshire Eagle*.
62–63. "O, my God," "Too bad, too bad," and "If your car got out of control,": *New York Sun*, September 4, 1902.
63. Pratt had a fractured skull: He later died of his injuries. Madden pled guilty to manslaughter and was sentenced to six months in jail and a fine of $500.
63. TR's surgery: *Washington Times*, September 24, 1902; *Indianapolis Journal*.
63. Repairs to the White House: *Washington Evening Star*, September 24, 1902.
64. Temporary White House: *Washington Times*, June 29, 1902; *Washington Evening Star*, September 24, 1902; U.S. General Services Administration.
64. "One of the most handsomely appointed houses": *Washington Times*, June 29, 1902.
64. Background on George Cortelyou: the Miller Center at the University of Virginia (Millercenter.org).
65–66. America's demand for coal had increased nearly forty-fold, and it constituted more than 70 percent of America's energy needs: Adams.
66. "Every basket [of coal]": Freese, 10.
66. Effects of coal strike on the poor: Freese, 142, 145.
66. Pennsylvania was mining more than eighty million tons of coal a year: Adams.

66. Miners' working conditions: Amsden and Brier; Freese, 47–49.
66. More than one hundred mine disasters in the last quarter of the nineteenth century: U.S. Department of Labor (arlweb.msha.gov). A disaster is defined as an accident taking more than five lives.
67. Accidents claimed more than fifteen hundred miners' lives every year: U.S. Department of Labor (arlweb.msha.gov).
67. Scofield mine disaster: In December 1907 that accident would be superseded by an explosion at Monongah, West Virginia, which claimed 362 lives and remains the most deadly mine disaster in American history.
67. Coal strike of 1900: Grossman.
68. Average coal miner's wages were $560 a year: Donald, 147–48.
68. "Anthracite mining is a business": Morris 2001, 133.
69. Hanna interceded again: *New York Times*, May 8, 1902.
69. "The worst enemy": *New York Times*, September 20, 1902.
69. Background on George Baer: *New York Times*, April 27, 1914.
69. 80 percent of coal mined by railroads: Wellman.
70. "[These men] don't suffer" and "the rights and interests of the laboring man": N. Miller, 371.
70. "A good many people think": Morris 2001, 137.
70. Fifty-five million tons of coal: Morris 2001, 134.
70. Geology of coal: Freese, 111–12.
70. Early history of anthracite industry: Freese, 110–22.
71. Factory boilers and home stoves adapted for anthracite: *New York Tribune*, October 5, 1902.
71. Industries and street railways began to burn bituminous: *New York Tribune*, June 4 and 18, 1902.
71. Brooklyn Bridge disappeared: *New York Tribune*, June 13, 1902.
71. Thirty thousand miners abandoned the region: Grossman.
71. Some twenty thousand men remained at work: Letter from TR to W. Murray Crane, October 22, 1902. Theodore Roosevelt Digital Library, Dickinson State University (theodorerooseveltcenter.org); the original is in the Theodore Roosevelt Papers, Library of Congress Manuscript Division.
71. Riot in Shenandoah: Morris 2001, 134.
72. "No power or duty in the matter": Morris 2001, 137.
72. The New York Board of Trade and Transportation called on the president to appoint an arbitration panel: *New York Evening World*, June 4, 1902.
72. History of state and federal mediation attempts: Barrett.
72. "Fight to the bitter end": *New York Times*, August 21, 1902.
72. "The nation's biggest union": Freese, 140.
72. "I do not know that I have ever had": Letter from TR to Anna Roosevelt Cowles, October 16, 1902. Theodore Roosevelt Digital Library, Dickinson State University (theodorerooseveltcenter.org); the original is in the Theodore Roosevelt Papers, Harvard College Library.
72. Mitchell's involvement in U.S. Steel strike: Strouse, 427–28.

73. "Do what was right": Strouse, 448.
73. JPM announced he had no plan to involve himself: *New York Evening World*, June 4, 1902.
73. JPM's effigy hanged: *New York Evening World*, June 7, 1902.
73. Speculation that JPM had returned to end the strike: *New York Tribune*, August 22, 1902.
73. "I don't know anything about the coal strike": *New York Evening World*, August 20, 1902.
73. JPM met with mine presidents: *New York Tribune*, August 21, 1902.
73. Operators weren't keen to see JPM intervene: Wellman.
73. "[Morgan] has a lot of unruly presidents": Strouse, 448.
73. Easley, Hanna, and Depew asked JPM to step in: Strouse, 449.
74. "His influence is so great": *New York Evening World*, August 25, 1902.
74. "I have not said I would interfere": *New York Tribune*, August 23, 1902.
74. "The issues do not admit of arbitration": *New York Tribune*, August 27, 1902.
74. "I wouldn't be surprised" and rumors that a settlement would soon be announced: *New York Evening World*, August 26, 1902.
74. "Price has become of little consequence": "The Famine Price Grows," *New York Tribune*, September 30, 1902.
74. Coal train attack: "A Coal Train Attack," *New York Tribune*, September 30, 1902.
74. Stick pins mounted with anthracite: "Sell Anthracite As Fine Jewel," *New York Evening World*, October 2, 1902.
74. Price of anthracite had quadrupled: *New York Sun*, September 29, 1902; *New York Tribune*, September 21, 1902.
75. Cost of other necessities had risen: "Coal Famine Sends Up Price of Bread," *New York Evening World*, September 30, 1902; "Poor Who Can't Buy Coal Scour Streets for Wood," *New York World*, October 2, 1902; "Hopes to End Coal Strike," *New York Tribune*, October 1, 1902.
75. Poor lived on ten dollars a week: "Poor Who Can't Buy Coal Scour Streets for Wood," *New York Evening World*, October 2, 1902.
75. "Unfortunately, the strength of my public position": TR to Henry Cabot Lodge, September 27, 1902. Theodore Roosevelt Digital Library, Dickinson State University (theodorerooseveltcenter.org); the original is in the Library of Congress Manuscript Division.
75. Second operation on TR's leg: *New York Tribune*, "A Second Operation," September 29, 1902; "Temperature Normal," *Washington Evening Star*, September 29, 1902; *Washington Times*, September 29, 1902.
75. "We have entered and are conducting this struggle": "Statement by Mitchell," *Washington Evening Star*, September 29, 1902.
76. Mitchell and four lieutenants met with mine owners: *New York Times*, September 30, 1902.
76. President met with Cabinet members: "Coal Strike Talks at White House," *New York Evening World*, September 30, 1902.
76. "The arrogance of the money power will bring a revolution": Strouse, 449.

76. American Federation of Catholic Societies petitioned TR: *New York Tribune,* "American Federation of Catholic Societies Sending Petition to TR Asking for Him to Use 'His Good Offices' to Settle the Strike," September 29, 1902.
76. Methodist Preachers' Meeting petitioned TR: *New York Evening World,* September 29, 1902.
76. "The welfare of a large section": Low to TR, October 2, 1902. Theodore Roosevelt Digital Library, Dickinson State University (theodorerooseveltcenter.org); the original is in the Library of Congress Manuscript Division.
76. "Unless you end this strike": Morris 2001, 151.
77. Anthracite had risen to thirty-eight dollars a ton and "the greatest economy": *New York Evening World,* October 6, 1902.
77. "I should greatly like to see you": "Operators Will Meet Roosevelt," *New York Evening World,* October 1, 1902.
77. Low's letter and Crane's visit finally pushed him to action, "untold misery," and "the certainty of riots": TR to Crane, October 22, 1902. Theodore Roosevelt Digital Library, Dickinson State University (theodorerooseveltcenter.org); the original is in the Library of Congress Manuscript Division.
77. "A necessity of life" and "under ordinary conditions": TR to Anna Roosevelt Cowles, October 16, 1902. Theodore Roosevelt Digital Library, Dickinson State University (theodorerooseveltcenter.org); the original is in the Harvard College Library.
77. "The invasion of a hostile army": Roosevelt 1913, 505.
78. "Elated" and Mitchell's response to TR's invitation: *New York Tribune,* October 2, 1902.
78. "Solution of Strike Seems Near at Hand": *New York Evening World,* October 1, 1902.
78. "General impression": "Hopes to End Coal Strike," *New York Tribune,* October 1, 1902.
78. "The plan to have these gentlemen": "Operators Will Meet Roosevelt," *New York Evening World,* October 1, 1902.
78. "Signs of lukewarmness": "Mr. Morgan Omitted," *Washington Evening Star,* October 2, 1902.
78. Conference between operators and union men, including travel details and their activities immediately before and after: *New York Sun,* October 4, 1902; *New York Tribune,* October 3 and 4, 1902; *New York Evening World,* October 3, 1902; *Washington Evening Star,* October 3 and 4, 1902; *Washington Times,* October 3, 1902; Wellman; also see specific citations below.
78. 4½ Street: This is now 4th Street.
78–79. Hotel Fritz Reuter and Prince Henry's dinner there: streetsofwashington.com.
80. "Be seated, gentlemen": *Washington Evening Star,* October 3, 1902.
80–81. "I wish to call your attention," "Mr. President" and "Before considering": *New York Sun,* October 4, 1902.
82. "Mr. President," "It will be a pleasure," and "I have prepared": *New York Sun,* October 4, 1902.
82. Baer's face shining with indignation: His anger is reported in Wellman.

82. "Abused, assaulted, injured" and rest of Baer's remarks: "Story of Conference," *New York Tribune*, October 4, 1902.

83. Cortelyou's interpretation of Mitchell's and TR's emotions: Wellman; Morris 2001, 620.

83. "At the conference this morning": *New York Sun*, October 4, 1902.

84. "I have listened with deep interest" and other remarks by operators, except exchange noted below: *New York Sun*, October 4, 1902.

84. "I did not say that!" and subsequent dialogue: Wellman.

85. "The charge by the gentlemen": *New York Sun*, October 4, 1902.

86. Meeting had hardened attitudes on both sides: TR to Robert Bacon, October 7, 1902. Theodore Roosevelt Digital Library, Dickinson State University (theodorerooseveltcenter.org); the original is in the Library of Congress Manuscript Division.

86. "There has been no settlement": *New York Evening World*, October 3, 1902.

86. "As a consequence": *New York Sun*, October 4, 1902.

86. "Mitchell behaved with great dignity": TR to W. Murray Crane, October 22, 1902. Theodore Roosevelt Digital Library, Dickinson State University (theodorerooseveltcenter.org); the original is in the Library of Congress Manuscript Division.

86. "If it wasn't for the high office I hold": Pringle, 190.

87. "Well, I have tried and failed": TR to Mark Hanna, October 3, 1902. Theodore Roosevelt Digital Library, Dickinson State University (theodorerooseveltcenter. org); the original is in the Library of Congress Manuscript Division.

87. "Men who have been maddened": TR to Robert Bacon, October 5, 1902. Theodore Roosevelt Digital Library, Dickinson State University (theodoreroosevelt center.org); the original is in the Library of Congress Manuscript Division.

87. The nation was facing its most urgent crisis since the Civil War: Roosevelt 1913, 514.

87. JPM announced that he would buy coal: "Morgan Gives 50,000 Tons of Coal to Poor," *New York Evening World*, October 4, 1902. Some writers have also credited JPM with setting up a coal distribution center on Manhattan's East Side in 1902, but this actually occurred in 1893. (See *New York Tribune*, September 21, 1902.)

87. Was JPM trying to shame the operators?: "Morgan Gives 50,000 Tons of Coal to Poor," *New York Evening World*, October 4, 1902.

87. The strike had become an embarrassment to JPM: Wiebe 1961, 247.

88. Stone ordered out the National Guard: *Scranton Tribune*.

88. TR's offer to the miners: TR to W. Murray Crane, October 22, 1902. Theodore Roosevelt Digital Library, Dickinson State University (theodorerooseveltcenter. org); the original is in the Library of Congress Manuscript Division.

88. Mitchell's rejection of TR's offer: *New York Evening World*, October 7, 1902.

88. Miners' vote to maintain strike: Strouse, 450.

88. Wooden boxes and barrels distributed to poor: *New York Sun*, October 5, 1902.

88. *World* burned furniture to keep presses running: *New York Tribune*, October 7, 1902.
88. Meetings of Odell, Penrose, Quay, et al.: "Conference to End Coal Strike," *New York Evening World*, October 9 and 10, 1902.
88–89. Meeting of Penrose, JPM, and "Mr. Morgan, some of the morning papers" and "it is not true": "Conference to End Coal Strike," *New York Evening World*, October 10, 1902.
89. Publicly JPM was disclaiming any right to involve himself: *New York Sun*, October 10, 1902.
89. JPM summoned Baer to the Corner to press him to resolve the walkout: "Conference to End Coal Strike," *New York Evening World*, October 10, 1902.
89. Root wrote JPM and asked for help: Pringle, 192.
89. TR walked on crutches for the first time: "Roosevelt Walks to His Carriage," *New York Evening World*, October 10, 1902.
89. TR's behind-the-scenes efforts to end strike: Roosevelt 1913, 514–15; TR to W. Murray Crane, October 22, 1902 (including "would form an evil precedent" and other quotations); Theodore Roosevelt Digital Library, Dickinson State University (theodorerooseveltcenter.org); the original is in the Library of Congress Manuscript Division.
90. Root's visit to New York and JPM's activities that day: *New York Evening World*, October 11, 1902; *New York Sun*, October 12, 1902; *New York Tribune*, October 12, 1902.
90. "Alive to the seriousness of the situation": TR to W. Murray Crane, October 22, 1902. Theodore Roosevelt Digital Library, Dickinson State University (theodore rooseveltcenter.org); the original is in the Library of Congress Manuscript Division.
91. "The managers" and rest of Root and JPM's draft agreement: The original document is in the Reading Room of the Morgan Library & Museum.
92–93. Mine owners' meetings, and word spread that the strike had been settled: *New York Evening World*, October 13, 1902; *New York Tribune*, October 13, 1902.
93. Baer was summoned to New York: *New York Tribune*, October 13, 1902.
93. JPM and Bacon's visit to Washington: *New York Sun*, October 14, 1902.
93. "The public" and rest of published agreement: *New York Sun*, October 14, 1902.
93. "Highest respect and admiration": *New York Sun*, October 15, 1902.
93. "I hope the miners will accept": *New York Evening World*, October 14, 1902.
93. Mitchell's reaction to owners' offer: *New York Sun*, October 14, 1902.
93. Mitchell's visit to Washington: "May Modify Terms," *New York Evening World*, October 15, 1902; *New York Evening World*, October 16, 1902; Roosevelt 1913, 507; TR to Henry Cabot Lodge, October 17, 1902. TR to W. Murray Crane, October 22, 1902. Both letters from Theodore Roosevelt Digital Library, Dickinson State University (theodorerooseveltcenter.org); the originals are in the Library of Congress Manuscript Division.

94. "It appeared": TR to W. Murray Crane, October 22, 1902. Theodore Roosevelt Digital Library, Dickinson State University (theodorerooseveltcenter.org); the original is in the Library of Congress Manuscript Division.

94. Bacon and Perkins's visit to Washington, including "nearly wild," "more and more hysterical," "violence and possible social war," and "at last I grasped": Roosevelt 1913, 508–9; TR to Henry Cabot Lodge, October 17, 1902. Theodore Roosevelt Digital Library, Dickinson State University (theodorerooseveltcenter.org); the original is in the Library of Congress Manuscript Division.

95. Failure to recognize Clark undercut the legitimacy of organized labor: Wiebe 1961, 248.

95. Cortelyou's press release, including "that for the purposes of such a commission": *New York Sun*, October 16, 1902.

95. Stocks rose sharply: *New York Tribune*, October 17, 1902.

95. Price of coal dropped by a third or more and TR received thousands of letters and telegrams: *New York Evening World*, October 16, 1902.

95. "I am delighted beyond words": Henry Cabot Lodge to TR, October 14, 1902. Theodore Roosevelt Digital Library, Dickinson State University (theodoreroosevelt center.org); the original is in the Library of Congress Manuscript Division.

95. "My dear Theodore": John Hay to TR, October 16, 1902. Theodore Roosevelt Digital Library, Dickinson State University (theodorerooseveltcenter.org); the original is in the Library of Congress Manuscript Division.

96. "If others had been as fair": Allen, 227.

96. "It really does begin to look": TR to JPM, October 16, 1902. Theodore Roosevelt Digital Library, Dickinson State University (theodorerooseveltcenter.org); the original is in the Library of Congress Manuscript Division.

96. Miners' return to work: *New York Evening World*, October 21, 1902.

96. Miners' celebrations: *New York Tribune*, October 22, 1902.

96. Mitchell Day: *New York Times*, October 30, 1902.

96. "We have to be satisfied": *New York Evening World*, October 16, 1902.

97. JPM, piqued, refused to donate to Republican candidates: "Morgan Shuts the Dough-Bag," *New York Evening World*, October 15, 1902.

97. 1902 election results: U.S. House of Representatives (history.house.gov) and U.S. Senate (senate.gov).

97. Work of the Anthracite Coal Commission: Grossman; Anthracite Coal Commission.

97. Recognition of the UMW wouldn't come for thirteen years: Wiebe 1961, 249.

97. Precedent set by coal strike arbitration: Grossman.

97. "Both kinds of federation": Roosevelt 1902.

98. Future federal efforts to mediate labor disputes: Grossman.

98. "The most important single incident in the labor movement": Gompers.

CHAPTER FOUR: "THE MIST OF MENDACITY"

99. Throughout this chapter, my principal source of information on the history of the Panama Canal was McCullough 1977; also see specific references below.

99. Treaty between New Granada and the United States: The full text is available online, including at jstor.org.
99–100. Construction of the Panama Railroad: McCullough 1977, 35; the figure of ten thousand lives lost has been widely reported.
100. De Lesseps's early involvement in the canal and the Congrès International d'Études du Canal Interocéanique: McCullough 1977, 60–84.
101. "Our work will be easier at Panama": McCullough 1977, 118.
101. French investment in the canal: McCullough 1977, 124–26.
101. JPM's role in the Panama Railroad Company and the Compagnie's American Committee: Carosso, 217.
101. French engineers' challenges: McCullough 1977, 130–31.
102. Bunau-Varilla's ingenious solution: Bunau-Varilla 1914, 79–86; McCullough 1977, 193–95.
102. Collapse of the Compagnie Universelle: McCullough 1977, 192–203.
102. Scandal in France around the canal: McCullough 1977, 204–41.
103. Commercial need for the canal: Irwin.
103. Projected British canal through Nicaragua: Carosso, 217.
103. Roosevelt's resistance to the no-fortification clause: McCullough 1977, 256–57.
103. "No single great material work": For the full text of his statement, see the website of the American Presidency Project (presidency.ucsb.edu).
104. Over the objections of bankers like Pierpont Morgan: Carosso, 216.
104. The Battle of the Canal Routes: Miner; McCullough 1977, 259–328. For those interested in delving into the "battle" in depth, Miner is a model of clarity, comprehensiveness, and accuracy.
104. The French had done 40 percent of the digging: Miner, 25.
105. "Reasonable time": Quoted in Miner, 123.
105. Rumors of a Panama Plot: McCullough 1977, 263.
105. Incorporation of the Panama Canal Company of America, including quotation: *New York Sun*, December 28, 1899; *New York Times*, December 28, 1899.
105. Cromwell's work for the Panama Railroad and early work for the Compagnie Nouvelle: Dean; McCullough 1977, 271–73; Miner, 76–77, 79, 92; Harding, 8–11; Newman.
106. Cromwell's background: Dean; Newman.
106. Cromwell's supposed contribution to Hanna: Miner, 78, 102–4.
107. TR said that Bunau-Varilla had the eyes of a duelist: Morris 2001, 274.
107. Bunau-Varilla's primary interest was the restoration of French honor: Bunau-Varilla 1940, 189; Bunau-Varilla 1914, 138.
107. "The vindication of the French genius": Bunau-Varilla 1914, 138.
107. Bunau-Varilla's background and his history on the canal: Bunau-Varilla 1914; McCullough 1977, 162, 180, 400.
108. Bunau-Varilla's role in the Battle of the Routes: Miner, 75–156; McCullough 1977, 277–88, 316–17, 323–24; Bunau-Varilla 1914.
108. "An official witness": Miner, 148.
108. Senate debate on the Spooner bill: Miner, 147–56; McCullough 1977, 318–24.

109. Negotiation of the Herrán-Hay Treaty: Miner, 140–42, 157–99, 399–407; McCullough 1977, 329–41.
110. Cancellation of the French contract: Miner, 57.
110. Colombian approach to the German government: Miner, 314.
110. "I am commanded by the President": Miner, 195.
111. Marroquín's domestic limitations: Miner, 162–73, 216–40.
111. Cromwell's outmaneuvering of Colombia concerning the amount of their indemnity: Miner, 207–13, 273.
111. U.S. and Colombian treaty negotiations: Miner, 273–334.
111. "Neither the canal nor the railroad company": Miner, 280.
112. "If Colombia should now reject the treaty": Miner, 285.
112. "I fear we may have to give a lesson to those jack rabbits": Diaz Espino, 67.
112. TR considered taking the canal by force: Roosevelt 1913, 563.
112. "President Roosevelt is determined": Miner, 294.
112. "Those contemptible little creatures": Miner, 308.
113. "It seems that the great bulk of the best engineers": TR to Hay, August 19, 1903. Theodore Roosevelt Digital Library, Dickinson State University (theodorerooseveltcenter.org); the original is in the Library of Congress Manuscript Division.
113. Prelude to revolution in Panama: Miner, 335–59; McCullough 1977, 341–60.
114. Weather for October 10, 1903: National Climatic Data Center (ncdc.noaa.gov).
114. Bunau-Varilla's meeting with TR, including dialogue: Bunau-Varilla 1914, 310–12.
116. Meeting between Bunau-Varilla and Hay, including dialogue: Bunau-Varilla 1914, 316–19.
117. Panamanian Revolution: McCullough 1977, 361–86; Miner, 335–70.
118. Negotiation, signing, and ratification of treaty between Panama and United States: McCullough 1977, 387–402; Miner, 371–93, Bunau-Varilla 1914, 368–76.
118. "What do you think, Mr. Minister?" and response: McCullough 1977, 390.
118. "Usurpation. . . . [Panama had] no more right": *New York Tribune*, December 10, 1903.
118. "Let us not deceive ourselves": *New York Times*, December 29, 1903.
119. "The most ignominious thing we know of": Morris 2001, 295.
119. "Not only in the strictest accordance": Roosevelt 1913, 569.
119. "No one connected with this government": Roosevelt 1904.
119. TR's psychology in dealings on Panama: Miner, 387–91; Roosevelt 1913, 566–69.
119. "I took Panama because Philippe Bunau-Varilla brought it to me": McCullough 1977, 384.
119. "Envoy Extraordinary and Minister Plenipotentiary": McCullough 1977, 387.
120. JPM's role as financial agent for Panama: McCullough 1977, 389, 399–400.
120. "The authorized party to make treaties": McCullough 1977, 388.
120. Negotiation of the Hay–Bunau-Varilla Treaty: McCullough 1977, 388–94; Miner, 374–78.
120. Cromwell's role as legal and financial representative of Panama: McCullough 1977, 393.

121. Panamanian emissaries' reaction to news that treaty was already signed: McCullough 1977, 395. Some accounts indicate that Bunau-Varilla was spat on instead of slapped.
121. Bunau-Varilla received Legion of Honor: *New York Tribune*, May 12, 1904.
121. JPM's role in transfer of canal to United States: Carosso, 525–26; McCullough 1977, 400; *New York Tribune*, April 28, May 4, and May 10, 1904; *New York Evening World*, May 3, 1904; *New York Sun*, May 10, 1904; Chernow, 111.
122. Official transfer of canal to United States: McCullough 1977, 402.
122. Expenses reportedly included generous payments to founding fathers: Diaz Espino, 177–78.
122. Cromwell's determining role in events: Miner, 386.
122. Payments to the Compagnie Universelle and Compagnie Nouvelle investors: Curtis, 26–28; McCullough 1977, 400–401.
123. Cromwell's fee for services: Harding, 63.
123. "Reliable information": *New York Evening World*, March 30, 1903.
123. Compagnie Universelle issued bearer bonds: Diaz Espino, 186.
123. "Lockjaw": *Washington Times*, February 28, 1906.
124. "Lying fabrication": Diaz Espino, 3.
124. Attempts to blackmail Cromwell: *New York Evening World*, February 17, 1909; *New York World* (book), 7–9; *New York Times*, February 18, 1909.
124. No evidence against Taft's brother or TR's brother-in-law: *New York World* (book), 9.
124. "Slander": Diaz Espino, 4.
124. "The stories were scurrilous and libelous": *New York World* (book), 14.
125. "If the World has libelled anybody": *New York Evening World*, December 16, 1908.
125. Government libel suit against *New York World*: *New York World* (book); Harding, 48ff; Peirce.
125. Indictment against the *World* et al.: *New York World* (book), 15.
125. The *News* was singled out: *New York World* (book), 11; Harding, 50.
125. "This persecution, if it succeeds": *New York Evening World*, February 18, 1909.
126. "I am not in accord with the Government": *New York World* (book), 16.
126. "I have never known in my lengthy experience": *The Story of Panama*, 328.
126. Cromwell's brief: Harding, 63.
127. "The plan seems to me good": Harding, front matter (unnumbered).
127. Original syndicate agreement and leather-bound book: Harding, 58–60.
127. Judge Anderson's verdict, including "to my mind that man has read": Peirce, 184.
128. "I have nothing to say": *New York World* (book), 82.
128. U.S. completion of canal: McCullough 1977, 405–615.
128. Canal navigable for eleven miles: McCullough 1977, 440.
128. Eradication of yellow fever: McCullough 1977, 500.
129. 1906 death rates: McCullough 1977, 501.
129. 1914 death rate: McCullough 1977, 581.
129. Total deaths during American phase: McCullough 1977, 585, 610.

129. Twenty-four thousand workers: McCullough 1977, 471.
129. Cost and time estimates for sea-level versus lock canal: McCullough 1977, 483–86.
131. Thirty-seven million cubic yards of earth: McCullough 1977, 530.
131. Nearly fifty thousand employees: McCullough 1977, 559.
131. Taft's visits to Panama: McCullough 1977, 445–46, 512.
131. Earthquake in Panama: McCullough 1977, 606.
131. Final cost and time for completion of canal: McCullough 1977, 610–11.
131. First transit of the canal: McCullough 1977, 609.
132. "One of the rather contemptible features": McCullough 1977, 617.
132. "By far the most important action": Roosevelt 1913, 553.

CHAPTER FIVE: "SEND YOUR MAN TO MY MAN"

133. TR's receipt of news on Northern Securities and his reaction: "President Vindicated," *New York Tribune*, March 15, 1904; *New York Sun*, March 15, 1904; Morris 2001, 314.
133. "Run amuck": *New York Evening World*, March 15, 1904.
133. Wall Street's reaction to Northern Securities decision: "Wall Street Unshaken," *New York Tribune*, March 15, 1904.
133. JPM's reaction to Northern Securities decision: *New York Tribune*, March 16, 1904.
133. "Crude, ill-considered, harsh": *New York Times*, March 15, 1904.
134. Popular and general press reaction to Northern Securities decision: Morris 2001, 316.
134. "Under this decision" and "politically": *Washington Evening Star*, March 15, 1904.
134. "Theodore thinks of nothing": Morris 2001, 319.
134. "That damned cowboy": This remark has been quoted widely.
134. Hanna and TR's détente: N. Miller, 436–37.
135. TR's 1903 coast-to-coast tour: Morris 2001, 214ff; Pringle, 242–43.
135. TR's outmaneuvering of Hanna: Pringle, 243–45; Brands, 493–95; Morris 2001, 232–33.
135. "Of course those who favor my administration": Pringle, 245.
135. "Duty" and "would only give the word": Beschloss, 147.
135. "The country has lost one of the greatest men": "Thousands See Body Removed," *Washington Times*, February 17, 1904.
135. JPM's attendance at Hanna's funeral: *Washington Times*, February 17, 1904.
136. The Dow shed nearly 24 percent: forecastchart.com.
136. "Undigested securities": *New York Evening World*, March 31, 1903.
136. "The financial situation here": Letter from TR to Henry Cabot Lodge, August 6, 1903. Theodore Roosevelt Digital Library, Dickinson State University (theodorerooseveltcenter.org); the original is in the Library of Congress Manuscript Division.
136. TR's efforts to win over Wall Street: Pringle, 246.

136. "Mr. Perkins tells me": Letter from TR to JPM, October 8, 1903. Theodore Roosevelt Digital Library, Dickinson State University (theodorerooseveltcenter.org); the original is in the Library of Congress Manuscript Division.
136. "I should like extremely to have an interview": Letter from JPM to TR, October 12, 1903. Theodore Roosevelt Digital Library, Dickinson State University (theodorerooseveltcenter.org); the original is in the Library of Congress Manuscript Division.
136. "There is no hurry whatever": Letter from TR to JPM, October 13, 1903. Theodore Roosevelt Digital Library, Dickinson State University (theodoreroosevelt center.org); the original is in the Library of Congress Manuscript Division.
136. Nomination of Charles Fairbanks: Brands, 504–5.
136. "The big New York and Chicago capitalists": Beschloss, 146.
137. "Most formidable Democrat" and "Pierpont Morgan and other Wall Street men": Letter from TR to Henry Cabot Lodge, May 23, 1903. Theodore Roosevelt Digital Library, Dickinson State University (theodorerooseveltcenter.org); the original is in the Library of Congress Manuscript Division.
137. JPM's efforts to recruit Cleveland: Strouse, 535.
137. Newspaper endorsements of Parker: Morris 2001, 342.
137. "Theodore! with all thy faults—": Morris 2001, 351.
137. Business's preference for TR: Pringle, 249.
137. Corporate contributions to TR's election campaign: Morris 2001, 360, 692; Strouse, 536; Pringle, 251.
138. Tillman Act: The statute had little effect, since it did not include any method of enforcement or restrict personal contributions by the corporations' stockholders or directors; the prohibition against contributions was later dropped. For a cogent, concise history of related legislation throughout American history, see Fuller.
138. "You have not kept the faith, Mr. President": Morris 2001, 356–57.
138. "Blackmail": Morris 2001, 362.
138. "Monstrous": Pringle, 250.
138. TR's instructions to Cortelyou to return Standard Oil contribution: Pringle, 251–52; Morris 2010, 361.
139. TR's trip to the polls: "How President Voted," *New York Tribune*, November 9, 1904.
139. "How they are voting for me!": N. Miller, 435.
139. 1904 election results: Morris 2010, 364; Pringle, 250; N. Miller, 441.
139. "My dear, I am no longer a political accident": N. Miller, 436.
139. TR's activities on election night: "Joy at the White House," *New York Tribune*, November 9, 1904; *Washington Evening Star*, November 9, 1904.
139. "I am deeply sensible of the honor": *Washington Evening Star*, November 9, 1904.
139. TR had been considering the decision for a long time, but he wished he could take it back: Brands, 514–17.
140. TR's second inauguration: *New York Sun*, March 5, 1905; *New York Tribune*, March 5, 1905 (including quotations from inaugural address); *Washington Times*, March 5, 1905.

141. "Tomorrow I shall come into my office in my own right": N. Miller, 441.
141. "Somehow or other": N. Miller, 451.
142. "The immediate and most pressing need": Roosevelt 1905.
142. Passage of the Hepburn Act: N. Miller, 456–62; Vietor.
142. For more on the significance of the Hepburn Act, see Milkis and Charnok, in Nelson.
142. "Chronic wrongdoing": Brands, 527.
143. "When it comes to finance": Pringle, 303.
143. Perkins's help in creating Department of Commerce and Labor: Kolko, 70.
143. "I know your interest": TR to George Perkins, December 26, 1902. Theodore Roosevelt Digital Library, Dickinson State University (theodorerooseveltcenter. org); the original is in the Library of Congress Manuscript Division.
143. "Already been at work" and "two gentlemen": Perkins to TR, December 27, 1902. Theodore Roosevelt Digital Library, Dickinson State University (theodoreroosevelt center.org); the original is in the Library of Congress Manuscript Division.
144. Creation of the Department of Commerce and Labor: N. Miller, 379–80.
144. "Your interest in the legislation": TR to Perkins, June 26, 1903. Theodore Roosevelt Digital Library, Dickinson State University (theodorerooseveltcenter.org); the original is in the Library of Congress Manuscript Division.
145. "The dull purblind folly of the very rich men": N. Miller, 452.
145. "You know that I have the highest hopes": Kolko, 71.
145. Gary's friendship with TR: Tarbell, 181–84; Kolko, 74.
145. International Harvester's accommodation with the government: Kolko, 74, 119–22; Wiebe 1959, 54.
146. Gary's meetings with officials from the administration: Kolko, 79–81; Wiebe 1959, 52–53; Tarbell, 184–86; Strouse, 542.
146. "I don't know, Mr. President" and subsequent dialogue: Tarbell, 184.
146. "The President tells me": Tarbell, 185.
146–147. "To cooperate with the government" and "by the president alone": Wiebe 1959, 52.
147. "I have no knowledge of any moral grounds": Kolko, 121.
148. Both sides' preference for behind-the-scenes negotiations: Strouse, 542–43.
148. "We have anticipated" and "looked upon in Washington": Wiebe 1959, 53.
149. Canton-Hankow Railway: Lee, 51–56, 76, 85; Strouse, 371, 541–43; Sinclair, 171–72; *Washington Evening Star*, August 9, 1905.
150. Root's activities after stepping down as secretary of war: Kolko, 84; Lee, 76.
150. Bacon's resignation: Strouse, 443.
150. JPM's visit to Sagamore Hill: Strouse, 541 (including "serious enough to make him," "a blow to our prestige," "now, my dear Mr. Morgan," and "insist that China shall carry out its side of the agreement"); *Washington Evening Star*, August 8, 1905.
151. Chentung Liang Cheng's visit to Sagamore Hill: *Washington Evening Star*, August 9, 1905.

151. JPM's second visit to Sagamore Hill and decision to sell railway: *New York Sun*, August 29 and 30, 1905; Lee, 78.

151. "Mr. Morgan has consulted with the Administration": *New York Sun*, August 30, 1905.

151. New York, New Haven & Hartford Railroad: Abrams. Louis Brandeis famously objected to the merger with the Boston & Maine; later the combined company would founder amid revelations of cooked books and a series of accidents caused by postponed maintenance to boost profits.

152. Gary dinners and "to maintain so far as practicable": Page.

152. Gary and Frick's arrival at White House: *New York Sun*, November 5, 1907; weather, *Washington Evening Star*, November 4, 1907, 1.

152. JPM's visit to White House in March 1907: *Washington Evening Star*, March 12, 1907; *New York Tribune*, March 12, 1907; *Washington Herald*, March 13, 1907; Satterlee, 439.

153. "I do not like to seem to talk": Pringle, 305.

153. "Allay the public anxiety": *Washington Evening Star*, March 12, 1907.

153. "On the run": Morris 2001, 498.

153. The Treasury released more than $35 million: Kolko, 155.

154. Gary and Frick's departure for the White House in November 1907: Tarbell, 200–201 (including dialogue between Gary and JPM).

155. Gary and Frick's meeting with TR in the White House: Roosevelt 1913, 478–81; Tarbell, 200–201 (including dialogue with Garfield).

156. "I understood the President to say" and subsequent correspondence: Tarbell, 202–3.

157. Aftereffects of the panic: Lowenstein, 66–68, 70.

157. Rumors that JPM had engineered the crisis: Lowenstein, 72.

157. "What Mr. J. P. Morgan represents": Allaway.

157. Criticism leveled at TR for his warm relationship with the trusts: Strouse, 542.

157. "The past has shown that in raising campaign funds": *New York Sun*, October 8, 1908.

157. "Had great and admitted wrongs to contend with": *New York Evening World*, November 3, 1908.

CHAPTER SIX: THE BULL MOOSE AND THE LION OF WALL STREET

159. TR's departure for Africa: *New York Tribune*, March 23, 1909; *New York Evening World*, March 23, 1909.

160. "Wall Street expects every lion": O'Toole, 15.

160. "Good-bye! Good-bye!": *New York Evening World*, March 23, 1909.

160. "My main reason for wishing to go to Africa": N. Miller, 500.

160. "Your most difficult task will come": Brands, 674.

161. "The most popular President" and "the most popular human being": Morris 2001, 430–31.

161. "Still, small voice": Morris 2001, 490.

161. Loeb persuaded TR to name a successor: Pringle, 353; N. Miller, 484.
161. Potential presidential candidates in 1908: Brands, 596.
161. "I would walk on my hands and knees": N. Miller, 484.
162. "I am the seventh son": N. Miller, 483.
162. "I have the profound satisfaction": Brands, 632.
162. Taft's advantages as a candidate: Chace, 32.
162. Wall Street's enthusiasm about Taft's candidacy: Wiebe 1959, 57.
162. The House of Morgan donated $150,000: Kolko, 202.
162. "Four, four, four years more," "final and irrevocable," and "impugn[ed] his sincerity": Brands, 627.
162. TR's and Taft's ovations: N. Miller, 489.
162. Taft's margin of victory: N. Miller, 491; Brands, 513.
163. "I always said it would be a cold day": N. Miller, 495.
163. "Always excepting Washington and Lincoln": Brands, 628.
163. "Conservative men who know what they are talking about": O'Toole, 76.
163. Perkins bragged that he had selected several of Taft's Cabinet, and "filled to our entire satisfaction": Strouse, 601.
164. Elimination of tariff on artwork: Lowenstein, 42, 95.
164. "The best tariff bill": N. Miller, 502.
164. Taft brought half again as many anti-trust suits as TR (65 versus 44): Kolko, 167.
165. Alaska Syndicate: Nasake, 90–93; Alaska Humanities Forum website (akhistory course.org).
165. "For filing a disingenuous statement": Nasake, 93.
165. "A very ungracious thing": N. Miller, 504.
165. "I very keenly share your disappointment": Brands, 672.
165. "Something more than a king": Morris 2010, 51.
166. "The national need before sectional or personal advantage" and other quotes from New Nationalism speech: Roosevelt 1912. Available online at teachingamerican history.org.
167. Taft threw a golf club: N. Miller, 515.
167. "Going quite beyond anything that he advocated": Goodwin, 645.
167. 1910 election results: Brands, 680.
167. "It is very hard to take all the slaps": Pringle, 387.
168. "More anxious for Taft's success" and "very much disappointed in Taft": Strouse, 602.
168. Senate investigation and "unless they were prepared": Kolko, 118.
168. "I would have been derelict in my duties": *Washington Evening Star*, August 5, 1911.
168–169. "Great and dangerous power," "was not made fully acquainted," and "had been fully advised": *New York Tribune*, October 27, 1911.
169. "Any statement that I was misled" and subsequent quotes: Roosevelt, 1913, 608, 615, 617.
170. "I really feel so blue and depressed": O'Toole, 136.
170. TR's reasons for challenging Taft: N. Miller, 520–21.

170. "As far as I know my own soul": Brands, 700.
170. Garfield and others' endorsements of TR: N. Miller, 520–22; Brands, 697.
171. "The letter to me": Brands, 701–2.
171. Republican governors' letter: *New York Tribune*, February 11, 1912.
171. "My hat is in the ring!": *New York Tribune*, February 22, 1912.
171. "Well, the fight is on": *New York Sun*, February 23, 1912.
171. "I will accept the nomination": *New York Tribune*, February 26, 1912.
171. "Justice between man and man" and other quotes from the speech: Pringle, 390–91.
172. "Theodore has gone off on a perfectly wild program": Auchincloss, 119.
172. "I have had my mishaps": N. Miller, 523.
172. "The Colonel and I have long since agreed to disagree": Morris 2010, 169.
172. "Frequently when asked to take another cup of coffee": Brands, 698.
172. Perkins's negotiations to head off Harvester suit: Kolko, 190–91.
174. "Roosevelt Halted Harvester Suit" and subsequent quote: *New York Tribune*, April 25, 1912.
174. "Heartily concurred" and "in all other cases of the kind": "Calls Harvester Charge Nonsense," *New York Tribune*, April 26, 1912.
174. "Dictator, who, once he received a third term": "President Bitterly Attacks Roosevelt," *New York Tribune*, April 26, 1912.
174. "I do not think that Mr. Taft means ill": *New York Tribune*, April 27, 1912.
174. "Demagogue," "dangerous egotist," "fathead," "puzzlewit": Brands, 712.
174. "Brains less than a guinea pig": N. Miller, 523.
175. "[Roosevelt] is essentially a fighter": Brands, 706.
175. "Roosevelt was my closest friend": Brands, 707.
175. Republican primary results: Gould, *Four Hats*, Appendix B.
175. Delegate counts at Republican convention: Gardner, 236; Gould, *Four Hats*, 67; Chace, 122.
175. "I care more for one button": Auchincloss, 120.
175. "As strong as a bull moose": This has been widely quoted.
176. "Colonel, we will see you through": O'Toole, 182.
176. Progressive Party's wealthy donors: Kolko, 193–94, 202; Chace, 204.
176. For more on Willard Straight, see Croly.
176. "Who is the representative of": *New York Times*, June 28, 1912.
176. Delegate counts at Democratic convention: Gould, *Four Hats*, 88.
177. "A strong national regulation" and other Progressive platform planks: "Progressive Party Platform of 1912."
177. "To special privilege and to monopoly" and other Republican Party platform planks: "Republican Party Platform."
178. Roosevelt compared to John the Baptist: Donald, 251.
178. "Dangerous changes in our present": Taft.
178. "Letting the people rule": Kolko, 200.
179. Herbert Satterlee's and Anne Morgan's support of TR: Strouse, 665.
179. Wilson was chagrined by support of *Harper's*: Chace, 133.

179. "Dominion by what is known as the money trust" and other planks of the Democratic Party platform: "1912 Democratic Party Platform."

179. Wilson's belief that women's suffrage and child labor should be decided by the states, his opposition to minimum wage, and "no government has ever been beneficent": Chace, 203.

180. "The trouble with Mr. Wilson": The full text of TR's speech is given in Gould, *Bull Moose*, 108–17.

180. "I want it distinctly understood" and rest of JPM's testimony: U.S. Senate, 437–53.

180. "If that is all he gave": *New York Times*, October 4, 1912.

181. "His complaint is that he did not get anything" and rest of TR's testimony: U.S. Senate, 469–527.

181. "The Clapp Committee behaved very well": *New York Times*, October 6, 1912.

181. "In the long list of unmitigated lies" and rest of Perkins's testimony: *New York Sun*, October 22, 1912.

182. Attempted assassination of TR: Helferich.

182. "Fake!": Helferich, 177.

182. "It takes more than that": Helferich, 178.

182. "That must have been a great speech": Helferich, 187.

183. "We propose to lift the burdens from the lowly and the weary" and other quotes from speech: Gould, *Bull Moose*, 187–92.

183. 1912 presidential election totals: Gould, *Four Hats*, 176–77, Appendix C; Chace, 238–39.

183. "The victory of Wilson": "The Great Wilson Victory," *New York Times*, November 6, 1912.

184. America was the leading industrial power of the world: Strouse, 5.

184. "Like all other good citizens": "Roosevelt Meets Defeat Buoyantly," *New York Times*, November 6, 1912.

184. "We have fought the good fight": Gardner, 280.

184. "I'll be very glad to ride down Pennsylvania Avenue": *New York Evening World*, November 6, 1912.

184. JPM's appearance before the Pujo Committee, including quotes: *Money Trust Investigation*, Parts 14 and 15, 1003–91; *New York Sun*, December 20, 1912.

185. "The trust of trusts": Strouse, 659.

188. "Dominating and yet not domineering": *New York Tribune*, December 20, 1912.

188. JPM's final illness, death, burial, and will: Strouse, 674–85.

189. "And to think he wasn't even a rich man": Strouse, 15.

189. "We may look upon Mr. Morgan's like again": *New York Times*, April 1, 1913.

189. TR's expedition to Brazil: Millard.

190. "The old lion is dead": This has been widely cited.

191. "Important and valuable part": *Report of the Committee Appointed Pursuant to House Resolutions 429 and 504 to Investigate the Concentration of Control of Money and Credit*, 159.

192. "There is an established and well-defined identity": *Report of the Committee . . .* , 129.

192. Five institutions holding 341 directorships in 112 corporations valued at more than $22 billion: *Report of the Committee* . . . , 89.
192. "If the arteries of credit now clogged": *Report of the Committee* . . . , 161.
192. United States had built the world's largest economy: Lowenstein, 48.
193. Establishment of the Federal Reserve: Lowenstein; Carosso, 548–49.
193. Jekyl Island: The spelling was changed to two *l*'s in 1929 (Lowenstein, 118).
194. Fed was the greatest accomplishment of Wilson's famously successful first term and one of the signal financial reforms of the century: Lowenstein, 265–66.
194. Benefits of the Fed: Lowenstein, 252–53.
196. For more on the history of campaign finance reform, see Fuller.

BIBLIOGRAPHY

The literature on the remarkable life of Theodore Roosevelt is vast, ranging from full biographies to works that delve more deeply into a single period. One possible starting place for readers in search of additional information is Edmund Morris's trilogy, *The Rise of Theodore Roosevelt, Theodore Rex,* and *Colonel Roosevelt.* For those wanting more about the life and career of Pierpont Morgan, Jean Strouse's *Morgan: American Financier* is the standard work on the subject. And readers wishing to learn more about the Morgan banking empire, including the time before and after Pierpont, would do well to pick up Ron Chernow's National Book Award–winning *The House of Morgan: An American Banking Dynasty and the Rise of Modern Finance.*

For more information about specific episodes related in this book, readers might consult the following works: on the Panama Canal, *The Path Between the Seas* by David McCullough; on the election of 1912, *1912: Wilson, Roosevelt, Taft & Debs—the Election That Changed the Country* by James Chace; on the relationship between Roosevelt and Taft, *The Bully Pulpit: Theodore Roosevelt, William Howard Taft, and the Golden Age of Journalism* by Doris Kearns Goodwin; and on the founding of the Federal Reserve, *America's Bank: The Epic Struggle to Create the Federal Reserve* by Roger Lowenstein. All are authoritative and eminently readable.

The collaboration between Theodore Roosevelt and Pierpont Morgan, and the relationship between government and business during the Progressive years, is explored in Gabriel Kolko's scholarly, thought-provoking *The Triumph of Conservatism.*

Finally, readers seeking a wider glimpse into the world of the early twentieth century may wish to consult the extensive online resources of the Library of Congress, which include a wealth of historical photos and, at the Chronicling America website, an unparalleled, searchable database of American newspapers published from 1789 to 1924.

In my research and writing, I've drawn on the books and articles listed below, nearly all of which are also cited in the Notes. Publications with a byline are alphabetized under the author's name; those with no byline appear under the title of the publication. Articles with no headline are listed chronologically under the name of the newspaper. Letters and websites are given in the Notes but do not appear in the Bibliography. My sincere thanks to all these authors, my unseen but invaluable guides to the era I've sought to capture in this book.

Abrams, Richard M. "Brandeis and the New Haven-Boston & Maine Merger Battle." *Business History Review*, Winter 1962, 408–30.
Adams, Patrick Sean. "The U.S. Coal Industry in the Nineteenth Century." Website of the Economic History Association (eh.net).
Allaway, H. "The Financial World." *New York Tribune*, November 3, 1907, 4.
Allen, Frederick Lewis. *The Great Pierpont Morgan.* New York: Harper & Row Publishers, Inc., 1948.
Amsden, Jon, and Stephen Brier. "Coal Miners on Strike: The Transformation of Strike Demands and the Formation of a National Union." *Journal of Interdisciplinary History*, Spring 1977, 583–616.
Anthracite Coal Commission. *Report to the President on the Anthracite Coal Strike.* Washington: Government Printing Office, 1903.
Auchincloss, Louis. *Theodore Roosevelt.* New York: Times Books, 2001.
Barrett, Jerome T. "The Origin of Mediation: The United States Conciliation Service in the U.S. Department of Labor." Friends of Federal Mediation and Conciliation Service History Foundation, 1995. Available online at mediationhistory.org.
Berkshire Eagle, "Eyewitness Talks of T.R.'s Pittsfield 'Outrage,'" August 20, 1960.
Beschloss, Michael. *Presidential Courage: Brave Leaders and How They Changed America.* New York: Simon & Schuster, 2007.
Bishop, Joseph Bucklin. *Theodore Roosevelt and His Time: Shown in His Letters.* Vols. 1 and 2. New York: Charles Scribner's Sons, 1920.
Brandeis, Louis D. *Other People's Money: And How the Bankers Use It.* New York: Frederick A. Stokes Company, 1914.
Brands, H. W. *T.R.: The Last Romantic.* New York: Basic Books, 1997.
Bruner, Robert F., and Sean D. Carr. *The Panic of 1907: Lessons Learned from the Market's Perfect Storm.* Hoboken, NJ: John Wiley & Sons, Inc., 2007.
Buffalo Illustrated Express. "Roosevelt Quickly Sworn In as President," September 15, 1901, 1.

Bunau-Varilla, Philippe. *Panama: The Creation, Destruction, and Resurrection*. New York: McBride, Nast & Company, 1914.

———. *From Panama to Verdun: My Fight for France*. Philadelphia: Dorrance and Company, 1940.

Carosso, Vincent P. *The Morgans: Private International Bankers, 1854–1913*. Cambridge: Harvard University Press, 1987.

Chace, James. *1912: Wilson, Roosevelt, Taft & Debs—the Election That Changed the Country*. New York: Simon & Schuster, 2004.

Chandler, Lester V. *Benjamin Strong: Central Banker*. Washington: Brookings Institution, 1958.

Chernow, Ron. *The House of Morgan: An American Banking Dynasty and the Rise of Modern Finance*. New York: Grove Press, 1990.

Croly, Herbert. *Willard Straight*. New York: The Macmillan Company, 1924.

Curtis, W. J. "The History of the Purchase by the United States of the Panama Canal; The Manner of Payment; and the Distribution of the Proceeds of Sale." Speech delivered before the Alabama State Bar Association, July 8, 1909.

Dalton, Kathleen. *Theodore Roosevelt: A Strenuous Life*. New York: Random House, 2002.

Daughtery, Greg, "Seven Famous People Who Missed the *Titanic*," *Smithsonian* website, March 1, 2012 (smithsonianmag.com).

Dean, Arthur H. *William Nelson Cromwell 1854–1948*. Privately published, 1957. New York Public Library.

Diaz Espino, Ovidio. *How Wall Street Created a Nation: J. P. Morgan, Teddy Roosevelt, and the Panama Canal*. New York: MJF Books, 2001.

Donald, Aida D. *Lion in the White House: A Life of Theodore Roosevelt*. New York: Basic Books, 2007.

Freese, Barbara. *Coal: A Human History*. New York: Penguin Books, 2004.

Fuller, Jaime. "From George Washington to Shaun McCutcheon: A Brief-ish History of Campaign Finance Reform." *Washington Post*, April 3, 2014. Available online at washingtonpost.com.

Gardner, Joseph L. *Departing Glory: Theodore Roosevelt as Ex-President*. New York: Charles Scribner's Sons, 1973.

Garraty, John A. *Right-Hand Man: The Life of George W. Perkins*. New York: Harper & Brothers, 1957.

Gompers, Samuel. *Seventy Years of Life and Labor: An Autobiography*. New York: E.P. Dutton & Company, Inc. (reissued 1943). Book IV, 126–27.

Goodwin, Doris Kearns. *The Bully Pulpit: Theodore Roosevelt, William Howard Taft, and the Golden Age of Journalism*. New York: Simon & Schuster, 2013.

Gould, Lewis L. (editor). *Bull Moose on the Stump: The 1912 Campaign Speeches of Theodore Roosevelt*. Lawrence: University Press of Kansas, 2008.

———. *Four Hats in the Ring: The 1912 Election and the Birth of Modern American Politics*. Lawrence: University Press of Kansas, 2008.

Grondahl, Paul. *I Rose Like a Rocket: The Political Education of Theodore Roosevelt*. Lincoln: University of Nebraska Press, 2004.

Grossman, Jonathan. "The Coal Strike of 1902: Turning Point in U.S. Policy." *Monthly Labor Review*, October 1975. Reproduced on the Department of Labor website (dol.gov).

Harbaugh, William Henry. *Power and Responsibility: The Life and Times of Theodore Roosevelt*. New York: Farrar, Straus and Cudahy, 1961.

Harding, Earl. *The Untold Story of Panama*. New York: Athene Press, Inc., 1959.

Helferich, Gerard. *Theodore Roosevelt and the Assassin: Madness, Vengeance, and the Campaign of 1912*. Guilford, CT: Lyons Press, 2013.

Hilpert, John M. *American Cyclone: Theodore Roosevelt and His 1900 Whistle-Stop Campaign*. Jackson: University Press of Mississippi, 2015.

Historical Statistics of the United States 1789–1945. Washington: Bureau of the Census, 1949. Available online at census.gov.

Indianapolis Journal. "President in Hospital." September 24, 1902, 1.

Irwin, Douglas A. "Explaining America's Surge in Manufactured Exports 1880–1913." *Review of Economics and Statistics*, vol. 85, issue 2, 2003, 364–76. Available online at Dartmouth.edu.

Jessup, Philip C. *Elihu Root*. New York: Dodd, Mead & Company, 1938.

Keating, George P. Letter to Louis L. Babcock, December 12, 1933. Reproduced in Wallace.

Knokey, Jon. *Theodore Roosevelt and the Making of American Leadership*. New York: Skyhorse Publishing, Inc., 2015.

Kohn, Edward P. (ed.). *A Most Glorious Ride: The Diaries of Theodore Roosevelt 1877–1886*. Albany: State University of New York Press, 2015.

Kolko, Gabriel. *The Triumph of Conservatism: A Reinterpretation of American History, 1900–1916*. New York: Free Press, 1977.

Lamont, Thomas W. *Henry P. Davison: The Record of a Useful Life*. New York: Harper Brothers Publishers, 1933.

Lee, En-Han. *China's Quest for Railway Autonomy, 1904–1911: A Study of the Chinese Railway-Rights-Recovery Movement*. Singapore: Singapore University Press, 1977.

Long, Clarence D. *Wages and Earnings in the United States, 1860–1890*. Princeton: Princeton University Press, 1960.

Lowenstein, Roger. *America's Bank: The Epic Struggle to Create the Federal Reserve*. New York: Penguin Press, 2015.

McCullough, David. *The Path Between the Seas: The Creation of the Panama Canal 1870–1914*. New York: Simon & Schuster, 1977.

——. *Mornings on Horseback*. New York: Simon and Schuster, 1981.

Milkis, Sidney M., and Emily J. Charnok. "History of the Presidency," in Nelson.

Millard, Candice. *The River of Doubt: Theodore Roosevelt's Darkest Journey*. New York: Doubleday & Company, Inc., 2005.

Miller, Nathan. *Theodore Roosevelt: A Life*. New York: William Morrow and Company, Inc., 1992.

Miller, Scott. *The President and the Assassin: McKinley, Terror, and Empire at the Dawn of the American Century*. New York: Random House, 2011.

Mills, Cuthbert. "The Financial World." *New York Tribune*, February 23, 1902, 4.

Miner, Dwight Carroll. *The Fight for the Panama Route: The Story of the Spooner Act and the Hay-Herrán Treaty.* New York: Octagon Books, 1966.

Minneapolis Journal. "Sen. Washburn's Strong Words," November 20, 1901, 1.

Money Trust Investigation: Investigation of Financial and Monetary Conditions in the United States under House Resolutions 429 and 504 before a Subcommittee of the Committee on Banking and Currency. Washington: Government Printing Office, 1913. Available online from publicintelligence.net.

Morris, Edmund. *The Rise of Theodore Roosevelt.* New York: Coward, McCann & Geoghegan, Inc., 1979.

———. *Theodore Rex.* New York: Random House, 2001.

———. *Colonel Roosevelt.* New York: Random House, 2010.

Nasake, Claus-M. and Herman E. Slotnick. *Alaska: A History of the 49th State.* 2nd Ed. Norman: University of Oklahoma Press, 1994.

Nelson, Michael (ed.). *The Presidency and the Executive Branch.* 5th Ed., vol. 1. New York: Sage Publications, Inc., 2013.

New York Evening World. "No Peril Ahead, Says Morgan." September 14, 1901, 1.

———. "Merger Action Angers Trust." February 20, 1902, 12.

———. "Big Railroads in Merger Suit." February 21, 1902, 10.

———. "Call on Roosevelt to Act for Peace." June 4, 1902, 3.

———. "Effigy of Morgan Hanged by Strikers." June 7, 1902.

———. "Morgan Holds Out No Hope to End Coal Strike." August 20, 1902, 1.

———. "Coal Magnates Ready to Hear Morgan's Plan." August 25, 1902, 1.

———. "Morgan Sends for Baer; Coal Strike May End." August 26, 1902, 1.

———. "Methodist Preachers' Meeting Voted to Ask TR to Intervene." September 29, 1902, 12.

———. "Coal Famine Sends Up Price of Bread." September 30, 1902, 1.

———. "Coal Strike Talks at White House." September 30, 1902, 1.

———. "Operators Will Meet Roosevelt." October 1, 1902, 1.

———. "Solution of Strike Seems Near at Hand." October 1, 1902, 1.

———. "Poor Who Can't Buy Coal Scour Streets for Wood." October 2, 1902, 2.

———. "Sell Anthracite As Fine Jewel." October 2, 1902, 2.

———. "No Settlement of Coal Strike, Says Mitchell." October 3, 1902, 1.

———. "Morgan Gives 50,000 Tons of Coal to Poor." October 4, 1902, 1.

———. "No Extra Session of Congress to End Strike." October 4, 1902, 2.

———. "Hard Coal Jumps to $30 and $38 a Ton." October 6, 1902, 2.

———. "Mine Leader Rejects Plan to End Strike." October 7, 1902, 1.

———. "Conference to End Strike Fails, Says Gov. Odell." October 9, 1902, 1.

———. "Conference to End Coal Strike." October 10, 1902, 1.

———. "Roosevelt Walks to His Carriage." October 10, 1902, 3.

———. "Root Has a Conference with J. Pierpont Morgan." October 11, 1902, 2.

———. "Mine Operators Now Ready to Advance Wages." October 13, 1902, 1.

———. "Miners Angry at Supposed Snub in Strike Plan." October 14, 1902, 1.

———. "May Modify Terms." October 15, 1902, 1.

———. "Morgan Shuts the Dough-Bag." October 15, 1902, 2.

——. "Famine Price of Coal at End; Big Drop To-Day." October 16, 1902, 1.

——. "Strike Commission to Meet on Friday." October 21, 1902, 1.

——. "Canal Payment No Menace Now." March 30, 1903, 9.

——. "J. P. Morgan Sees Good Times Ahead." March 31, 1903, 14.

——. "Government Will Not Run Amuck, Says Knox." March 15, 1904, 1.

——. "Morgan Winds Up Panama Deal." May 3, 1904.

——. "Bankers Send Messengers to See Roosevelt." November 4, 1907, 1.

——. "Bluffed to a Standstill." November 3, 1908, 10.

——. "The World Cannot Be Muzzled." December 16, 1908, 16.

——. "Cromwell Talks of Blackmail." February 17, 1909, 4.

——. "A Political Persecution." February 18, 1909, 16.

——. "Great Guns Roar Good-by Salute As Roosevelt Sails." March 23, 1909, 1.

——. "Taft to Practice Law in Cincinnati; Is Not Depressed." November 6, 1912.

New York Sun. November 5, 1882, 7.

——. "New Panama Canal Company." December 28, 1899, 2.

——. "Sent Stock Prices Down." September 14, 1901.

——. "Our President." September 15, 1901, 1.

——. "Safeguard the President." September 16, 1901, 5.

——. "London Views of Ship Combine." April 21, 1902, 1.

——. "President in Crash." September 4, 1902, 1.

——. "Coal Expected to Go Higher." September 29, 1902, 2.

——. "Coal Strike Goes On." October 4, 1902, 1.

——. "Ship Combine Imports Coal." October 5, 1902, 1.

——. "Talk Sans Result." October 10, 1902, 1.

——. "Root on a Mission." October 12, 1902, 1.

——. "To Arbitrate." October 14, 1902, 1.

——. "May Modify Terms." October 15, 1902, 1.

——. "End of Strike." October 16, 1902, 1.

——. "Merger Illegal." March 15, 1904, 1.

——. "The $40,000,000 Warrant Paid." May 10, 1904, 9.

——. "Roosevelt Is Inaugurated." March 5, 1905, 1.

——. "Mr. Morgan Sees President." August 29, 1905, 1.

——. "China Gets Canton-Hankow." August 30, 1905, 3.

——. "Bankers Long in Conference." November 4, 1907, 1.

——. "Steel Men at White House." November 5, 1907, 1.

——. "The President and the Republican Treasury." October 8, 1908, 6.

——. "Now Col. Roosevelt's Stripped to the Buff." February 23, 1912, 1.

——. "Say T.R. Planned His Race in 1911." October 22, 1912, 6.

——. "No Money Trust, Mr. Morgan Says." December 20, 1912, 1.

New York Times. "Metropolitan Art Museum." March 15, 1871, 2.

——. "The Museum of Natural History." November 10, 1875, 8.

——. "The Wall Street Rally." November 5, 1876, 10.

——. "Candidates in the Field." October 30, 1881, 1.

——. "Republican Nominations." November 1, 1881, 2.

——. "The Contest in the City." October 12, 1882, 5.

——. "Theodore Roosevelt's Views." August 1, 1884, 1.

——. "Big Panama Canal Plans." December 28, 1899, 5.

——. "Mr. Roosevelt Is Now the President." September 15, 1901, 1.

——. "Senator Hanna Tries to Avert Coal Strike." May 8, 1902, 1.

——. "President Mitchell Sees No Peace Signs." August 21, 1902, 2.

——. "President's Landau Struck by a Car." September 4, 1902, 1.

——. "Mitchell Warns Men Against Violence." September 20, 1902, 3.

——. "Miners and Operators in Conference." September 30, 1902, 1.

——. "'Mitchell Day' in the Anthracite Region." October 30, 1902, 6.

——. "Stolen Property." December 29, 1903, 8.

——. "Unlawful Restraint of Trade." March 15, 1904, 8.

——. "Bankers Confer with Mr. Morgan." November 4, 1907, 1.

——. "Indict Five Editors for Panama Libel." February 18, 1909, 2.

——. "Bryan Fails in Plan to Oust Ryan and Belmont; Clark and Wilson Cheered More Than an Hour Each." June 28, 1912, 1.

——. "Calls Morgan a 'Tightwad.'" October 4, 1912, 5.

——. "Mr. Roosevelt's Testimony." October 6, 1912, 16.

——. "Roosevelt Meets Defeat Buoyantly." November 6, 1912, 1.

——. "The Great Wilson Victory." November 6, 1912, 14.

——. "A Great Financier." April 1, 1913, 10.

——. "Geo. F. Baer Dead; His Illness Brief." April 27, 1914.

New York Tribune. "The News This Morning." November 6, 1881, 6.

——. "The Vote for Assemblymen." November 10, 1881, 2.

——. "Club Women Discreet." November 16, 1900, 5.

——. "New York's Grief Great." September 14, 1901, 1.

——. "Roosevelt Now President." September 15, 1901, 1.

——. "The City Draped in Black." September 15, 1901, 3.

——. "Views of Governor Van Sant." November 28, 1901, 14.

——. "Message in Congress." December 4, 1901, 1.

——. "Morgan at White House." February 24, 1902, 7.

——. "Meets Industries' Captains." February 27, 1902, 1.

——. "The Passing Throng." March 25, 1902, 7.

——. "Americans to Control." April 20, 1902, 1.

——. "News of Two Capitals." April 27, 1902, 1.

——. "Health Department Sending Out Notices of Complaints." June 4, 1902, 2.

——. "Smoke Clouds Shut Out View." June 13, 1902, 14.

——. "Manhattan Men in Court." June 18, 1902, 16.

——. "Operators See Morgan." August 21, 1902, 14.

——. "Morgan and the Coal Strike." August 22, 1902.

——. "Mr. Morgan and the Strike." August 23, 1902, 14.

——. "Baer Calls on Morgan." August 27, 1902, 1.

——. "Morgan's Gift of Coal to Poor." September 21, 1902, 5.

——. "A Second Operation." September 29, 1902, 1.

——. "American Federation of Catholic Societies Sending Petition to TR Asking for Him to Use 'His Good Offices' to Settle the Strike." September 29, 1902, 2.

——. "The Famine Price Grows." September 30, 1902, 1.

——. "A Coal Train Attacked." September 30, 1902, 5.

——. "Hopes to End Coal Strike." October 1, 1902, 1.

——. "Progress on Coal Famine." October 1, 1902, 1.

——. "Pleased with Plan to Discuss Strike in Washington." October 2, 1902, 4.

——. "Ready for Conference." October 3, 1902, 1.

——. "Story of Conference." October 4, 1902, 1.

——. "Strike Not Settled." October 4, 1902, 1.

——. "Nuisance in Soft Coal." October 5, 1902, 1.

——. "Old Furniture As Fuel." October 7, 1902, 2.

——. "Odell Still Hopes for Peace." October 10, 1902, 1.

——. "Root Here to See Morgan." October 12, 1902, 1.

——. "Some Hope of Resumption." October 13, 1902, 1.

——. "The Day's Operation in Stocks." October 17, 1902, 12.

——. "Pleased with Ship Trust." October 19, 1902, 6.

——. "The Coal Strike Ends." October 22, 1902, 1.

——. "Morgan to the Attack." December 10, 1903, 3.

——. "Stolen Property." December 29, 1903.

——. "President Vindicated." March 15, 1904, 1.

——. "Wall Street Unshaken." March 15, 1904, 3.

——. "To Obey the Law." March 16, 1904, 1.

——. "Panama Canal Transfer." April 28, 1904, 2.

——. "In Possession of Canal." May 4, 1904, 3.

——. "Panama Warrant Paid." May 10, 1904, 3.

——. "Sail with Panama Canal Deed." May 12, 1904, 2.

——. "Roosevelt Wins Tremendous Victory." November 9, 1904, 1.

——. "How President Voted." November 9, 1904, 3.

——. "Joy at the White House," November 9, 1904, 3.

——. "Roosevelt and Fairbanks Inaugurated." March 5, 1905, 1.

——. "Roosevelt Inaugurated." March 5, 1905, 2.

——. "To Hear Railway Men." March 12, 1907, 1.

——. "President on Finance." October 23, 1907, 3.

——. "Relations with Japan." October 27, 1907, 1.

——. "Thanksgiving Nov. 28." October 27, 1907, 9.

——. "Bankers in Session." November 4, 1907, 1.

——. "J.P. Morgan a Bull." December 11, 1908, 1.

——. "Ready to Sail." March 23, 1909, 3.

——. "Government Sues to Dissolve Steel Trust As Illegal Combination in Restraint of Trade." October 27, 1911, 1.

——. "Demand Roosevelt Run." February 11, 1912, 2.

———. "'My Hat Is in the Ring!' Says Col. Roosevelt." February 22, 1912, 1.

———. "'I Will Accept the Nomination,' Says Roosevelt." February 26, 1912, 1.

———. "Roosevelt Halted Harvester Suit." April 25, 1912, 1.

———. "Calls Harvester Charge Nonsense." April 26, 1912, 1.

———. "President Bitterly Attacks Roosevelt." April 26, 1912, 1.

———. "Roosevelt Calls Taft Falsifier." April 27, 1912, 1.

———. "Money Trust Impossible, Says Morgan on the Stand." December 20, 1912, 1.

New York World. The Roosevelt Panama Libel Case Against the New York World. New York: Press Publishing Company, 1911.

Newman, Roger K. *The Yale Biographical Dictionary of American Law.* New Haven: Yale University Press, 2009.

"1912 Democratic Party Platform." Available online at the website of the American Presidency Project (presidency.ucsb.edu).

O'Toole, Patricia. *When Trumpets Call: Theodore Roosevelt After the White House.* New York: Simon & Schuster, 2005.

Page, William H. "The Gary Dinners and the Meaning of Concerted Action." *SMU Law Review,* Spring 2009, 597.

Peirce, Clyde. "The Panama Libel Cases." *Indiana Magazine of History,* June 1937, 171–86.

Pringle, Henry F. *Theodore Roosevelt.* New York: Harcourt, Brace and Company, 1931.

"Progressive Party Platform of 1912." Available online at the website of the American Presidency Project (presidency.ucsb.edu).

Report of the Committee Appointed Pursuant to House Resolutions 429 and 504 to Investigate the Concentration of Control of Money and Credit. Washington: Government Printing Office, 1913. Available online at publicintelligence.net.

"Republican Party Platform of 1912." Available online at the website of the American Presidency Project (presidency.ucsb.edu).

Roosevelt, Theodore. "Second Annual Message to Congress." December 2, 1902. Full text available on the website of the Miller Center at the University of Virginia (millercenter.org).

———. "Special Message." January 4, 1904. Available online at the American Presidency Project (presidency.ucsb.edu).

———. "Fifth Annual Message to Congress." December 5, 1905. Available online at the American Presidency Project (presidency.ucsb.edu).

———. "New Nationalism Speech." August 31, 1912.

———. *Theodore Roosevelt: An Autobiography.* New York: The Macmillan Company, 1913.

Satterlee, Herbert L. *J. Pierpont Morgan.* New York: The Macmillan Company, 1939.

Schwantes, Carlos Arnoldo. *Going Places: Transportation Redefines the Twentieth-Century West.* Bloomington: Indiana University Press, 2003.

Scott, James Brown. *Robert Bacon—Life and Letters.* Garden City, NY: Doubleday, Page & Company, 1923.

Scranton Tribune. "All State Troops Are Ordered Out." October 7, 1902, 1.

Sinclair, Andrew. *Corsair: The Life of J. Pierpont Morgan.* Boston: Little, Brown and Company, 1981.

The Story of Panama: Hearings on the Rainey Resolution Before the Committee on Foreign Affairs of the House of Representatives. Washington: Government Printing Office, 1913.

Strouse, Jean. *Morgan: American Financier.* New York: Random House, 1999.

Sullivan, Mark. *Our Times: The United States 1900–1925.* Vol. 2, *America Finding Herself.* New York: Charles Scribner's Sons, 1927.

Taft, William Howard. "Speech of William Howard Taft Accepting the Republican Nomination for President of the United States." August 1, 1912. Available at archive.org.

Tarbell, Ida M. *The Life of Elbert Gary: A Story of Steel.* New York: D. Appleton and Company, 1925.

U.S. General Services Administration. *A History of 736 Jackson Place,* 1995. Available online at clinton4.nara.gov.

U.S. Senate. *Campaign Contributions: Testimony before a Subcommittee of the Committee on Privileges and Elections.* Part One. Washington: Government Printing Office, 1912. Available online at babel.hathitrust.org.

Vietor, Richard H. K. "Businessmen and the Political Economy: The Railroad Rate Controversy of 1905." *Journal of American History,* June 1977.

Wallace, David H. *The Ansley Wilcox House and Its Furnishings.* Harpers Ferry: National Park Service, 1990. Available online at nps.org.

Washington Evening Star. "Week Ending Feb. 22, 1902." February 22, 1902, 3.

———. "Dinner to Prince." February 25, 1902, 10.

———. "President's Hurt." September 24, 1902, 1.

———. "President Is at Home." September 25, 1902, 12.

———. "Temperature Normal." September 29, 1902, 1.

———. "Statement by Mitchell." September 29, 1902, 17.

———. "Mr. Morgan Omitted." October 2, 1902, 1.

———. "The Coal Mine Magnates." October 2, 1902, 2.

———. "Ringing Words." October 3, 1902, 1.

———. "Looking for Relief." October 4, 1902, 1.

———. "Editors on Decision." March 15, 1904, 6.

———. "Roosevelt's Pledge." November 9, 1904, 8.

———. "China Road Concession." August 8, 1905, 8.

———. "The Hankow Railroad." August 9, 1905, 14.

———. "Mr. Morgan Sees President." August 29, 1905, 11.

———. "Morgan's Hasty Trip." March 12, 1907, 1.

———. "Frequent Visitor Here." November 5, 1907, 1.

———. "Steel Deal Story by Col. Roosevelt." August 5, 1911, 1.

Washington Herald. "Ask Roosevelt's Aid." March 13, 1907, 2.

———. "Walks in the Rain." October 28, 1907, 1.

———. "Cortelyou Returns to Desk." October 28, 1907, 2.

———. "Roosevelt and Morgan." November 5, 1907, 6.

Washington Times. "Activity at the Expense of Values." February 21, 1902, 8.

———. "Millionaires Dine." February 23, 1902, 2.

———. "Senator Depew a Host." February 23, 1902, 7.

———. "Supreme Court Denies Minnesota Suit." February 25, 1902, 4.

———. "Temporary White House Well Placed." June 29, 1902, 17.

———. "President Operated On and Abandons His Western Trip." September 24, 1902, 1.

———. "President Spends a Restful Night." September 24, 1902, 1.

———. "President Resting in Comfort Here." September 25, 1902, 1.

———. "Second Operation on the President Found Necessary." September 29, 1902, 1.

———. "Details of Conference at the White House." October 3, 1902, 1.

———. "Members of Federation Attend Obsequies." February 17, 1904, 2.

———. "Thousands See Body Removed." February 17, 1904, 2.

———. "Great Pageant Passing Up Avenue Cheered by Thousands." March 5, 1905, 3.

———. "Cromwell's Case of Lockjaw Bad, Declares Morgan." February 28, 1906, 1.

———. "Finance Leaders Confer 17 Hours at Morgan Home." November 4, 1907.

Wellman, William. "The Inside History of the Great Coal Strike." *Collier's*, October 18, 1902, 6.

Wiebe, Robert H. "The House of Morgan and the Executive, 1905–1913." *American Historical Review*, October 1959, 49–60.

———. "The Anthracite Strike of 1902." *Mississippi Valley Historical Review*, September 1961, 229–51.

Wilcox, Ansley. "Theodore Roosevelt, President." October 1902. Available on the National Park Service website (nps.gov).

Wister, Owen. *Roosevelt: The Story of a Friendship*. New York: The Macmillan Company, 1930.

Wood, Frederick S. *Roosevelt As We Knew Him: The Personal Recollections of One Hundred and Fifty of His Friends and Associates*. Philadelphia: The John C. Winston Company, 1927.

INDEX

·

About the Author

Gerard Helferich is the author of the widely praised *Theodore Roosevelt and the Assassin: Madness, Vengeance, and the Campaign of 1912*; *Stone of Kings: In Search of the Lost Jade of the Maya* (both from Lyons Press); *Humboldt's Cosmos: Alexander von Humboldt and the Latin American Journey That Changed the Way We See the World*; and *High Cotton: Four Seasons in the Mississippi Delta*. A member of the National Book Critics Circle, he publishes reviews in the *Wall Street Journal*, and he has contributed to the Fodor's travel guides to Mexico and Guatemala. For the past fifteen years, he has been on the faculty of the Columbia Publishing Course at the Columbia Journalism School. Before turning to writing in 2002, he was an editor and publisher for twenty-five years at companies such as Doubleday, Simon & Schuster, and John Wiley & Sons. He lives in Jackson, Mississippi, and San Miguel de Allende, Mexico, with his wife, the writer Teresa Nicholas. Please visit his website, gerardhelferich.com.